SOCIAL SOURCES OF CHURCH GROWTH

Korean Churches in the Homeland and Overseas

GIL SOO HAN

UNIVERSITY
PRESS OF
AMERICA

Lanham • New York • London

Copyright © 1994 by
University Press of America,® Inc.
4720 Boston Way
Lanham, Maryland 20706

3 Henrietta Street
London WC2E 8LU England

Library of Congress Cataloging-in-Publication Data

Han, Gil Soo.
Social sources of church growth : Korean churches in the homeland
and overseas / Gil Soo Han.
p.   cm.
Includes bibliographical references and index.
1. Australia—Church history—20th century. 2. Koreans—
Australia—Religious life. 3. Korea—Church history. I. Title.
BR1480.H36   1995
279.4'082'089957—dc20   94–31101 CIP

ISBN 0–8191–9758–0 (cloth : alk. paper)

Contents

PART I

PART III:
THE GROWTH OF KOREAN ETHNIC CHURCHES IN SYDNEY

Chapter 9   The Economic Dimension of Korean Churches in Sydney 143

PART IV

Chapter 10 Summary and Conclusion

Bibliography

Index

About the author

List of Diagrams

List of Tables

Abbreviations

GDP   Gross Domestic Product

KCYF
  Korean Christian Youth Fellowship (Chaeho Kidok Ch'ongnyŏnhoe)

KRC   Korean Resource Centre (Han'guk Minjok Charyosil)

NCC   (Korean) National Christian Council

SEM   Society for Ethnic Mission (Sosu Minjok Sŏn'gyowŏn)

TOEFL   Test Of English as a Foreign Language

UCA   Uniting Church in Australia

UNESCO   United Nations Educational, Scientific
                                        and Cultural Organization

WCC   World Council of Churches
YMCA   Young Men's Christian Association

Foreword

The discussion of the reasons for the rapid development of the Christian Church in Korea has been an ongoing issue amongst missionaries, missiologists and Christians in general since the first generation of Protestant missionaries began work in the Korean peninsula at the end of the nineteenth century. The rapid acceptance of Protestant Christianity by Koreans of virtually all social strata stood in marked contrast to the rate of acceptance of Christianity in neighbouring countries such as China and Japan. Many historical, political, cultural and social factors have been used in the examination of Korean church growth to explain the reasons for this remarkable phenomenon. Within the last two decades, the classic studies of Korean church growth in Korea have been augmented by studies of the growth of Christianity amongst the recent Korean immigrant population in the United States. However, there has been virtually no work done on the Korean immigrant churches in other parts of the world.

Gil Soo Han's examination of the phenomenon of the growth of the Christian churches amongst the immigrant Korean population in Australia is a pioneer work of scholarship. In this book, Han examines three factors relevant to the development of Christianity amongst Korean Australians, the dimensions of ethnicity, politics and economics. This aspect of his research sets the question of church growth firmly within its proper social context. The unique aspect of this book is, however, its comparison of the growth of Christianity in Korea with church growth amongst Koreans in Australia. This feature of the work enables the author to illustrate what is uniquely characteristic about the Australian case. Han's work is to be commended for its emphasis on both the social context of church growth and its comparison with the growth of Christianity in the homeland. If other scholars were to conduct further research of this type, we would be able to have a clearer view of church growth amongst immigrant populations.

Dr. James H. Grayson
Director of Korean Studies
The University of Sheffield

Preface

This book would not have been completed without the invaluable assistance of the following people, to whom I acknowledge my appreciation.

Firstly, I wish to thank Associate Professor Alan Black and Dr. Steven Thiele of the Department of Sociology, University of New England, for their intellectual guidance which has influenced the direction of my thought.

I am grateful to my fellow Koreans in Sydney for their encouragement and cooperation during the data collection. They include journalists, Christian ministers and Buddhist masters in the Korean community in Sydney.

A considerable gratitude is also due to Ruth Nicholls and Erle Robinson for their extensive help in the intricacies of English style and expression.

I acknowledge my thanks to the Korean National Commission for UNESCO and the Australian Folklore Association for permissions to reproduce much of the material from chapters 6 and 7, originally published in *Korea Journal* 35 (2): 67-76 and in *Australian Folklore* 9: 162-173 respectively.

Finally, to my friend and wife, Sŏngsuk, for her constant and unselfish support — without her support, this study would never have come to fruition. I would also thank Joy, my five-year-old daughter, who has missed much of fatherly care while I put my time and effort into this study.

PART I

Chapter 1

Introduction

The Problem

The influx of Asian migrants into Australia has been steadily increasing since the 1960s. This has led Australian society to become more diverse than before, not only in its ethnic composition but also in the kinds of religions practised. Since 1974 Koreans have also contributed to the process. By the time of the 1986 Census, the number of Koreans in Australia had reached 9,284; by the time of the 1991 Census, 20,997. The Korean Consulate in Sydney (quoted in *Kŭrisch'yan Ribyu*, Jan. 1991) estimates that the number of Koreans in Sydney reached 25,000, including offsprings born in Australia, as of early 1991. What is of interest in this book is that there are a number of peculiarities about Koreans in Australia. One of the most interesting features is that the religious composition of these Koreans is significantly different from that of the population of their country of origin. Koreans share this peculiarity with two other Asian groupings (see Table 1.1).

Christians constitute a higher proportion of the first generation of those in Australia who have come from Japan, Indonesia or Korea than they do of the population in their homelands. This gives rise to the question as to what extent this difference is due to a greater propensity for Christians to migrate than for followers of other religions from these countries; or to what extent it is due to a process of church involvement after migration. The latter is a key question to be explored in this study, with particular reference to Koreans. Christians constitute an overwhelming majority of Koreans in Australia, but not of the Japanese or Indonesians. It is also the case that Koreans attend church at a far greater rate than the Australian or Japanese average: about 20 per cent of the adult Australian population attends church each week and about 60 per cent[1] of Koreans in Sydney do so (*Kŭrisch'yan Ribyu*, Jan. 1991).

Table 1.1: Religious composition (percentages) of (a) four Asian countries, and (b) the first generation within the same Asian ethnic categories in Australia

| KOREANS | | JAPANESE | | RELIGIOUS AFFILIATION | FILIPINO | | INDONESIAN | |
Korea	Aust.	Japan	Aust.		Philip.	Aust.	Indon.	Aust.
20.6	75.1	0.009	11.5	Christianity	94.2	98.1	9.6	40.5
20.1	3.0		28.4	Buddhism	0.0007		1.0	2.0
				Hinduism			1.9	4.1
				Muslim	5		86.9	46.9
		72.8		Shintoism				
1.19				Confucianism				
0.00137			3.2	Others			0.6	
57.5	21.7		56.9	No Religion		1.6		6.1
99.39	99.8		100	IN TOTAL	99.2	99.7	100	99.6
	7.0		12.3	Not Stated		3.9		4.9

Sources: (a) from *The Far East and Australasia 1992*, 23rd edition
(b) from Charles A. PRICE. 1991. *Religion and Ancestry in Australia* (based on 1986 Census)
The figures of (b) are concerned with the first generation of each ethnic group, excluding those who have "not stated".
Figures slightly vary from one source to another. I have decided to rely on the above two sources in order to provide relatively consistent information to the reader, thinking that using one source for one group and a different source for another can be misleading. They lack some data (*e.g.*, Japanese), but provide enough for present purposes. Moreover, the three Asian ethnic groups of Japanese, Filipino and Indonesian are chosen on the basis of the availability of data from the above two sources for the same time period.

What is also intriguing is that the number of Korean churches in Australia has sharply increased since 1974, reaching over seventy by early 1993. Most of the churches maintain Korean educated and ordained ministers, except a few of them which are served by theological graduates who are not yet ordained as ministers. No other ethnic group in Australia has established as many churches as Koreans have in this period. It is in the Sydney metropolitan area, where over two-thirds of Koreans in Australia have settled, that this can most readily be observed.

Korean immigrants in Sydney, no matter what their religious status prior to emigration, as is indicated in the above paragraphs, have tended to form churches. Most activities among Koreans in Sydney are actually centred around their churches (Macken, 1993: 37, 42). This has been the case for the last two decades in Sydney. In order to answer the central question of this book, it is important to study two broad areas: first, the enormous expansion of Christianity in Korea and second, the growth of Korean churches in Sydney. While attempting to explain these, I will argue throughout this study, that the significance of the church within an immigrant community is determined by both the culture of the country of origin and the social context of the new country.

Definition of Terms

In most cases, key concepts will be defined at the point where they are introduced. However, there are two for which early definition is required, namely church and church growth. In this book, the term "church" is used in the generic or everyday sense to refer to a Christian collectivity. The term "temple" is used to refer to Buddhist and Confucian collectivities.

When thinking of church growth, there are at least three kinds: (1) An increase in the total number of people associated with an individual congregation; (2) An increase in the total number of congregations; (3) An increase in the total number of people associated with all congregations. The term "church growth" should be regarded as including all three of the above, unless a specific dimension of growth is mentioned.

Sources of Data

The data used in this study have been collected from a number of sources. The analysis of church growth in Korea is largely based on secondary sources such as books, journals, newspapers and government publications. For the analysis of Korean churches in Sydney, I have undertaken participant observation, interviews with laity and clergy of both Christian and Buddhist organisations, and with those who are not members of either. Semi-structured interview schedules were used. The *Kŭrisch'yan Ribyu*, a monthly magazine, and Korean ethnic newspapers, all of which have been published in Sydney, have also provided important information[2].

Book Organisation

In chapter 2, I will review studies on church growth in Korea, Korean churches in the United States, Korean churches in Sydney and some relevant theories of church growth and decline. Then I will present a model of understanding the central question of the study in chapter 3. In chapters 4 and 5, which form Part II of this book, selected aspects of church growth in Korea will be analysed, as they have contributed to the growth of overseas Korean churches. In chapters 6 to 9, which make Part III, Korean churches in Sydney will be examined. This study concludes with chapter 10 or Part IV, which briefly summarises the main conclusions.

Notes

[1] Surveys have varying figures on this, depending on whether or not they have considered that some do not attend church every week.

[2] In Part II of the book, the names of individuals or churches are sometimes withdrawn or changed to protect their rights.

Chapter 2

Literature Review

The Literature on Church Growth in Korea

For the last few decades, the Korean church has grown enormously, not only in Korea but also overseas. There have not been as many sociological writings about this as one would have expected, given that there has been a great deal of literature on the issue of church growth in general. For this reason the study of this phenomenon is of particular interest. A number of reasons why the Korean church has grown have been set out. Some of these issues will be addressed in later chapters. According to Han Wansang (1983), the involvement of the Christian church in social justice, nationalism and human liberation contributed significantly up to the time of national independence in 1945 (Han Wansang, 1983: 152). Han goes on to argue that since then a fundamentalist type of belief has limited interest in social issues like human liberation and that church growth in Korea has been achieved mainly through continuous schism. These schisms have occurred because of two of the most significant characteristics of Korean Christians: namely, their fundamentalistic and shamanistic beliefs (Han Wansang, 1983: 139). He also argues that a fundamentalistic approach tends to sharply distinguish the "pure" from the "un-pure" and the "orthodox" from the "heterodox" and that this tendency has led churches in Korea to split continually, and, consequently, to an increase in the number of churches. This has eventually contributed to an increase in the number of churchgoers, for the churches that experienced split tend to put an effort into increasing their membership size. Scholars such as Han Wansang (1983: 125) argue that a Christian fundamentalism has been formed in Korea since the 1930s, and that this fundamentalism has been partly responsible for church splits in Korea. Although Han's argument is good as far as it goes, the social sources of church schisms (cf. Niebuhr, 1957) and related factors need to be further investigated.

From a sociological point of view, the most pertinent study of church growth in Korea is that by Kim Byong-suh (1985). This study takes issues such as industrialisation and urbanisation, social instability, and political insecurity into consideration. Other writers (*e.g.*, Harold Hong, 1983; B. Ro, 1983) have tended to leave out such matters. Kim Byong-suh (1985: 62) suggests that "an understanding of church growth requires an analysis of the social, political and economic background as well as the motivational aspect of the individual converts". Before he deals with more recent expansion in church membership, he discusses church growth between 1940 and 1960. According to him, this earlier growth paved the way for the later expansion. He points out that church growth was brought about by the structure of Korean society in the period between 1940 and 1960, despite the unstable condition of this society after independence from Japanese colonialism. Kim (1985: 64) also argues that the American military force has generally been regarded as the major factor in Korea's gaining independence and not being swallowed up by communist power. Koreans considered the military force closely associated with Christianity. In addition, president Syngman Rhee and his aides, who were mostly American-educated, offered Korean Christianity a politically and culturally favourable climate. When Kim goes on to explain church growth in Korea after 1960 he contends that it has been fostered by the heavy wave of industrialisation that has been very much growth oriented rather than stability oriented. Therefore, he argues, Koreans suffering from instability and stress or anomie have been in search of their ultimate concern, self-identity, and the social meaning of reality through church activities (Kim, 1985: 69, 71), which has consequently brought about church growth.

But, he asks, why has there been no enormous church growth in other developing countries such as Taiwan, the Philippines, and Indonesia? According to him, along with the instability of Korean society during this period, some particular characteristics of the Korean church have contributed to its explosive growth. First of all, a prevalent tendency of the Korean church itself is that it tends to be shamanistic, and that it accommodates indigenous belief systems such as totemism, shamanistic fetishism and other kinds of nature worship, which are much inclined to seek blessings in material wealth, good health, and other forms of personal and financial well-being. In the process of industrialisation, Koreans have attempted to achieve a better life by any means possible, one of which was to attend church where some clergy have stressed, and offered them, a better life "here and now", not merely in the "hereafter". This has appealed not only to the poor but also to the middle class who suffer from a firm sense of relative deprivation compared to those of higher status.

Secondly, Kim maintains that the church in Korea has kept up a tradition of human liberation, being deeply involved in struggling for the independence of the nation and the development of education and social welfare. Thus, the church has been able to attract people disenchanted with the authoritarian and bureaucratic system of government. Third, together with individualism as a basic characteristic of industrialisation and urbanisation, the so-called Nevius mission policy[1] from an early period of missionary activities in Korea has injected an independent nature into Korean churches. Fourth, Christianity was introduced at the historical juncture in which Koreans, the Confucian rulers in particular, began to question the Confucian value system as they saw Japan's victory over China in the Sino-Japanese War of 1894-95 with the Westernised military system and weaponry (Kim Byong-suh, 1985: 62). Fifth, the missionaries popularised the use of Korean phonetic script and started education for the masses (Han Wansang, 1983; Ro Bong-rin, 1983: 159; H. Hong, 1983).

While Kim's (1985) study considers many important sociological factors, his analysis has deficiencies. First, when examining church growth in Korea, denominational and church splits should be taken into consideration. This is because they have been among the most significant phenomena of the Korean church. Despite the fact, as Kim Byong-suh (1981) noted in an earlier form of the article, that there were 261 Protestant denominations in Korea as of 1981, no attempt was made by him to show the link between schisms and church growth. Yi Sanggyu (1986: 104) and Han Wansang (1983) have argued that splits in the church in Korea have brought about a membership increase both in churches that have experienced schism and in the new churches formed as a consequence.

Here, other questions are raised: whether a minister is available to minister to a newly founded church, or whether the church has to wait for a while until another minister arrives. If the split has occurred within a church served by two or more ministers, at least one of whom accompanies those who split off and forms a new congregation or denomination, another minister may not be required. Korea has over-produced theological college graduates who specifically look for church ministry: over 6,500 of them are produced every year (*Saenuri Sinmun*, 15 Feb. 1992). The ways in which they have contributed to church growth in Korea are overlooked in Kim's (1985) study. Church splits may not necessarily lead to an eventual increase in the number of churchgoers. However, such an increase has occurred in Korea partly due to the hard work of ministers in recruiting new members. In turn, this is linked to the way in which ministers are supported financially by church members.

Second, Kim (1985) argues that the strong bureaucratic system of the Korean government has maintained law and order in the process of rapid urbanisation and that the Korean church has adopted such tight bureaucratic control to help its expansion. This view appears to be narrow rather than comprehensive. Few scholars deny that there is a pervasive authoritarian bureaucratic structure throughout most institutions in Korea and that this has largely come from an indigenised Confucianism. In fact, it has been suggested that this has virtually formed the Korean personality over the last several centuries (Daniels, 1979). Kim Byong-suh (1984: 126-128) elsewhere argues that Confucianism in Korea is responsible for Korean individual churches' excessive interest in expansionism. One of its emphases is "respect for parents" which has led Korean life to be "family oriented" and consequently to clearly discriminate "them" from "us" with respect to their belonging to organisations such as church. This in turn has contributed to the pervasive tendency of church and denominational schisms. However, he does not fully consider the implications of Korean Confucianism when attempting to explain church growth.

Third, deep involvement in human liberation has not been a general feature of the Korean church. It is true that the churches in Korea which have been concerned about human liberation have achieved a significant growth since 1960, but this appears to be of relatively minor significance in the process of church growth. Korean churches have experienced a "bigness syndrome" (Kim, 1985: 71), and have concentrated on an expansion of membership, budget, and church buildings. Involvement in the issues of social welfare and justice has, since 1960, actually been of concern to only a small portion of those in the Korean church members (Han Wansang, 1983; Kim Hyŏngsŏk, 1983), whereas such involvement had been of interest to a majority of Korean church members prior to the 1960s when the industrialisation process started. In other words, industrialisation has led to most churches taking expansion as their major goal (An Pyŏngmu, 1983: 346; Han Pyŏngok, 1986: 31).

Fourth, the Nevius mission policy was indeed a catalyst for the growth of the Korean Presbyterian church especially when the policy was first introduced. Another major denomination, the Methodists, did not adopt it and this seems to be a reason why its growth was not as great as that of the Presbyterian church (Kim Ill-soo, 1985: 230). Although the significance of church polity in the growth of the church has been taken into consideration, it has probably been over-stated by Kim Ill-soo. Fifth, although Kim Byong-suh (1985) is largely successful in explaining how Korean Christianity has gained a large number of people, he has failed to show how more and more congregations and denominations have come to be established. A large number of people going to church does not necessarily lead to an increase in the number of churches, although these factors are sometimes inter-related.

A brief appraisal of Kim's (1985) study is that while he has considered the possibility that the social contexts around the church can lead on to, decline or growth, he has not fully considered some of the most pervasive phenomena within the church as well as in Korean society and their inter-relations. So he has not provided a full account of church growth in Korea. Some studies refer to schisms in Korean Christianity as one of the most pervasive phenomena. For example, Kim Ill-soo (1985) rightly observes that "For better or worse, these [Christian] religious schisms in Korea stimulate the growth of church membership partly because a splintered church or a group of splintered churches struggles to increase its membership". However, Kim Ill-soo (1985) and other scholars (Yi Sanggyu, 1986; Barret, 1982; Ji Won-yong, 1965; Chang Hyŏngil, 1991; Pak Sun'gyŏng, 1985) of Korean Christianity have not been able to provide a full picture of why schisms have been pervasive in Korea.

Other studies (*e.g.*, Ro, 1983) point out that political insecurity caused by a constant threat of communist attack during the Cold War has led Koreans to join churches and to look for spiritual security and that political, social, cultural and religious circumstances have also been favourable for church growth. These studies (*e.g.*, Nelson, 1983a; H. Hong, 1983) provide us with descriptive and general information for the present study. However, they do not provide a comprehensive explanation of church growth in Korea. Some other studies emphasise spiritual factors as a cause of the explosive church growth (Oh Pyeong-seh, 1983; Kang Shin-myung, 1983; Nelson, 1983b). Such studies largely leave unanswered the question as to why church growth has occurred mainly in the last thirty years. They also tend to stress the religiosity of the Koreans in a way which privileges a Christian world view. A typical statement in these studies is that "We see church growth as both God's blessing and the result of hard work by the Christians" (Nelson, 1983a: 189). The first part of this statement is interesting but it is beyond the scope of a sociological study. Whether Koreans are more religious in some general sense is a sociological question, but it will not be a major focus of this book.

There have been a few other studies about Korean churches before the 1960s when church growth was not as explosive. However, some of these studies are important for this study, in particular the study by Palmer (1967), who advocated the "religious saga thesis" (Yun Sung-bum, 1963). According to this thesis, the rapid growth of Christianity in Korea (up to the 1960s) was largely due to the fact that the shamanistic Koreans found a mirror of their own "true" god in the Christian religion. It is generally agreed, as stated earlier, that Korean Christians tend to be shamanistic in their belief (Palmer, 1967; Yun Sung-bum, 1963; H. Hong, 1983; Han Wansang, 1983; Yoon Yee-heum, 1992; Choi Joon-sik, 1992). The religious saga thesis may help to explain church growth since the 1960s as well. However, advocates of the thesis have focused on Pentecostal churches, largely neglecting other denominations, which have also expanded enormously.

To conclude this section, church growth in Korea has been a consequence of the complex inter-relations between society and the churches. Three broad questions to be answered remain: (1) What is the historical background of the Korean church? (2) What have been the most pervasive economic, political and ideological phenomena of Korean society at least for the last several decades, and what have been the ways in which they have been related to church growth in general and the over-supply of ministers in particular? (3) Do Korean Christians have a relatively high tendency to migrate from Korea compared to non-Christians?[2] The church should be examined with specific reference to these phenomena: that is, the way in which various social factors influence church growth needs to be explored. To put this in different terms, although a number of scholars have acknowledged and examined various aspects of the church in Korea (*e.g.*, political, religious and economic ones by Kim Byong-suh, 1985 and Kim Ill-soo, 1981: 190), no sociological study has been able to describe them in a systematic and comprehensive way. This is mainly because no clear analytical framework to understand the growth of the church in Korea has been developed.

The Literature on the Growth of the Korean Church in the United States

It is interesting to observe that the Korean church has grown enormously, not only in Korea, but also in many other parts of the world, *e.g.*, the United States, Canada, Australia, and Argentina. There were only 75 Korean churches in the United States in 1970, but the number had increased to 2,000 by 1990 (Hurh and Kim, 1990). About three-quarters of the Koreans in the United States are affiliated with Korean churches (Hurh and Kim, 1984a, 1988; Min, 1988). By contrast, less than five per cent of the Koreans are associated with Buddhist temples (Hurh and Kim, 1990), whereas about a quarter of the population of Korea are so associated (Korean National Bureau of Statistics, 1985). Korean immigrants show a higher level of affiliation with churches than any other ethnic group in the United States (Min, 1990: 9). A relatively small proportion of Chinese-Americans and Japanese-Americans are churchgoers (Kim Bok-lim, 1978). About 85% of Filipino-Americans are Catholics (Pido, 1986), but most of them attend ordinary Catholic parishes rather than specifically Filipino churches (Min, 1990). Mangiafico (1988: 174) found that only 17% of Filipino-Americans are associated with ethnic churches. The interesting questions here are whether there is any relationship between church growth in Korea and the growth of overseas Korean churches and how such an enormous growth has been possible in the United States.

Most of the studies on overseas Korean churches are about the United States where most Korean migrants have settled, especially since the liberalisation of immigration laws in 1965. Although there have been various studies on Korean immigrant churches in the United States, most of them have been highly descriptive rather than sociological (B. Kim, 1937; W. Kim, 1971; Shim, 1977; Choy, 1979; Kim Ill-soo, 1981). These descriptive studies do, however, provide much useful historical data on the activities of Korean immigrants. They illustrate many of the political aspects of Korean ethnic churches because of the importance of the struggle to achieve Korean independence from Japanese imperialism during the Second World War. However, none of these studies have conceptualised this political dimension as an aspect of the church seen as a multi-dimensional institution. Most scholars note that American missionaries took a vital role in encouraging Koreans to emigrate to Hawaii (Kim T'aekyong, 1979; Choy, 1979; Patterson and Kim, 1977; Deshler[3], quoted in Kim Hyung-chan, 1977b: 49; Min Pyong-gap, 1990). Korean immigrant churches in Hawaii built up a tradition of providing Koreans with both Christian and ethnic fellowship and have consequently been maintained as the key centres of the general Korean immigrant community of the United States (Choy, 1979; Patterson, 1988). By contrast, there were only a few Christians among the early Chinese and Japanese immigrants, so that, in contrast, their ethnic organisations are mostly centred around regional and kinship ties. Without this historical background, the enormous growth of Korean churches in the United States over the last three decades would not have been possible. The Christian tradition of the early Korean immigrants was further strengthened by the arrival of new Korean immigrants who since the 1960s have mostly been drawn from an urban middle-class background (Kim, 1981).

A pertinent study of Korean churches in the United States has been made by Hurh and Kim (1990). According to them, about half the Korean Christians[4] in the U.S. were Christians (predominantly Protestants) prior to their emigration; most of the rest become Christians after arrival in America. After reviewing writings about Korean ethnic churches in the United States and theories on the immigrant churches in general, Hurh and Kim (1990: 22-23) offer four propositions to be tested empirically. Their data are from first generation Korean immigrants living in the Chicago area. Their first proposition is that for Korean immigrants "religion becomes a way of life" (Hurh and Kim, 1990: 22). Generally speaking, immigrants participate more strongly and in greater numbers in religious activities in the new country than in the old. Going to church is one of the most significant processes of adjusting their lives to the conditions in the United States (Handlin, 1973: 105; cf. Greeley, 1972; Smith, 1978). Their second proposition is that "religion provides meaning, belonging and comfort" (Hurh and Kim, 1990: 22). Third, they suggest that the mental health or life satisfaction of immigrants is positively related to their church participation (p. 23). Lastly they propose that "religion either promotes or slows mobility/assimilation" (p. 23). The first two propositions were generally supported by Hurh and Kim's data, the mental-health theories only by the data from their female sample, and the fourth was not supported at all.

It is important to note Hurh and Kim's (1990: 29) inclusion of the background of Korean immigrants prior to emigration as an explanatory factor. This is because the growth of Korean churches in the U.S. is closely related to that in Korea. They suggest that: "the new immigrants' Christian/urban middle-class background" (Hurh and Kim, 1990; Kim Ill-soo, 1981) indicates that a religious motive is a significant reason for the Korean immigrants' attendance at ethnic churches. This view is also supported by earlier work done by Hurh and Kim (1984a). It is interesting to note that both their studies (1984a,

1990) discuss the religious motive as one of the reasons why Korean immigrants are actively involved in church participation. Other writers (*e.g.*, Kim Ill-soo, 1981; Min, 1990) tend to take it for granted that religious motives are a major cause of the growth of the Korean immigrant church and then quickly turn to other aspects (*i.e.*, "secular" or "non-religious") of the church. While not denying the importance of the purely religious motive, this study will also give particular attention to other aspects of the church.

While Hurh and Kim's (1990) data reveal that nine ordained Protestant ministers were represented in their sample of 622 Korean immigrants (20 years and older residing in the Chicago area where there are currently 70,000 Koreans), how the minister/laity ratio is so high, compared to other ethnic groups, is yet to be explored. This issue takes us to at least two further issues: the over-supply of ministers in Korea and their emigration from Korea. This is one of the core themes of the present study. There were only three Korean Catholic churches, and five Korean Buddhist temples in the Chicago area as of 1989, despite the fact that Buddhism is a major religion in Korea together with Christianity. Although the historical background of Korean churches in the United States (Hurh and Kim, 1990; Choy, 1979; Kim Hyung-chan, 1977b) and the ethnic functions of the Korean church partially explain why there were 155 Korean Protestant churches in the Chicago area, a full account of such a difference needs to be delivered (cf. Min, 1990). Hurh and Kim (1990) note that many ethnic groups actively participate in immigrant churches, but they also point to the unique tradition of the Korean church in the United States which developed from its beginnings in 1903. This explains the increase in membership of churches to a large degree. However, it leaves out the matter of the increase in the number of churches that has taken place simultaneously with a membership increase in existing churches.

The rise in the number of churches cannot be explained without looking at schism in Korean churches in the United States. Therefore, Hurh and Kim's (1990) study (which does not consider how religion or church services come to be "supplied") remains deficient. The matter of schism is significant because this is a factor not shared by other ethnic churches. Church schism in Korean churches in the United States has been a pervasive and accelerating phenomenon from around 1970. What needs looking at is whether there is any link between church schism and the large number of Korean Protestant churches in the United States. Schism has been a pervasive phenomenon of Christianity in Korea as well, so it is likely that this will affect Korean Christianity in the United States. Hurh and Kim (1990) acknowledge that there has been an abundant supply of ministers available to establish immigrant churches (also see Shin and Park, 1988), but the ways in which these are established are left out of their discussion. This is where the issue of schism is important. Moreover, the relationship between church participation of Korean immigrants and an increase in the number of churches and denominations requires investigation.

Shin and Park (1988), in their sociological study of the growth of overseas Korean churches, argue that schisms in Korean churches in the United States have been one of the main means of increasing membership and that the schisms partially result from an abundant supply of ministers (Kim Ill-soo, 1981: 198) and partially from competition among these ministers to ensure their livelihood. The significance of their research is that it implicitly or explicitly acknowledges the economic dimension of the church. This point has also been emphasised by Kim Ill-soo (1981: 198), when he argues that "the meaning of each [Korean] minister's existence in both an idealistic and a materialistic sense is directed toward creating and leading his own ethnic church". As far as I am aware, no research on the Korean immigrant church looks at the reason for the over-supply of ministers. This is a matter I intend to address in depth later under the rubric of "religio-economic entrepreneurship"[5].

Hurh and Kim's (1990) view that Korean churches in the United States have an ethnic dimension has been widely supported by other scholars (Choy, 1979; Min, 1990). Choy (1979), for instance, contends that: it "(1) functions as a social centre and a means of cultural identification (specifically for language and traditional values); (2) serves an educational role by teaching American-born Koreans Korean language, history and culture; and (3) keeps Korean nationalism alive". Min (1990) has more fully explored these points. He observes that those Korean immigrants who are affiliated with a church tend to be "as Korean as", or even "more" Korean than, those not affiliated, whereas "Christians in Korea are on the average less Korean than other Koreans" (Min, 1990: 29). The former case suggests that the Korean church encourages affiliates to maintain a high level of ethnicity. Min (1990) aptly points out that Korean immigrants from middle-class background are not generally satisfied with their "middle man" minority status (Bonacich, 1973) and they suffer from "status inconsistency" or "a sense of alienation" (Hurh and Kim, 1984a; Kim Ill-soo, 1981; Min Pyong-gap, 1984; cf. Dearman, 1982), so they become active in church participation. However, the scope of the study is narrow and the question of church growth is largely overlooked. Min (1990) also tends to regard the Korean church as solely a site of ethnic gathering instead of recognising other dimensions. In doing so, the focus of his study has been on the inter-ethnic relationship between Koreans and other

Americans. This leads him to mistakenly argue that a characteristic of the Korean church, its small-sized congregation, is due to Korean immigrants wanting to be part of a small group (Min, 1990). He leaves out all discussion of schism. Further, he does not suggest why ethnic services are provided particularly by the church rather than by other organisations. Min's (1990) rather weak explanation is that non-religious ethnic organisations do not have frequent meetings.

What the Korean church in the United States has offered particularly for Korean immigrants has been obviously a constant force to lead them to the church so as to expand Korean churches. This leads us necessarily to the migration issue. Why do people emigrate in the first place? Why does church affiliation become important for immigrants? This requires a further investigation. When the Korean immigrant church provides Korean immigrants with ethnic roles, this activity is more than merely preserving Korean ethnicity. That is, the Korean church is constantly struggling for a better economic and political status for Korean immigrants in the wider society. Kim Ill-soo (1981: 199-207), for example, notes that the Korean immigrant church not only serves as "a pseudo-extended family" but also functions as "a broker between its congregation and the bureaucratic institutions of the larger society".

As Korean immigrant churches have expanded much more rapidly than any other ethnic churches, this may be due to features unique to Korean society/culture, including, of course, the place of the church in Korea. The ethnic functions of the Korean church in the United States have, as I mentioned above, been investigated by a number of scholars. However, the ways in which the church has been involved in the economic and political status of Korean immigrants, in addition to providing religious services, need to be further explored.

The linkage between the growth of the Korean church in the United States and that in Korea certainly needs to be made clear. This is part of what I intend to do in later sections. While Kim Ill-soo (1981) and Hurh and Kim (1990) point out that a large proportion of Korean immigrants in the United States were affiliated with the church prior to emigration, Kim Ill-soo (1981: 190, 207) also argues that a large number of Christians fled from North Korea to South Korea around the time of the Korean War. Without strong kin and regional ties in South Korea they tend to immigrate to the United States in greater proportion than the general population of South Korea (Kim Ill-soo, 1981; Min, 1990); thus church growth has come about in the Korean community in the United States and a large number of Korean ministers in America are of North Korean origin. This view which has not been supported by any statistical data, may partially explain the growth of Korean churches during the 1960s or 1970s, but does not by any means explain the continuous growth after this time. In fact, none of Kim Ill-soo's (1981: 198) three categories[6] of Korean ministers in America seems to indicate that they are of particularly North Korean origin.

To sum up, although there have been various studies of the Korean church in the United States which suggest that the Korean church has multiple dimensions, no study provides a clear analytical framework for understanding the Korean immigrant church and no comprehensive sociological study of the growth of the overseas Korean church has so far been undertaken. The influence of church growth in Korea on the growth of overseas Korean churches has also been largely neglected.

The Literature on the Korean Church in Sydney

There have been two major studies of Korean churches in Australia. The first is Kim Man-young's (1983) *A Theology of and Strategy for Ministry among Korean Immigrants in Australia*. The second is Lee Sang-taek's (1987) *Exploring an Appropriate Church Structure for Korean Speaking Congregations Which are Members of the Uniting Church in Australia*. Both have been written from primarily ministerial and theological points of view[7]. Lee's dissertation was later published as *New Church, New Land: The Korean Experience* (Lee, 1989a). Although this study contains some sociological insights into the situation of Korean immigrants in Sydney, his sociological view tends to be based exclusively on theories of marginality. Lee (1989a) argues that the life of Korean immigrants in Sydney is a marginalisation process, particularly suffering from status inconsistency. This aspect should certainly be taken into consideration, and some of his arguments regarding this issue will be raised in a later chapter of this study. However, his study raises a number of questions he does not answer. For example, are Korean immigrants the only ethnic group that are marginalised in Australia? Are they more marginalised than other ethnic groups? If the answer to both is no, the question as to why there has been an enormous growth of the church among Koreans in Sydney when this is not a feature of ethnic groups in Australia has not been answered. The answer must relate not just to the immigration experience but also to something brought from Korea.

In addition, various writings and reports about Korean churches in Sydney have appeared in Korean ethnic newspapers over the last ten years. *Kŭrisch'yan Ribyu*, a monthly magazine of these churches, carries useful information for this study. The tradition of catering for fellow immigrants from Korea developed among Korean immigrant churches in the United States at the turn of the century and it was an important factor in bringing about enormous church growth there since the 1970s. Korean immigrant churches in Sydney have had a much shorter history. Korean immigration into Australia only started in 1974 and Korean churches started to grow almost immediately.

The Concept of Conversion

As mentioned above, "the new immigrants' Christian/urban middle-class background" (Hurh and Kim, 1990) partially explains Korean immigrants' level of church participation. However, there is still a large proportion of people who were not churchgoers prior to emigration, but who became church attenders after their arrival in their new countries (Min, 1991). What is the reason for this? One explanation is that they convert in a religious sense to Christianity. According to the work of Balch (1985), three important areas to look at in studying religious involvement are *recruitment, conversion,* and *commitment.* Recruitment refers to "joining a group", whereas conversion means a change in belief and personal identity (Balch, 1985: 28). Commitment is "the level of intensity of participation". The scarcity of sociological studies dealing directly with conversion, recruitment, and commitment in regard to more traditional or mainstream religious groups is conspicuous (Richardson, 1978: 8). Most of the sociological studies concerned with these three issues focus on exotic new religious movements (*e.g.*, Snow and Phillips, 1980; Lofland, 1977b). These are not particularly relevant for the present study. This is because these movements (*e.g.*, the Unification Church, the Buddhist Movement in America, the Hare Krishna Movement) are significantly different from the phenomena of interest in the present study.[8]

Nevertheless, some insights can be derived from existing studies of religious conversion. There have been a number of perspectives proposed, though little consensus exists because of the complexity of the conversion process in different situations. Richardson (1985) has categorised the studies on conversion into two: the passive and the active paradigms of conversion. The passive paradigm (or traditional, old or deterministic view) of conversion derives from the common interpretation of the conversion of Paul on the road to Damascus. The Pauline conversion has been perceived to be sudden, dramatic, and emotional, lacking a definite rational quality (Richardson, 1985: 105). This passive paradigm, often pictured as a more or less "forced" conversion, has been adopted by a number of scholars (*e.g.*, Berger, 1963; Singer, 1979; Clark, 1979; Conway and Siegelman, 1978;

Nolan, 1971; Marin, 1972; Foss and Larkin, 1978). This perspective
has received further support not only from theorists of deprivation and
strain like Smelser (1963) and Glock (1964), but also from the
secularisation theory of religion, for these theories tend to view
individuals as passive objects (Richardson, 1985: 106, 107).

Another view is more humanistic. Its focus is on "active"
conversion. People are viewed as active agents who take the initiative
in regard to self-affirmation which occurs through rational decision
making (Lofland, 1977a; Strauss, 1976, 1979; Downton, 1980;
Lofland, 1977b; Balch and Taylor, 1977; Lynch, 1977). Decisions such
as "intellectual conversion" through reading a book (Lofland and
Skonovd, 1981) or "coming to agree with friends" (Lofland and Stark,
1965) are presented as an active search for meaning or relevant life-
styles.

I would argue that a combination of the passive and active
paradigms shares much similarity with a supply/demand congruence
theory of church growth and that the combination would enable us to
better understand religious conversion in general. The reason for the
latter is that although the Pauline conversion as a passive paradigm is
typically sudden and dramatic, most passive conversion experiences are
likely to involve some degree of conscious decision-making. The extent
to which one may be passive or active in the process of conversion
varies. A person may seek religious conversion actively, but if social
circumstances do not favour it, then conversion may not occur. By
contrast, although a person may be less interested in conversion (*i.e.*,
have a passive attitude towards it), it may nevertheless take place under
social circumstances or cultural factors which are supportive of
conversion. Most anthropologists have considered social circumstances
(*e.g.*, migration, war) or cultural factors extremely important in the
process of conversion (Rambo, 1982: 147). Here, the commonly agreed
motives of conversion have to be considered, namely, meaning and
belonging. Some scholars have given more emphasis to meaning
(Weber, 1958; Berger, 1967; Berger and Luckmann, 1966) and some to
belonging (Durkheim, 1965). One person might be primarily interested
in belonging to a group, which may be achieved through conversion.
However, someone else may be more interested in searching for
meaning.

It should not, however, be assumed that people who go to a
Christian church have converted to Christianity. This follows directly
from the position, central to this study, that the church is multi-
dimensional. Why people go to church is an open question. It is here
that the distinction between conversion and recruitment becomes
crucial. People are recruited into a church for many reasons and they

may or may not be converted. For the purpose of this book, it is more important to study the recruitment process than to study when or if any individual converts to Christianity. Just as conversion takes place actively as well as passively, recruitment can also be active or passive.

The Concepts of Church and Religion

The notion of an ethnic church brings together two concepts: religion and ethnicity. The church has often been understood as primarily a religious institution. This view has been adopted by many researchers such as Bellah (1970), Yinger (1970) and Berger (1979). This is problematic from a sociological point of view. The definition of religion adopted in this book is not far from its generally accepted meaning of "a system of concepts, feelings, attitudes and practices with a supernatural, sacred[9] or ultimate point of reference" (Black, 1978: 282). This is a substantive definition. If church refers to a religious institution in the sense that only religious matters are dealt with within the church, "church as a religious institution" is not problematic. However, religious activity is only a part of what a church is and does, for it is a complex social institution. In other words, a church is a multi-dimensional institution.

There have been numerous studies of ethnic churches, especially regarding the relationship between religion and ethnicity. However, the concepts religion and ethnicity tend not to be used carefully. For example, Lewins (1991) argues that one can be simultaneously Irish and Catholic; Swedish and Lutheran; Greek and Orthodox; and Polish and Catholic. This is to say that an individual can identify with both religion and ethnicity and be involved in activities associated with both of them. A relevant question is that, for example, if Irish immigrants tend to be more closely attached to the Irish Catholic church in a new nation than they were in the old, does this mean that Irish ethnicity has led them to further *Catholicism* (a religion) or that Irish ethnicity has led them to be more closely attached to an *Irish* (an ethnic) institution where they can pursue not only their Irish identity or ethnicity but also religion?

The primary focus of many existing studies (Greeley, 1972; Handlin, 1973; Smith, 1978; Herberg, 1955) which claim to focus on religion and ethnicity in the ethnic churches has been on inter-ethnic relations rather than on the ethnic church as such, although I do not deny that they are related to each other. The types of inter-ethnic relations vary from being integrationist to conflictual (McKay and Lewins, 1991; McKay, 1989). Such studies are relevant to the present study only in so far as they throw light on the ways in which inter-ethnic relationships influence church participation.

The Concept of Ethnicity

Ethnic churches tend to be agents for maintaining ethnicity, but the ways in which ethnicity is maintained vary from one immigrant group to another. The notion of ethnicity is notoriously confused. I wish to draw attention to two different conceptualisations of ethnic identity and behaviour. The first view is that ethnicity is largely determined by common cultural traditions and a sense of identity based largely on the country of origin (Gordon, 1964; Barth, 1969; Schermerhorn, 1970; Greeley, 1971; Isajiw, 1974; Cohen, 1974; Glazer and Moynihan, 1975; Wallman, 1977; Yinger, 1985; Black, 1991). In other words, a group of immigrants may feel, for example, that it is their eating habits, using their mother tongue, and participating in particular customs, that distinguishes them from other groups and which characterises their ethnicity (Barkan, 1991: 95; Alba, 1990). This form of ethnicity derives from clear cultural differences that often stand out after immigration. In this stage, an immigrant group which sustains the culture of the country of origin can be called an ethnic group solely on this basis. It is simply an aggregate or grouping sharing common cultural characteristics.

However, there are other dimensions to the notion of ethnicity which flow from the way in which an ethnic group of the above kind comes to deal with their situation in the host country. This may involve a change from living a culture to one of seeing a culture in new ways. When an immigrant group mobilises for the purpose of gaining advantage in the political processes of the host country, it may become an ethnic group of a different kind. The resulting organisation/ideas may well be something new, even alien, culturally speaking, to the original culture of the immigrants. This may occur when an immigrant group begins to see culture as an abstract political symbol rather than as something to be lived (or merely living it). In this way, the sense of being an ethnic (having an ethnic identity) can be sustained even as the original culture of the ethnic group declines, changes or disappears. This is usually an inter-generational phenomenon.

For example, an Italian immigrant who sustains a way of life brought with him/her from Italy (but who may not even identify as an Italian) is quite different from his/her third generation descendant who has a strong sense of being an Italian in Australia but whose life-style is shaped by specifically Australian as well as Italian norms and practices, although an image of what it means to be Italian in the "old way" will often be strong. Thus, ethnicity can be used to "denote a particular ideological configuration of self-conscious cultural practices" (Eipper, 1983), as well as referring to an immigrant group gathered around a collective ancestry and having a shared past as attributes of the group. To put it in other terms, immigration of people with a shared culture is generally necessary for ethnicity to develop but ethnicity in altered forms can continue long after the immigration process has lost significance (Roosens, 1989).

In this respect, "ethnicity as process" (Lewins, 1975) is a helpful concept, as it offers a way of understanding the complexity of the migrant experience, including the two types of ethnicity mentioned above. According to Lewins (1975: 17), the study of ethnicity needs to take account not only of the nature of the situation of the migrant in the country of origin (also see Matiasz, 1989: 219; Barkan, 1991: 95 and cf. Alba, 1990) but also of the complexity of the migrant's situations in the host society (cf. Aldrich and Waldinger, 1990: 132). Seen in this way, ethnicity is a continuing process in which the migrant generally struggles to achieve better economic and political status (cf. Roosens, 1989). The process of some members in one ethnic group may be one that is oriented towards the country of origin (Hansen, 1952; Abramson, 1975; Alba, 1976; Clark *et al.*, 1976; Gans, 1979; Goering, 1971; Goldstein and Goldscheider, 1968; Greeley, 1974; Isajiw, 1975; Johnson, 1976; Laumann, 1973; Masuda *et al.*, 1970; Masuda *et al.*, 1973; Matsumoto *et al.*, 1970; Nahirny and Fishman, 1965; Roche, 1984; Russo, 1969; Yancey *et al.*, 1976), and sometimes towards the host society (McKay, 1989) or towards something new. The ways in which migrants run through the process vary from one ethnic group to another, depending on the background of the country of origin and the situations in the new country.

While ethnicity among Korean immigrants in Australia needs to be seen as a process where different types of ethnicity are existing, it must be remembered that immigration has only been occurring for two decades. Therefore, the second type of ethnicity has not had a great deal of time to develop and is not of great significance for this study.

Some Theories on Church Growth and Decline

This section is not an attempt to provide a general theory of church growth, but rather an attempt to examine existing church growth theories. The aim is to assist in developing an approach to explain the particular case of church growth among Korean immigrants in Sydney.

Insights will be taken from Currie *et al.* (1977), and also from Hoge and Roozen's (1979a) four-fold categorisation of factors: local institutional factors, local contextual factors, national institutional factors, and national contextual factors (see Diagram 2.1). However, the most important task of this review will be to show the significance of the supply/demand congruence theory of church growth in this study. Further, only relatively short-term trends will be looked at in this study because the central phenomenon of interest in this study has only occurred since the mid 1970s. Moreover, it is not considered necessary to discuss secularisation as a factor influencing church growth during the last few decades, mainly because this study does not equate the church with religion and because a church can grow even as the significance of religion declines.

First of all, the four-fold categorisation of factors will be briefly reviewed, and various other studies regarding church growth will be categorised in a general way under these headings. These studies will be critically assessed and their applicability to the present study examined. Then I will move on to identify what those four factors are in regard to the present study, show how they are inter-connected and how they affect the growth of the Korean immigrant church, and then show the significance of the supply/demand congruence theory of church growth. In so doing, variables and perspectives will also be introduced.

One of the most discussed books in the area of church growth has been *Understanding Church Growth and Decline: 1950-1978* (Hoge and Roozen, 1979b). I will begin here. All the contributors to this book generally agree that multiple factors cause church growth. They make a distinction between two types of factors: those internal to the church (*e.g.*, leadership, theology, evangelism); and those external to the church (*e.g.*, social change, migration), the latter often called contextual factors. Hoge and Roozen (1979c) come to the conclusion that the contextual factors are relatively more important in explaining membership growth or decline. This theory appears to be a general theory one may adopt in explaining the growth of the church in general or the immigrant church in particular. This is because the theory pays particular attention to the influence of the wider society on the church. How applicable, then, is this theory to the present study and does it need to be supplemented?

A problem of Hoge and Roozen's (1979b) book is that it does not recognise that internal factors are not always clearly distinct from external factors. They are often intertwined. Also internal factors are generally considered insignificant. The issue of how institutional factors and external factors influence each other is not explored and the role of the pastor is not given enough importance. Moreover, although various conclusions have been drawn by the different authors in this book, the editors tend to simplify the results. This means that it is misleading in a sense, or at least does not reflect the rich and diverse results of the many researchers in an accurate way. One result is that institutional factors are largely underestimated. After examining research on church trends including McGavran's (1980), Kelley's (1972) and Wagner's (1979, 1981) works, I tend to agree with Hoge and Roozen (1979c: 327) to a large degree, that "action-oriented church analysts and consultants tend to estimate the weight of local institutional factors more highly than the best research would warrant". Nevertheless, I would argue that Hoge and Roozen's underestimation of institutional factors needs to be corrected.

In conceptualising the possible factors influencing church growth or decline, Hoge and Roozen suggest four categories (see Diagram 2.1). This categorisation is primarily based on the general agreement that some variables are relatively more changeable by the intention of church members. These are classified as institutional. Others, beyond their control, are classified as contextual.

Diagram 2.1: Four-fold categorisation of factors influencing church growth as proposed by Hoge and Roozen (1979c)

Local-Institutional Factors Type of leadership, program, management of tensions, life-style of the local congregation, *etc.*	**Local-Contextual Factors** Affluence of the community, presence of middle-class residential neighbourhoods near the church, *etc.*
National-Institutional Factors Denomination-wide characteristics (*e.g.*, polity, theological orientation, moral teachings and standards)	**National-Contextual Factors** Demography, secularisation. industrialisation, urbanisation economic conditions, politics, *etc.*

Research Emphasising Local Institutional Factors [10]

Local institutional factors are composed of the life-style of a local congregation, type of leadership and program, and management of tensions, *etc.* — over which members have some degree of choice.

The homogeneous unit principle (motivation for growth, growth orientation). This homogeneous unit principle was enunciated by McGavran (1970, 1980) and further developed by Wagner (1979).

McGavran and Arn (1976: 76-77) point out that "Growing congregations are usually composed primarily of the 'same kind' of people, with others, of course, cordially welcome. The conglomerate church made up of different segments, about equally distributed, is generally a non-growing church." McGavran and Arn (1976: 115) also suggest that those churches intending to grow apply the knowledge of the world — of sociology, geography, *etc.* — in line with biblical principles. They seem to suggest that the whole motivation or drive derives from God but that church growth can be achieved by utilising this-worldly knowledge. Sociologically speaking, it seems clear that the intention or motivation to grow is a factor growing out of those *people*, instead of God, who are ambitious to expand their church — which is internal to the church — whether or not they claim that there is a heavenly command or support for the growth. That McGavran and Arn's theory tends to cling to theological problematics becomes evident, in their dealing with evangelism and social action, when they argue that

> People say that unless we solve these problems, we don't have a credible witness. I have difficulty with that argument. It overlooks the meaningful Christian witness in our country, perhaps particularly in suburbia. I grant you there are problems in North America — poverty, prejudice, hatred — but we get nowhere by overstating the matter. ... Let "Suburban Church" continue social action but not make the capital mistake of saying, "We can't do any evangelism until we do a lot more social action." "Suburban Church," to have the greatest joy in Christian life, should be passing on Christ. *It must do more evangelism.* (1973: 166, 167, my italics)

The emphasis on evangelism by McGavran and Arn (1973: 167) and later by Wagner (1981) leads us to Kelley's (1972, 1977) "strict church" approach, which argues that evangelical or strict churches grow. This will be discussed shortly. All of these writers tend to concentrate on institutional factors rather than contextual ones. The theory of the homogeneous unit principle, that is, a church is more likely to grow if the members share socio-cultural homogeneity, has received much criticism from the Christian ethical point of view, as it can rule out the "other kind of people" and accept only "our kind". Nevertheless, the situation predicted by this can be observed among Korean immigrant churches in Australia and elsewhere, where with a few exceptions no one from other ethnic backgrounds is found.

Along with Kelley's "strict church" approach, Roof *et al.* (1979: 216) agree that "demands on members and conservative theology relate positively to growth", but their general conclusions do not support Kelley's thesis. For example, they argue that isolation from the wider culture, this being a critical aspect of Kelley's concern for the church's distinctive meaning system, can be negatively associated with growth. The growing Presbyterian congregations studied by Roof *et al.* have been closely identified with the culture and community of which they are a part. Roof *et al.* also mention that "overall satisfaction of the laity with church worship and program, and congregational harmony and cooperation" are influential factors in the growth of Presbyterian congregations in the USA. According to Carroll (1978: 80), such satisfaction has to do with "the pastor's preaching, leadership of public worship, sensitivity to people's needs, capacity to generate enthusiasm, ability to deal with conflict, and spiritual authenticity and maturity".

As people in Korean society generally pay high respect to the learned, better qualified ministers tend to attract and maintain more members, something which has produced the tendency to pursue doctoral studies among Korean ministers. According to a survey carried out by *Mokhoe-wa Sinhak* (or *Ministry and Theology*, cited in *Tonga Ilbo*, 5 Aug. 1990) with a sample of 246 Protestant churchgoers in Korea, the pastor's preaching is considered the most important factor in selecting a church: (37.8%). Other factors are: the church's involvement in social service and charity (20.3%); the church's interest in evangelism and mission (17.5%); the mood of the service (14.2%); and geographical closeness of the church (10.2%). Olson (1989: 445) finds, however, in his study of five Baptist congregations in the United States, that although satisfaction with the quality of preaching is a significant predictor of continued attendance, the role of friendships made at church is also significant; but, it is not easy to draw a close link between Olson's study and this study. This is because Olson has been able to compare growing churches with declining churches, and also to compare long established churches with newly organised ones, whereas most Korean churches in Sydney have not been long established, and have been steadily growing. Nonetheless, the expansion of Korean immigrant churches appears to depend in part upon the minister's capacity, and the quality of preaching may be important here. The role of church friendships should also be considered as an influential factor in the growth of Korean churches in Sydney, as they are one of the most important centres where the development and maintenance of friendships among Koreans occurs.

Stark and Bainbridge (1985, 1987) and Bainbridge (1990: 1288) offer a similar view. According to what they call social bond theory, individuals associate with particular congregations and stay there as a result of establishing strong attachments to fellow members. Similarly,

Roof's (1978) local-cosmopolitan theory of religious plausibility maintains that the stability of social relationships encourages faith and church membership, and thus that church membership rate will be high where rates of geographical mobility are low. A further prediction of Roof's theory is that in smaller cities there should be higher church membership than in larger ones. However, church growth among Korean migrants has been observed mostly in large cities in the USA, Canada, and Australia. Once they have reached Australia, the great majority of Korean immigrants reside in Sydney and they are not highly mobile geographically. The latter factor is presumably conducive to the growth of Korean ethnic churches.

The importance of the clergy needs to be stressed once again. Roof *et al.* (1979: 222) argue that "given the complexities of the factors involved, clergy should not be singled out as primarily responsible for the trends in question". However, the clergy are significant in explaining the central issue under examination in this study. Many researchers, such as Wagner (1979: 270-287), have indicated the significance of pastoral leadership in the life of congregations. Wagner concludes that church growth is due to the motivation of the clergy to expand the church and their willingness to pay the price, the laity's commitment to outreach and congregational activities, a large enough size of congregation to perform the functions required by church members, socio-cultural "homogeneity" among the church members, and an involvement in evangelistic efforts directed at culturally homogeneous groups. Wagner's conclusion describes many aspects of the churches in Korea and overseas Korean churches. It is important to note that institutional factors are not always completely free from contextual factors, but are inter-related with them. As will be shown later, the roles of pastors within each congregation have been unusually significant in the process of church growth among Koreans and these roles have been largely determined by external factors. In other words, it is actually national contextual factors which have brought about the phenomenon of religio-economic entrepreneurship[11].

Some scholars have discarded local institutional factors, but, as has been discussed above with reference to the growth of the churches in Korea and overseas Korean churches, this is unwarranted. This also applies to national institutional factors.

Research Emphasising National Institutional Factors

National institutional factors include denomination-wide characteristics such as organisational structure, theological orientation, moral teachings and standards, new church development, and mission emphases. Some observers point out that such factors are crucial in explaining denominational growth or decline.

The "strict church" theory of growth. Kelley's (1972, 1977) theories of church growth, mainly concerning why liberal churches have stopped growing, have been of much interest to those inquiring into church growth. He is firstly concerned with whether churches are organisationally strong or weak. He argues that organisational strength or vitality is closely related to growth and derives from traits of strictness, whereas traits of indulgence are associated with organisational weakness.[12] Absolutism, conformity, and fanaticism are observed among strict churches; relativism, diversity, and dialogue among liberal churches. Members of conservative churches have missionary zeal, with an eagerness to deliver the "good news" to all persons. Liberal denominations, on the other hand, have only a "dilute and undemanding form of meaning." According to Kelley, the ecumenical movement, which most liberal leaders have supported, is itself a sign of the dilution of meaning in the liberal churches. He argues that mainline churches have failed to meet the needs of their members and have offered ambiguous answers to questions considered ultimate. Strict churches, by offering certitude, tend to grow.

In contrast to Kelley's argument, Carroll (1978: 80) contends that there is little evidence that "growing local congregations are more conservative theologically than declining ones". Hadaway (1980) suggests that conservativism is somewhat more strongly associated with "sharing faith" than with higher levels of recruitment and that neither strictness nor intolerance, by themselves, explains church growth. Further, the most serious limit of Kelley's thesis is that his theorising is concerned purely with institutional factors, virtually ignoring the social or historical context or any other contextual factors (Hoge, 1979: 180). Kelley (1972: 91) does, however, at least at one point, simply note the possibility that changes in the whole social context may have affected some denominational stances. In fact, Kelley (1977: vii) himself reports in the preface to the second edition of his book that in 1973 three conservative denominations — the Presbyterian Church in the U.S., the Lutheran Church-Missouri Synod, and the Christian Reformed Church — peaked in membership and began to decline. Hoge and Roozen (1979c: 329) also argue that membership decline had occurred among some Protestant denominations of moderate and conservative theology during the last few years of the 1970s. This indicates that the situation is more complex than is acknowledged in Kelley's main thesis about strictness.

Currie *et al.* (1977: 37, 98) argue that

> ... while each church is itself a factor in determining its own growth by its specific recruitment policies, standards of discipline, and so on, the environment in which it operates is a still more influential factor. ... Church policy does therefore seem to be only one, and perhaps not the most significant, factor in church growth. Indeed it seems probable that, whatever efforts are expended by a church, increased recruitment cannot be obtained in unfavourable exogenous conditions.

Institutional factors do have some explanatory power, but I shall show that they only partially explain church growth among Koreans in Sydney. In addition, while institutional factors are heavily influenced by contextual ones, this study attempts to draw out the sources of the growth of Korean churches from Korean ethnic cultures as well as from the social contexts of Australian society. The latter are important because they largely influence the ways in which Koreans are forced to adjust after migration.

Research Emphasising Local Contextual Factors [13]

As mentioned earlier, local contextual factors are those beyond the control of the congregation. The local contextual factors contributing to mainline Protestant church growth are, for example, "affluence of the community, presence of middle-class residential neighbourhoods near the church, percent homeowners near the church, absence of minorities in the neighbourhood, and absence of other Protestant churches nearby" (Hoge and Roozen, 1979c: 324). Hoge (1979: 193) aptly points out that contextual factors should be seen as causally prior to institutional ones. Institutional factors, of course, also influence contextual ones to a degree.

Roof *et al.* (1979: 207), in their study of the growth and decline of United Presbyterian Churches, have similarly pointed to several important contextual variables positively influencing church growth: congregations located in affluent rather than in poor communities; overall demographic increase (*i.e.*, increasing numbers of young people, families, newcomers); the location of congregations in primarily residential areas rather than in the areas of, or near, public schools, banks or markets; and less interdenominational competition. Roof *et al.* have suggested that "affluence" and "favourable demographic shifts" are relatively more important than others. More direct support comes from Olson (1989) who finds, in a study of five Baptist congregations, that the fastest growing church was located in one of the fastest growing suburbs, but that none of the non-growing churches was located in a growing community. Significantly, the rate of church growth in Korea has been greatest in the expanding metropolitan areas. Whether Korean ethnic churches in Sydney have been in areas experiencing population growth is a matter which requires examination.

Research Emphasising National Contextual Factors

Numerous observers such as Weber (1963), Niebuhr (1957), and McGavran (1970) note that in modern church history there is a correlation between the age of a denomination and the lack of growth. Similarly, Currie, Gilbert, and Horsley (1977: 37) argue that contextual factors are more important than institutional factors in explaining this. This is because the life of a congregation or denomination reflects its socio-historical context.

Roozen and Carroll (1979: 21-41), Hoge and Roozen (1979b: 315-333), and Bodycomb (1984) have pointed to "functional alternatives" as a profound contextual factor which influences church trends. In seeking to explain why theologically conservative churches have continued to grow while liberal churches have declined since the mid-1960s, Roozen and Carroll (1979: 38) state that "the mainline denominations, long without much sway over members' beliefs, are losing persons to competing, more secular sources of fellowship or belonging."

A study by Currie *et al.* (1977) shows that institutional factors such as church policies and recruitment strategies can make a difference in the short term, but, in the long run, contextual factors such as demography, secularisation, industrialisation, urbanisation, economic conditions, politics and war are more important. Although Currie *et al.* (1977: 41) occasionally recognise the importance of institutional factors, for example, when they argue that church growth is often the consequence of the combinations of endogenous and exogenous factors, they underestimate institutional (endogenous) factors. In this regard, Currie *et al.* share many ideas with Hoge and Roozen (1979c). While emphasising contextual factors, Currie *et al.* argue that periods of social stress do not produce great church growth and that there can be growth at times of social stability. Interestingly, Korean immigrant churches have grown when the members have been under stresses, although Australian society has been relatively stable. This makes it important to discuss the experiences of immigrant Koreans and the ways in which these experiences contribute to the growth of their churches. I will ask questions such as: what has the Korean church offered Korean immigrants in Sydney and what are Korean migrants seeking through participation in church activities?

Currie *et al.* (1977: 8, 39, 43, 44), on the basis of their statistics, stress that church growth displays a cyclical pattern: depression, activation, revival, deactivation, and declension. The growth of Korean churches in Sydney, however, has taken place constantly since the start of immigration in 1974, and it is thus premature to predict what kind of cycles will occur. Although the history of the growth of Korean churches in the United States is somewhat longer than that in Sydney, they too have grown more or less constantly. This in part suggests that any decline of the Korean immigrant churches may be some way off.

Church historians have also examined social and cultural changes that seem to help explain church trends. The works of Ahlstrom (1970; 1972; 1978) and Marty (1976) are examples. Ahlstrom's *A Religious History of the American People*, is an attempt at a history of American religious life during the four-hundred-year period from the time when the Reformation was more or less established until the 1960s. He seeks both to set his religious theme in a specifically social context and to reassess the whole of American religious experience. The diversity of American religious movements is portrayed with specific reference to the social contexts — demographic, economic, political, sociological and psychological — which influence their development. What makes his writing significant for this study is that Ahlstrom looks not only at the national contextual factors but also at the international level within the frame of world history. Likewise, in this study I will argue that the growth of Korean ethnic churches in Sydney cannot be properly understood without reference to processes occurring within Korea, as well as to contextual factors within Australia.

Another Explanation of Church Growth: Supply/Demand Congruence Theory [14]

Supply/demand congruence theory derives from a market metaphor and has some similarities to those approaches emphasising local contextual factors, especially the effects of community demographics (Roof *et al.*, 1979; McKinney, 1979; Walrath, 1979; Hadaway, 1981; McKinney and Hoge, 1983) where demographics refers to a "market", "the pool of potential churchgoers available to a congregation" (Olson, 1989: 432). On the other hand, it differs from those studies in that it more fully considers the interaction between internal and external factors. Currie *et al.* (1977: 119) note that "It can be argued that a church's very existence is the product of demand for it, however unconsciously and incoherently expressed, by a part of a population."

While an understanding of growth cannot be reduced entirely to supply/demand factors, I shall argue that these are of considerable importance in explaining the growth of Korean ethnic churches. Indeed, supply/demand congruence theory can incorporate many of the points already discussed.

The increase in demand for the need of the church (irrespective of whether the demand is from churchgoers or from non-churchgoers) would lead churches to supply more services or result in the establishment of more churches. Although Bodycomb (1984: 206) argues that a high degree of supply/demand congruence (that is, both supply and demand are high) brings about church growth and a high degree of incongruence produces stability or decline,[15] demand, as is the case with the economic principle of supply/demand, may be manipulated by controlling supply. For example, when there is an adequate supply of ministers to meet new demand, and they establish churches and provide appropriate services or functions, the church will grow. This approach has been extensively discussed by Currie *et al.* (1977: 7) who argue that

> in so far as church-membership growth can be attributed to a supply-and-demand relationship, in which membership facilities are supplied by a church and demanded by a recruitable population, the external constituency probably acts on the church to produce demand-induced supply, while the church probably acts upon the internal constituency to produce supply-induced demand.

One significant matter is the supply of ministers. Ministers may be over-supplied because of various reasons. Churches in Korea have been often established because of an over-supply of ministers, especially after 1960. In many cases, theological colleges have admitted students who have failed to get into the non-theological colleges of their choice (Clark, 1986: 27). Most of the students have been in their early twenties and some of them have not chosen theological training out of a sense of mission. They know, however, that to be a member of the clergy in Korea carries some economic and social status. Furthermore, in Korean society, a student's future career is often directed by his/her parents rather than by himself/herself. This makes some Christian parents strongly urge one or two of their sons to undertake theological training and become members of the clergy. To put it simply, there has been not only much demand from people in Korea for ministers, but an abundant supply. The reasons why Koreans have been responsive to Christianity will be discussed in Part II. Theological graduates have kept on establishing churches and they have been able to recruit members from other established churches or through conversion. This has been largely due to the hard work of the minister and the laity involved.

Wuthnow (1987: 62) correctly points out that when studying the growth of a religious group one should consider both the demand side and the supply side. An increase in church membership is not only the result of successful recruitment of newcomers and of an increasing demand from the mass, but also the result of establishing new churches and of recruiting more members into existing churches. However, the supply/demand congruence approach seems to have remained largely in the form of a theoretical assumption without being employed in detail in empirical study, the main exception being the work by Currie *et al.* (1977). In this study, I will look at the kinds of social contexts under which demand for, and supply of, the church or its services bring about growth.

The supply/demand approach seems to go a considerable way towards explaining why so many Korean ethnic churches have come to be established. It is also important to examine the question of why and how they have been able to maintain and increase their membership. In order to answer this question, it is necessary to examine the supply of, and demand for, functions served by the churches. We need especially to look at the Korean church as an organisation with political, ethnic, religious, and economic dimensions as has been mentioned in this chapter. It is necessary to find out what functions have been served by the churches, and the extent to which church members have been attracted by these. Some of these functions will be discussed later. As will be shown, the supply/demand approach offers some key variables in explaining the central phenomenon under examination.

Notes

[1] The aim of this policy was to lead churches in the mission field to be "independent, self-reliant, and aggressive native churches" (cf. Kim Ill-soo, 1985).

[2] This question requires a comparative study of those Koreans (Christians and non-Christians) who have migrated and those who have not migrated.

[3] David W. Deshler was one of the agents who recruited labourers to work on Hawaiian sugar plantations. He was responsible for the immigration of the first group of Koreans to Hawaii in 1903 (Kim Hyung-chan, 1977b).

4 Christians here refer to a) nominal Christians or b) people going to Christian churches.

5 Economic aspects of Korean ethnic churches in the United States were also acknowledged by Dearman (1982: 175) when she argues that "the fact that a high percentage of the churches were established by ministers again demonstrates the high level of religious entrepreneurship among the immigrants". However, what she means by religious entrepreneurship is not entirely clear, although one could assume that it refers to ministers' high level of interest in church ministry.

6 They consist of a) those who arrived in the US as theology students and obtained their higher education in American seminaries, b) ministers who immigrated at the invitation of the Korean churches in the US and c) "visitors to the higher denominational institutions in the US" (Kim Ill-soo, 1981: 198).

7 Both dissertations were submitted for the degree of Doctor of Ministry, San Francisco Theological Seminary.

8 Although those subject matters were once understood as the earliest form of the sect-denomination-church development process (Nelson, 1968; Yinger, 1970), they are now understood as separate and distinct types of religious phenomena (Becker, 1932; Nottingham, 1971; Hargrove, 1979; McGuire, 1981).

9 In my adoption of Black's definition, "sacred" is not used in Durkheimian terms. The society is not considered sacred in this thesis, whereas it is so in the work of Durkheim (1965).

10 It is not easy to distinguish those studies emphasising local institutional factors from the studies emphasising national institutional factors, because there is a close interaction between national and local institutional factors (especially the former influencing the latter).

11 What I mean by this was briefly indicated in the section of the growth of the Korean church in the US in this chapter. More careful definition will be given in the following chapter. One may regard "religio-economic entrepreneurship" as an institutional factor. But, a significant aspect of this research is that it attempts to show the ways in which institutional, contextual, national, and local factors are inter-linked in the case of Korean churches.

12 These factors are related to the religious and political dimensions of a church which were discussed above.

13 Hoge and Roozen (1979b: 373) classified family size as contextual, since their "research has identified some strong determinants of family size not easily influenced by churches." However, family size is excluded from the discussion, because it seems that this factor has not influenced the growth of churches in Korea and overseas Korean churches at least for the

last few decades — though the birthrate among the members of Korean immigrant church may influence church trends in the future.

[14] Bodycomb (1984) notes this approach as a macro-level approach. It could be applied at micro-level too.

[15] If both supply and demand are low (*i.e.*, another way of being congruent), non-growth or decline may be observed.

Chapter 3

Theoretical Perspective and Methodology

The Church as a Multi-Dimensional Institution and the Consequences for Church Growth

I noted, in chapter 2, that growth comes about because the church provides a diversity of services (practices, ideas, income, helping a family to adjust to a new place, maintaining ethnicity, *etc*.) and because people pursue these through church participation. To put this differently and to use an economic analogy, church growth is most likely to occur when the degree of both demand for, and supply of, church services, is high. Religious services are only part of what a church supplies (Hertzler, 1948; Winter, 1962: 97, 99; Moberg, 1962; Winter, 1968). Consequently I will grant religion no ontological or epistemological priority in this study. Instead I will regard the church as a multi-dimensional institution. As noted earlier, many writers have presented the church as an institution with diverse dimensions. However, this has not been clearly conceptualised in a way which brings out the relevance of this for inquiry into church growth and decline.

A church can be the site of, for example, religious, ethnic, political and economic activity or a combination of these. Most churches are concerned not only with faith, hope, and charity, but also with education, welfare and health care (Boylen, 1991: 10). When the church is part of the daily life of its members, it is not possible to separate religious activity in the church from economic, political, and other activities (Yinger, 1970: 412). To put this differently, what a church is, or what a church generally does, cannot be understood by an examination of religious activities alone nor by just looking at socio-political activities (cf. Thung, 1977: 163). These dimensions are often not easily distinguishable, but an attempt at this needs to be made for analytical purposes.

To clarify how the church is a multi-dimensional institution I will use the university as an analogy because it is more widely regarded as a complex institution. A university is generally seen as an educational institution, but not as a centre of *education* only. Some students come to the university out of academic interest without any concern for their present or future income, some come to gain a credential for an occupation, some to have a good time or because their parents force them, and some for a mixture of these reasons. Some people work there as academics who may be primarily interested in their salary and career rather than teaching. Some people are employed as gardeners and some as administrators. Some locals living around the university are interested in having access to the sports facilities of the university. Some executive officers, although they might have been involved in teaching and research in the past, now focus on administrative or political matters, and have relatively little interest in things academic. Similarly, churches have a number of dimensions, of which four will be focused on in this study: the religious, the ethnic (specifically in the case of ethnic church), the economic and the political (cf. Hong Pansik, 1986: 8; Moberg, 1962: 134, 135).

Each dimension, or a combination of them, will influence whether a church grows, declines or is stable. Whilst the church is multi-dimensional, its different dimensions (or functions) can be used to look at sources of growth. The church's diverse dimensions show us what churchgoers seek (the demand aspect) as well as what a church provides for its members and why this is provided (supply aspect).

The Religious Dimension

As mentioned earlier, religion in this study refers to "a system of concepts, feelings, attitudes and practices with a supernatural, sacred or ultimate point of reference" (Black, 1978: 282). Some of the religious aspects or activities that occur within a church are: listening to sermons, praying, other ritual activities (*e.g.*, baptism, holy communion, hymn singing), and religious experiences (*e.g.*, conversion). Some of these activities are purely religious in their motives, but some are not always necessarily so, depending on the person and the situation.

Just as religion can be fully integrated into the cultural, economic, and organisational way of life for some people (Driedger, 1989: 207-208), a church often has implications for the life of a group. Take, as an example, a sermon about a matter relevant to this study. Often sermons may regard the life of immigrants as similar to that of prophets, like Jesus, Jacob, or Moses, who had to migrate. In doing so, the sermon encourages the immigrants to overcome the difficulties that stem from migration. There is a migrant theology which entails such a perspective (Hong Kŭnsu, 1986; Hong, 1988; Lee Sang-taek, 1988). Such a theology is not just religious, but is often also about ethnicity, economic survival or political resistance.[1] The religious side of church activity should not, however, be under-estimated (cf. Currie *et al.*, 1977: 6).

Smart (1984) suggests that religion generally has the following aspects: doctrinal, mythological, ethical, ritual, experiential, and social. These six aspects are observed not only in Western religions but also in other world religions.

The first three aspects deal with what are broadly called "beliefs" and "express a religion's claims about the nature of the invisible world" and about its aims for how people's lives ought to be shaped (Smart, 1984: 10). The *doctrinal* aspect recognises that the world religions draw some of their living power from their successful display of a total picture of ultimate reality, through a coherent system of doctrines. The *mythological* aspect consists of sacred stories in one form or another. Smart (1984: 15) notes that there are two aspects to the mythological dimension: historical myths, that is to say, stories concerning the sacred which have an anchorage in history; and non-historical myths, those that have no such anchorage. The term "myth" is not used to imply that the content is false. Though the distinction between the doctrinal and the mythological dimension is not easy to draw, the mythological aspect is typically more colourful, symbolic, picturesque, and story-like than the doctrinal one. The third dimension, the *ethical* dimension, concerns beliefs about a code of ethics, moral duty, the values an adherent is taught to live by, and so on.

The next three aspects suggested by Smart deal with what can broadly be called "practices" (Black and Glasner, 1983: 183). The *ritual* aspect has to do with activities like worship, fasting, offerings, prayers,

participation in special sacraments, and the like, through which religion
is often expressed. Rituals range from the very simple to the highly
elaborate. The *experiential* aspect comprises such experiences,
emotions, or feelings as conversion, divine illumination, spirit
possession, and so on. For example, a pious Christian believes that
God speaks to people in an intimate way and that the individual can and
does have an inner experience of God (Smart, 1984). The *social* aspect
refers to the various social structures and interpersonal relationships
involved in the transmission and maintenance of the other aspects of
religion.

For purposes of analysis, I treat Smart's first five aspects as all
part of the religious dimension of the church. I examine his sixth aspect
(*i.e.*, the social aspect) in terms of three dimensions of the church: the
ethnic, the economic and the political.

The Ethnic Dimension

The issue of ethnicity arises in this book because the case study is
of a church which consists of immigrants. Ethnicity is the setting of
one group off from others in a particular way. This may involve a focus
on such features as heritage, national origin, and language. Religion is
often involved here, so the distinction between ethnicity and religion is
sometimes a difficult one to make in practice. Sometimes religion is at
the core of ethnicity (*e.g.*, Judaism in the Jewish community in the
United States[2]). Whether religion itself has an ability to sustain
ethnicity has not been clear (Alba, 1990; Herberg, 1955). However, an
ethnic religious *institution* or ethnic church seems to be able to do so at
least for a few generations of an ethnic group. The sort of ethnicity
observed within the Lutheran church in Australia or in its relationship
with the larger society differs from that in Germany or in other
countries. A church can act as an agency to preserve the culture of a
group, to maintain friendships among people of a similar background,
or to enable them to sustain an identity (cf. Driedger, 1989: 55). Some
ethnic activities are confined within the church, while some are intended
to influence, or to express ethnicity to, the wider society. Both of these
need to be kept in mind. As ethnic resources differ from one immigrant
community to another, it is useful to examine the ways in which the
ethnic church uses its resources to react to the needs or interests of the
immigrants and their children. The demands immigrants make on the
church and their attempts to shape it in various ways are also
important. Further, it is useful to look at what sorts of ethnic resources
make the immigrant church of one ethnic group distinctive from those
of other ethnic groups.

The church can be an institution through or within which the ethnicity of immigrants is maintained. Greeley (1972: 125) argues that "[i]n the United States the churches came to serve an ethnic role; they helped sort out 'who one was' in a bewilderingly complex society. As a result the various denominations have been immeasurably strengthened, as they serve not only a religious need, but a social [ethnic] one as well."

The kinds of ethnicity which are seen to be important to maintain differ from one ethnic group to another. Jupp (1988: 165) argues that "different [ethnic] communities [in Australia] may variously define their 'core values'. Poles or Ukrainians stress language maintenance, Greeks and Jews stress in-marriage, Chinese and Italians the family structure, and Irish and Lebanese religious denomination". The ethnicity of different immigrant groups is based on the origin of nationality to a large degree (Alba, 1990). In other words, ethnicity often overlaps with nationalism, and the ethnicity of the descendants of immigrants is often linked to the original nationality of their forebears. While the church reinforces the cohesion and identity of immigrants, it may slow down the process of getting access to the central social institutions and the resources that go with this; thus the ethnic church may work as a "mobility trap" (Greeley, 1972; Hurh and Kim, 1990). While the church is the most significant centre of ethnic cohesion for some migrants, it is not so for other migrants. When the Lutheran church was first established in Australia, "Germanness" used to be vividly observed within the church[3]. However, going to a Lutheran church today is much like going to an Anglo-Australian church in terms of whether we can observe a particular ethnic identity. That is, the ethnic dimension of the Lutheran church is now of minor significance. This shows that the ethnic aspect of church life is subject to change.

Briefly, a church can be an institution which maintains the culture or identity of an ethnic group (*i.e.*, churchgoers) and/or an institution for enhancing a particular ethnic group's interest against others. A church may also be employed to represent an ethnic group in the wider society. In such a case, how a church acts, how it is perceived or treated by the wider society, can greatly affect it, including whether it grows or declines.

The Political Dimension

A church is an organisation which always has a political dimension. The linkage between church growth and politics (internal or external) is complex. Sometimes an authoritarian style of administration will lead to growth, sometimes not. When the church is

linked to a successful political movement, growth may result, only to
drop when the movement becomes successful. For example, Polish
churches in which political mobilisation was a central interest of the
church members during the 70s and 80s have been declining recently.

It is not easy to establish and maintain a distinction between the
political and the economic dimension. The latter often appears to be
political because economic concerns are expressed or negotiated through
political procedures. The financial aspects of a church are closely related
to, and sometimes dependent upon, internal and external politics. In this
book, the political dimension of the church has to do, for example,
with struggles to stop a dictatorship, or to change national policy, or to
bring about a different type of governing structure or church polity. The
church's economic dimension concerns such matters as church finances,
the minister's wage, charity, financial support for the poor, economic
equality/inequality, poverty, economic recession, and attempts to
change national economic policy.

I will look at various aspects of the political dimension. Churches
maintain some political aspects (*e.g.*, church polity) for the sake of
maintaining their own order. Ministers of organised churches spend a
bulk of their time on various types of decision-making and control of
administration. An ordained minister today is often a director rather than
just a preacher or priest (Winter, 1962: 100). H. R. Niebuhr *et al.*
(1956: 90) have aptly described such a pastor as a "pastoral director" or
a "democratic pastoral administrator". The way in which the church
performs these aspects or expresses the characteristics of, say, church
polity, varies from church to church and from denomination to
denomination and also from one era to another (Yinger, 1970: 362;
Bouma, 1991).

The church doctrines may be shaped not only by religious concerns
but also by a political agenda. When a church is deeply concerned with
justice and extends this concern to the wider society, the political
aspects of the church are outwardly expressed. The church may also
stand against an oppressive regime, and fight for political freedoms and
human rights.

Some church activities may be oriented to local or national
political activities. Churches sometimes function as a political pressure
group within the larger society. For example, some church groups try
to use the state to enforce a particular moral principle (cf. Berger, 1961:
70). The so-called Moral Majority in the United States, especially
during the Reagan period, tried to get the state to legislate in line with
their morality. To take another example, when a church is the central
site of the ethnic activities of an immigrant group, it tends to represent
the ethnic group in a political form in the larger society.

The Economic Dimension

Another significant aspect of the church is its economy. The economic dimension of a church is important not only for its own existence but also for its involvement in society at large. Churches react to the economic conditions of the society in which they exist. Members of society sometimes get involved in church activities for economic reasons (Douglass and Brunner, 1935; Winter, 1962, 1968; Yinger, 1970). Church growth may be closely related to economic aspects.

Now, I will discuss the internal aspect of the church's economic dimension. The church, for its own well-being, needs some form of income to maintain staff and buildings, and to support the activities it undertakes. The ways in which churches manage these matters vary from one to another. In their sermons or teaching to their members, some churches heavily emphasise members' financial contributions whereas others hardly mention such matters. Some depend almost entirely on tithing or direct giving from members, while others derive a significant part of their income from investments of one kind or another.

A church can also function as a place which caters to its members' economic or financial needs or as a place in which members interact with each other for their mutual financial benefit. In some cases, the primary reasons for attending church may be to attract more customers or maintain friendly relations with other members in order to become more prosperous. Some businessmen seek employees in the ethnic church as they are interested in cheap labour or particular skills such as language or employing people they trust. Church members are often more prepared to work for a fellow churchgoer and some businessmen may be interested in employing those who hold a "Christian belief".

A number of commercial businesses (*e.g.*, radio stations) are owned by churches (Boylen, 1991: 11) sometimes for religious reasons or economic gain or both, or for political influence. The Catholic, Anglican, and Uniting Churches and the Salvation Army in Australia employ a paid work force of more than 200,000 (quoted in Boylen, 1991: 10), including clergy, religious staff, and those who work for hospitals, schools.

The church is an institution from which clergy and others make their living. Some churches offer clergy a generous income, whereas others do not or cannot afford to. This can bring about a change in the attitudes of pastors or priests towards their ministry or affect those who plan to be involved in the ministry. This does not imply that financial reward is the only factor which influences attitudes of clergy or potential clergy.

The chance of securing a position in the ministry after necessary theological training may be easily available in one society but be very competitive in another. The profession of the clergy is more attractive in one society than in another. Such conditions can characterise some of the economic aspects of the church.

Non-believers who have tried to benefit from attending a church may soon leave the church with or without economic gain; it is also possible that they become regular members of the church irrespective of any economic gain. They may eventually come to experience religious conversion or remain as recruits or be drawn into ethnic or political activities.

Churches are often also concerned about economic matters in the broader society. Poor people who oppose the economic structure of the wider society may be attracted to, or encouraged to join, a church that puts much emphasis on liberation theology. The role of capitalism has been under attack from many churches for a long time. This may be illustrated by Yi Sam'yŏl (1984) who suggests that the modern economy tends to exploit human labour, which leads to dehumanisation, and it is up to the church to point out the problem. In other cases, various churches have advocated capitalism.

Churches can be places where people go to solve basic but significant practical problems, such as finding accommodation, employment, and various community services (including interpreting services in the case of some immigrants). Some of these may be solved through the help of other members of a church who have found ways to cope (cf. Jenkins, 1983; Jenkins, 1988: 2). These instrumental needs are closely related to economic interests.

Religio-Economic Entrepreneurship as a Significant Factor in Church Growth

In this section, I will outline what is meant by "religio-economic entrepreneurship" in this book. Religio-economic activity is a combination of religious and economic activities undertaken by professional clergy and members of a church. The term "religious entrepreneurship" has been used by Dearman (1982: 175) in her study of the Korean immigrant church in the United States, where she argues that "the fact that high percentage of the churches were established by ministers demonstrates the high level of religious entrepreneurship among the immigrant ministers". However, as mentioned in chapter 2, she does not develop this idea in any detail.

It has been a tradition of many churches to meet the clergy's financial requirements by extracting a portion of the laity's income. Religious aspirations often combine with non-religious, financial or ownership aspirations among the clergy (Yinger, 1970: 353). Turner (1983: 90) notes that Weber's view of religion involves the assumption that "there is an exchange relationship [both economic and religious] between the virtuosi and the mass" (my addition). Thus, the clergy serves the "mass" and the "mass" contributes various forms of payment to the clergy who do, therefore, not have to make a living in the market place. Of course, the clergy's ministerial service is not necessarily religious only, but can be ethnic, political or economic as well.

Luhmann (quoted in Thung, 1977: 152) suggests that because it employs functionaries such as clergy and administrators, the church can be regarded as an organisation in which a market situation prevails between the functionaries and the members (also see Iannaccone, 1992). Sometimes, the clergy may feel that the standard of living possible with their income and their social status are insufficient. Accordingly, not many people may regard the occupation of clergy as an attractive career. In other cases clergy may be well paid or have considerable prestige and the competition to get into this occupation may become high. The extent to which the occupation is seen as prestigious or not varies from one society to another, from one church to another, and also from one era to another. In other words, it largely depends on the socio-economic, cultural and historical background of each society. What is argued here is that the birth of religio-economic entrepreneurship depends on the social settings of each society.

Some theological graduates may be forced to get involved in a church ministry to make a living despite their ambition to follow a different career, because of the specialisation of theological training which makes it minimally relevant for other careers. Whether or not this really does apply and whether or not a theological graduate would be easily absorbed into occupations other than religious or theological sectors are again dependent upon the social contexts of each society.

Religio-economic entrepreneurship shares some of the characteristics of the modern marketing promoted in the 1950s. This is because, apart from the usual meaning of "marketing" which conjures up selling, influencing and persuading, the core of this concept of marketing is to serve and satisfy the needs of the customer (Kotler and Levy, 1969: 15; Levitt, 1960: 45-46), just as meeting the needs of churchgoers is an important task of the religio-economic entrepreneur. "The Entrepreneur Model" of cult innovation in the article, "Three

Models of Cult Formation" (Stark and Bainbridge, 1985: 178-188), throws some light on religio-economic entrepreneurship. Members of cults are usually keen to recruit people in order to sustain their organisation or to invite others to religious conversion. Door-to-door visits or friendship networks are often used for this purpose. However, the entrepreneurial model seeks the origin of cult formation or growth by looking primarily at the business or entrepreneurial aspects of cults, thus neglecting or under-estimating the religious aspects of the groups. The perspective of religio-economic entrepreneurship adopted in this book seeks to avoid this by taking into account both the religious and the business/financial aspects of churches.

Wilken (1979: 59) suggests that it is possible to delineate types of entrepreneurship other than economic entrepreneurship. What type of entrepreneurship is involved would be determined by the factors that are combined in the process and by the consequences that are achieved. He indicates, for example, that

> Political entrepreneurship will involve the combination of *political* factors of production, whatever they may be, and the achievement of political consequences. Economic entrepreneurship involves the combination of *economic* factors of production — land, labor, capital, and technology — and economic consequences, usually the production of goods and services (his italics).

It is proposed here that religio-economic entrepreneurs:

> (1) contribute to, and are influenced by, the supply of and demand for religious services; (2) apart from offering religious services and getting rewarded for this, can also be engaged in various social services (*e.g.*, ethnic or political) as the necessity occurs; (3) regard the religious organisation as the main site where they work; (4) seek social status, financial power and security as well as religious rewards; and (5) ideally consider both the religious and economic aspects in their ministry equally important; however, the balance between these aspects may vary.

Methodology

The primary aim of this study is to explain the enormous growth of Korean immigrant churches in Sydney. Being interested in explaining the phenomenon I have come across sociological theories on conversion, migration, assimilation, and intrinsic/extrinsic religiosity, as well as general theories of church growth. Some aspects of these theories are useful, but they need refinement, synthesis and extension to provide a satisfactory answer to the primary question of the study.

To put the matter differently, I initially tried to look at "what happened to Koreans since their immigration" which is what, I thought, leads Koreans to join the church and helps church growth amongst them. I assumed that Korean immigrants in Sydney, mostly well educated but currently employed in relatively low status jobs, suffer from status anxiety to a large degree (cf. Lee, 1989a) and that this would explain their involvement in church activities. In this respect, theories on marginality were once considered to be very significant in answering the central question. Then, a question arose: why has there not been such significant church growth amongst migrants from other parts of Asia? I have come to consider that church growth among Koreans in Sydney might be closely related to aspects of Korean society as well as to their immigrant life.[4]

This point was significant in my designing a research strategy and led me to realise that at least two broad sets of factors should be put into the analysis, *viz.*, church growth in Korea and the growth of Korean churches in Australia. The growth of Korean churches in Australia came about only after the enormous growth of churches in Korea. A pilot survey by interviews with lay persons, ministers, and Buddhist masters in the Korean community of Sydney suggested that account should be taken of factors both in Korea and in Australia. The survey was particularly supportive of the concept of the church as a multi-dimensional institution and the notion of religio-economic entrepreneurship, which form a central part of the over-arching framework of the study, *i.e.*, the supply/demand congruence theory of church growth. The examination of church growth in Korea led me to be aware that it is not only church growth in Korea but also the culture and economy of the Korean society that have significantly influenced church growth among Koreans in Sydney.

The chapters on church growth in Korea are based largely on secondary sources such as journals, books, and newspapers. Other instruments of data collection for the chapters were considered not necessary. This was because the purpose of these chapters was to shed light on the ways in which some aspects of Korean society and of church growth in Korea enhanced church activities amongst Koreans in Sydney. I have analysed not only some studies of church expansion in Korea but also relevant aspects of the wider society, such as industrialisation, education, Confucianism.

In addition to using documentary material, interviews and participant observation proved to be valuable for the analysis of Korean churches in Sydney. I developed semi-structured interview schedules for various categories of Koreans in Sydney. As this project has proceeded, more questions have arisen. I have been able to get back to the field with those questions. In attempting to achieve the aims of this study, obtaining reliable information from knowledgeable informants was considered much more important than interviewing a large number of Koreans or sending off a bunch of questionnaires to hundreds of people as a strategy for data collection.

Notes

[1] People may pray not only for repentance but also for money. The sermon may be sometimes about sins, and about social justice at other times. In this regard, almost all activities of the church are multi-dimensional.

[2] Of course, there are many people who strongly identify as Jewish who are not religious, in the United States, Israel, *etc.*

[3] This was probably only the case when "being German" was a problem.

[4] I am indebted to Alan Black for this suggestion.

PART II:
THE GROWTH OF THE CHURCH IN KOREA

Introduction: Church Growth in Korea and its Link to the Growth of Overseas Korean Churches

There is more than a grain of truth in the saying that "wherever Koreans go, they start a church". This is what they have been doing in Australia, the United States, Argentina, West Germany, Brazil and Japan. In seeking an explanation for this phenomenon, an obvious place to begin looking is in Korea itself to see if the drive to start churches among overseas Koreans has its origins in Korea, or in the immigration process, or in the places to which Koreans migrated. The position taken in this book is that the main factors are the first two. During the last three decades, there has been a tremendous growth in Korea of both liberal and conservative denominations (see Han Yŏngje, 1986). This is different from what is happening in many other countries, where only conservative denominations are growing (see Kelley, 1972). Part II of the book analyses the causes of church growth in Korea, as a precursor to the examination in Part III of the impact of this phenomenon on the growth of Korean churches in countries such as Australia.

I will examine the situation in Korea on the basis of the following hypothesis. Confucianism[1] and the process of industrialisation in Korea have been major causes of rapid growth. I suggest that, first, one religion (Confucianism) has accelerated the growth of another religion (Christianity); second, that industrialisation, usually assumed to cause a decline in religion, has helped church growth; third, that industrialisation and Christianity in Korea have been strongly influenced by close relationships between Korea and the United States; and fourth, that conflicts among religious leaders have been important.

The main time period covered in Part II is that of the last thirty years. However, some aspects of Korean Christianity before 1960 will be discussed in order to provide a broader perspective. I will now look at a number of important variables that should be considered.

Korean society has been heavily influenced by Confucianism from as long ago as the fourteenth century. The ethic of Confucius is deeply rooted in the minds of many Korean people. It is the philosophy which still tends to underlie the Korean personality and provide the central maxims of Korean life. Some of these are: that children are encouraged to obey their parents, that wives should be submissive to their husbands, that people should have a ruler and obey him, that students should respect their teachers, that juniors should respect seniors, and that the male should be superior especially in the family. Confucianism was adopted by the Chosŏn Dynasty (1392-1910). Scholars increasingly adopted Confucian culture, and the families of scholars and high-ranking officials began observing Confucian rituals in their daily lives. In particular, Yi T'oegye, one of the eminent Confucian scholars of the Chosŏn Dynasty, systematised and elucidated Chinese scholar Chu Hsi's dualism of *li* and *chi*. The Sŏnggyun'gwan, the headquarters of Confucianism in Korea, was established in Seoul in 1397 by King T'aecho who founded the Chosŏn Dynasty in 1392. Its purposes were to propagate Chinese literature and the teachings of Confucius, to scout for able young men, to foster scholars, and to educate people in the spirit of Confucian morality. The Sŏnggyun'gwan still exists in Seoul (six hundred years later) and serves as the major Confucian research institute in Korea. Although Confucianists, *i.e.*, people who identify themselves openly and strongly as Confucianists, were only 5 per cent of the Korean population by 1984, Confucian teaching still remains deeply influential. Confucianism in Korea has been a religion and the foundation of the systems of education, ceremony, and civil administration. With the passing of the monarchy in the early 20th century, only the first function remained important. However, the deeply ingrained Confucian mode of manners and social relations is still a major factor in the way Koreans think and act.

As Confucianism regards scholarship and aesthetic cultivation as pre-requisites for those in governing or official positions, Koreans have paid great respect to teachers and learned people. This is why many young people struggled to obtain higher education even during the Japanese colonial period (1919-1945). After the Korean Government introduced the Five Year Economic Development Plan in 1962, Korea established additional universities. Increasingly, more students have been admitted to higher education, including theological institutions, so as to supply college graduates for the plan as well as to meet the desire for education. As I will argue later, all these factors have helped to bring about labour-intensive religio-economic entrepreneurship.

Some important aspects of religio-economic entrepreneurship are as follows. It is often possible in the West, or in other nations, for theological college graduates to find jobs in non-religious areas. This is uncommon in Korea. Furthermore, unemployment, especially of university graduates, has steadily increased in Korea since the 1960s. Despite this, young people are still anxious to have a university education. There were, according to official figures released by the Culture-Information Ministry, Seoul: 4,110 Protestant clergy in 1962; 17,652 in 1973; 33,851 in 1981; and 43,468 in 1986. As theological college graduates have few employment alternatives, they often take a lengthy period to establish a church to which they can minister and from which they can make a living. Theological college graduates and ministers in Korea are very determined to be successful in their ministry, not only on a religious basis but also in economic terms. There has been extremely high competition to get into the ministry among the thousands of theological college graduates produced every year. This has been also the case in all other areas of professional life.

Another factor that has helped church growth in Korea is the co-operation which exists between ministers and laity. As ministers are often regarded as God-sent preachers and as respected teachers according to Korean Confucian culture and practice, the laity have been extremely cooperative with church ministers. Most of what they do is on a completely voluntary basis. They are active in such things as recruiting members, often through door-to-door visits to non-believers of up to four or five times a week. Such door-to-door visits by ministers and associates have been popular because of the widely recognised status given to teachers. When active members come to church, they spend much time in prayer and discussion about how their church can bring about "spiritual revivalism", which usually involves achieving quantitative growth as well. They usually work out detailed practical strategies. As Korean culture is based on Confucianism, married women have not been encouraged into full-time paid work, at least until recently. Women tend to stay home and do housework, and hence they are often approached during the day by recruiters from different churches and denominations. Actually, early Presbyterians in Korea gave priority to manual workers and women as the subjects of proselytisation (Cho Yohan, 1984: 39). The competition by members of a few churches in a region to encourage non-believers, especially women, to join has been very strong. These factors are associated with the development of religio-economic entrepreneurial leadership in Korea.

One Korean immigrant minister in Los Angeles (quoted in Steve S. Shim, 1977: 51) gave three major factors for the mushrooming phenomenon of Korean churches in Southern California:

> Firstly, it is part of the self-image of Korean ministers that each
> minister believes himself to be the best preacher (called by God)

and feels compelled to preach; secondly, they are without any other vocational skills; thirdly, the Korean community is readily responsive to the small churches where intimate interaction among church members is possible.

Another possible source of church growth in Korea has been conflicts among church leaders which cause church splits. There were a total of 67 Protestant denominations in the nation at the end of 1980 and 69 at the end of 1983 (Han Yŏngje, 1986: 198), rising to 120 in 1991 (Chang Hyŏngil, 1991). According to other sources, Korean Protestantism consisted of a total of 188 denominational bodies in 1978 (Barrett, 1982). Each Protestant denomination generally maintains at least one theological college. This has accelerated the supply of ministers, resulting in further church growth. Ji Won-yong (1965: 6) speaks of "a mental, spiritual and religious vacuum among the people" as a factor that gave rise to "sects"[2] which have their origin in the Christian churches in Korea. He goes on to argue that "the world was constantly changing and rapidly advancing, but the churches were almost static in their relations with the people and in their communication of the Christian message to a sophisticated secular world" (Ji Won-yong, 1965: 6). Ji's argument remains within the perspective of deprivation theory on church growth. Although such a perspective is of some relevance for the present study, a question remains as to why churches (as distinct from "sects") also grew so rapidly in Korea over the last thirty years. This issue is addressed in Part II.

Notes

[1] This study regards Confucianism as a religion (cf. Smart, 1984). A detailed examination as to whether or not Confucianism should be regarded as a religion is outside our theme.

[2] Most sects within Korean Protestantism have originated from mainline denominations. Once a group after splitting from a denomination forms a sect and comes to attract and gather followers around key leaders, it often settles down to form another denomination. This has been widely discussed in the literature. The reasons for church splits will be discussed later in the book. Making a distinction between sect and church is not an issue here. What may be known as a "sect" is generally included in the term "church" in this study.

Chapter 4

The Growth of the Church in Korea up to 1960

Although there was church growth in Korea before 1960, the growth rate was not as great as in the period from 1960 onwards (see the figures by Grayson, 1985: 126; also Samuel Moffet's figures, quoted in Kim Byong-suh, 1985: 60-61). Why the year 1960? It was 1960 when the Korean Government introduced the Five Year Economic Plan which started rapid industrialisation and urbanisation. In brief, 1960 was the year from which Korea started to achieve a development that had, in the west, taken several centuries. Before considering that in detail, I will first look at the coming of Christianity to Korea.

The Hermit Kingdom, the Advent of Christianity and the Opening Up of Modern Korea

Catholicism has been in Korea since 1784 and Protestantism since 1884. Christians tried to persuade the government officials of the Chosŏn Dynasty (1392-1910) that Christian teachings were not against Confucianism, the government-advocated religion (quoted in Chŏn T'aekpu, 1987: 35, 59). However, Christians were initially persecuted in Korea on the grounds that Christianity was opposed to

Confucianism, especially to ancestor worship, a key part of Korean Confucian practices[1]. Moreover, as Christianity taught the equality and the brotherhood of mankind, it was considered dangerous to the preservation of Confucian loyalties and hence to the then existing political regime. The Chosŏn Dynasty actually banned Christianity in 1785. The martyrdom of many Korean Christians including a Chinese priest followed shortly after. Three French missionaries and their Korean followers were also executed. Three bishops, seventeen priests, and numerous Korean Christians were put to death in 1866 (Kim Hyung-chan, 1977b: 48). Uraka (quoted in Chŏn T'aekpu, 1987: 44) in his *Religious Martyrdom in Korea* tells us that about 10,000 Catholics were martyred during the first hundred years after Catholicism was introduced to Korea (Chŏn T'aekpu, 1987: 49). Christianity struggled for a long period to gain a foothold in Korea, but it gradually began to play a significant role in the modernisation of Korea (Hong Kyong-man, 1983: 18). Confucian scholars during the Chosŏn Dynasty despite their antagonism to Western religion were attracted to Western science and technology, and sometimes even to the socio-political systems of the west. Because of these scholars' curiosity about Western civilisation, their perspective on social life built upon Confucianism began to weaken. Some Confucian intellectuals came to accept Christianity (Kim Hyŏngsŏk, 1983: 6). Yi Pyŏk, a noted Confucian scholar, came across some books from China in 1779, some of which were about Christianity. He came to be very enthusiastic about Christianity and wanted more literature. He persuaded Yi Sŭnghun, the son of an ambassador to China, to meet Western missionaries in China. Yi Sŭnghun learned Christian rituals and brought back literature on Christianity after a visit to China in 1783. Following Yi Sŭnghun's return, Yi Pyŏk carried out research on the books and publicised his study. This invigorated Korean Catholicism. Yi Sŭnghun was killed in 1786 and treated as a martyr by the Catholic church later.[2]

The arrival of Protestantism in Korea accelerated the opening of the hermit kingdom. Christian churches contributed to this process particularly through their institutional activities. The first Western style secondary school was founded by a missionary. Among the youth movements Christianity initiated, the YMCA was the first and the most influential. Protestant missionaries in what is known as the "social gospel approach" also engaged in social welfare work and set up medical services (cf. Cho Yohan, 1984: 10; Dearman, 1982: 168). The *Yangban* (upper class) and the *Sangmin* (lower class) in the old rigid class system came to the church and worshipped together without class distinction (cf. Cho Yohan, 1984: 43). In addition, Bibles were printed in *Han'gŭl* (Korean alphabet which tended to be neglected by the upper class and the dynasty), thus contributing not only to the revival of the alphabet in the twentieth century but also to education being directed to all social groupings. To ensure that all believers could use the Bible, church members were strongly encouraged to learn to read (Moffett, 1973: 11).

There were also fortuitous circumstances. In 1884 there was a conflict between the conservatives and progressives as to whether or not Korea should maintain a policy of seclusion. The queen's nephew, Min Yŏngik, who was a leader of the conservatives, was seriously injured during the conflict. An American physician, Dr. Horace Allen, was called upon to give him medical attention, which led to his recovery. This incident gave Allen, with special permission from the king Kojong, the opportunity to establish the first modern medical institution in Korea. Dr. Allen became the king's personal physician and, as a consequence Christianity came to earn royal approval more quickly. This proved to be of significant value to succeeding American missionaries in their dealings with the Korean court.

During the late 19th century, which was the last stage of the Chosŏn Dynasty, conflicts between the conservatives and progressives were ongoing. These had become more acute after Japan's victories in the Sino-Japanese War of 1894-95 and Russo-Japanese War of 1904, as these provided the conqueror with the justification to colonise Korea and as the conservatives and progressives maintained different policies towards Japan. A large number of the progressives were imprisoned. When a few Christians who were deeply involved in running the schools were put in jail, many missionaries worked to have them released. They also supplied them with books on politics, history, philosophy and Christianity[3]. This led a significant number of political leaders and intellectuals in prisons (who were mostly from the high class of the Chosŏn Dynasty) to convert to Christianity. Although this broke the class barrier, thereby causing conflict between Christians from different class backgrounds, it also became a strong factor in organising people against Japanese imperialism (Han'guk Kidokkyosa Yŏn'guhoe, 1989: 266). The latter will be discussed shortly.

Following the turn of the century, when Russian political influence was rising, Dr. Horace Underwood, an American physician and missionary, was approached by the nobility of the Chosŏn Dynasty, with a request that he assist them to establish "a State Presbyterian Church in Korea". Being in dread of the power and influence of Russia, the Emperor and his court feared the possibility of being forced to join the Russian Orthodox Church. This would have virtually put them under the control of the Czar (Underwood, 1918, quoted in Palmer, 1967: 61).

The Great Revival in 1907, which was a massive religious movement, tends to be regarded as a key event in the history of the growth of Korean Christianity. It was a time when the religious components of the church strengthened and the rate of conversion increased. Korean churches grew rapidly in the thirteen years between 1898 and 1910. The social reasons for this growth have not been fully explored, although church historians tend to argue that it had much to do with the religious interest of Koreans (Yi Man'yŏl, 1980; Chŏng Taewi, 1980, both quoted in Chŏn T'aekpu, 1987). From the theoretical perspective of this study, what they argue is that the church growth for the period was overwhelmingly religious rather than political or economic.

Table 4.1: Some statistics on Protestant religious bodies in Korea in 1918

	Presby-terian	Northern Metho-dist	Southern Metho-dist	Episcopal, Salvation Army, Seventh Adventist, Evan-gelical	Total of Available Figures
No. of Churches	2,005	652	238	?	2,895
No. of Clergy	169	70	14	?	253
No. of theology graduates to be ordained or *Chŏndosa*	659	263	32	?	954
No. of Believers	160,919	41,044	10,740	12,000	234,703
No. of Sunday School	2,655	412	138	?	3,205
(Teaching Staff)	(13,756)	(2,133)	(482)		(16,371)
(Students)	(147,953)	(26,640)	(5,911)	(180,504)	
Boys Schools Established by	423	75	26	?	524
(No. of Students)	(15,573)	(4,070)	(986)		(20,629)
Girls Schools	132	58	40	?	230
(No. of Students)	(5,041)	(3,214)	(1,145)		(9,400)
No. of Theological Students	174	?	20	?	

Source: Chŏn T'aekpu, 1987: 205

By 1910, there were 2,250 private western-style educational institutions, 796 of which had been established by Christian missionaries, 501 Presbyterian, 158 Methodist, 4 Church of England, 2 Seventh Adventist, 46 Catholic, and 85 others (P'yo Sŏnil, quoted in Son Insu, 1980: 78-79). Some of the basic statistics of Protestantism and the number of educational institutions in 1918 are set out in Table 4.1.

American Impact on Korean Christianity: The Growth of Korean Churches in the United States and International Relations between the Two Nations

It is important to note how Americans, including missionaries, had an impact on Korean Christianity. The United States was the first country from the west to open diplomatic relations with Korea and to send Christian missionaries. Presumably, this is where American influence stems from. The arrival of Horace Allen in Seoul in 1884 to later become the first resident Protestant missionary, occurred at a time when a set of circumstances that proved favourable to the expansion of Christianity existed. These circumstances developed over a long period of national isolation and conflict with other nations (Palmer, 1967: 51). The coming of missionaries was just a part of American expansionism occurring from the late 19th century (Yi Man'yŏl, quoted in Han'guk Kidokkyosa Yŏn'guhoe, 1989: 175; Palmer, 1967: 48, 49). "The Treaty of Amity and Commerce between the United States of America and Corea [sic]" was signed on 22 May 1882.[4] American missionaries in China and Japan emphasised that missionary work through medicine and education would be productive in Korea (Paik Lak-Geoon George, quoted in Han'guk Kidokkyosa Yŏn'guhoe, 1989: 176).

The elite and the lower class looked on Christianity favourably: the former were interested in increasing national power and self-reliance; the latter, oppressed by the corrupted Chosŏn Dynasty, came to see Christianity as a haven and a form of resistance[5] (Yi Man'yŏl, quoted in Han Wansang, 1983: 122).

During the late 19th century missionaries, focusing their activities on education and medical services, left aside direct involvement in proselytising. This was only to be expected, for the government officials (who were Confucianists) did not want the new religion to become socially pervasive. Hospitals were established in many parts of the nation around the turn of the 20th century (Pak Hyosaeng, 1986: 101-102). While receiving medical services and education, many people were converted to Christianity. The missionary H. Underwood came to

Korea in April 1885 and established a college which grew into the present Yonsei University. It produced a large number of leaders in various sectors of the Korean society. It has also been one of the few Korean universities to become well-known in the United States. The graduates of this university have tended to be well recognised by American universities, so many have been interested in pursuing their higher studies there (*Korea Journal*, 1962a: 22; 1962b). This has resulted in Korean education and Korean society being heavily under the influence of the United States. Because of the recommendations of the missionaries, Koreans began to go to the United States for university education. In 1900 Esther Park was the first Korean to return with the degree of doctor of medicine. Koreans with American degrees have often been leading figures in Korean society during the last hundred years.

Christian missionaries were also active in translating the Bible, and in publishing religious and general magazines. These magazines reported western church news and theological trends and introduced western culture, farming techniques, and child-rearing practices. According to the Nevius Plan, which was strongly advocated by American Presbyterian missionaries in Korea, students in theological seminaries received primary knowledge about the Bible, but without scholarly or professional training. This has led Korean theology to be dependent upon the west, and Korean Christianity to be western oriented at the cost of Korean traditional culture.

American missionaries have been deeply involved in many facets of Korean life. Missionaries also tended to display the life-styles of their home country and Koreans were often curious and envious. Introducing "advanced" American culture to Koreans, the missionaries tried to convince them quickly that Christianity was the core of advanced culture (Harrington,[6] quoted in Pak Sun'gyŏng, 1985: 33). They imported commercial goods and supplied them to markets in Korea and put much effort into advertising them. Some missionaries provided American exporting companies (*e.g.*, Townsend Company) with items in demand. One missionary, H. Underwood, brought in petroleum, coal, and farming tools from which he derived commercial profit. Another example is Horace Allen, who in the years between 1897 and 1905 obtained contracts to build electric railways, power stations, waterworks, telephone facilities, and government offices, and sold the contracts to Americans. He stated that any constructing business in which a huge sum of money is involved belongs to Americans (quoted in Pak Sun'gyŏng, 1985: 34). Allen also assisted Americans to obtain gold mining rights in Wonsan. Only one tenth of the profits from the mining was returned to the Korean government and the miners took out US$15,000,000 during the forty years before 1939 when they sold the mining rights to a Japanese company for $8 million. Allen's obtaining of these mining rights was the high point of American imperialism in Korea during the early part of this century. Allen expressed this imperialism personally in his contemptuous attitudes towards Korea. He argued that Korea needed to be subject to another country as it always had been (Harrington, quoted in Pak Sun'gyŏng, 1985: 35). Such a superiority complex was pervasive among American missionaries and other westerners in Korea (Pak Sun'gyŏng, 1985: 35).

As already mentioned, Japan's victory in the Russo-Japanese War was crucial in Japan's move to annexe Korea. The English-Japanese Treaty of Alliance in 1902 legally justified this Japanese imperialism. The United States and the United Kingdom provided Japan with financial support during the Russo-Japanese War. The American president, Roosevelt, once stated that "we [Americans] are proud of Japan's victory as she fought for us" (Kang Man'gil, quoted in Pak Sun'gyŏng, 1985: 35). The United States came to support Japan in its efforts to colonise Korea through a secret agreement. This was based on Japan remaining indifferent to American colonialism in the Philippines. Japanese colonialism followed this agreement and the United States unilaterally abrogated the "Treaty of Amity and Commerce between the United States of America and Corea [sic]" (Harrington, quoted in Pak Sun'gyŏng, 1985: 35). Japanese imperialism and Western expansionism, partly through Christianity, went hand in hand in Korea. Some Korean Christians actually came to be pro-Japanese although many remained opposed to Japan during the colonial period.

The relationships between Korea and the United States that developed around the turn of the century were the firm base for the present diplomatic and economic ties. The United States has been the most popular choice of destination among potential migrants from Korea and the largest proportion of them have settled there since World War II.

Christianity and the Independence Movement

When Japan annexed Korea in 1910 and began to suppress the church, which was a centre of continuing Korean patriotism and education, the church's growth slowed considerably. Some of the strengths of Korean Christianity were its high level of organisation within the country and its links with churches abroad (Kang Wi-jo, 1987). The Japanese colonial authorities realised that the church was the one free Korean organisation they could not easily control.

Large-scale rebellions against the Japanese commenced around the time of the abdication of the emperor Kojong in 1907. From that year the Japanese openly claimed that the uprisings were under the direction of ambitious Christian missionaries attempting to increase their power. However, the overwhelming threat posed by the Japanese policy tended to push the Koreans and the missionaries together (Palmer, 1967: 68). This does not mean that the missionaries strongly protested against Japanese imperialism in Korea. The missionaries, in fact, who were mostly fundamentalist at the time, encouraged Korean Christians to focus on religion instead of getting involved in political issues.

During the colonial period (1910-1945) the Japanese tried to destroy all Christian associations and related educational institutions. Schools were not allowed to teach the Bible or to run prayer meetings (Chŏn T'aekpu, 1987: 189). Private educational institutions were severely suppressed. There were 2,080 private schools in Korea at the time of colonisation in 1910, but the number gradually decreased to 1,045 in 1916, 868 in 1917, and 649 in 1923. Determined to expel all anti-Japanese sentiment and action, the governor-general and his aide fabricated a charge against 123 Korean Christian leaders in the north. The charge was that they had attempted to kill the governor-general, Terauchi, around 27-28 December 1911, while he was going to Shinŭiju to celebrate the construction of a bridge across the Yalu River. When the truth was revealed, it actually strengthened the faith of pastors and elders and brought an even greater friendship between missionaries and leaders of the church (Moffett, quoted in Palmer, 1967: 64).

In order to counter Christianity, the Japanese tried to revive Buddhism, which had been officially discouraged during the Chosŏn Dynasty. Japanese Buddhism restored Korean temples and attempted to transplant some of the Japanese Buddhist sects (such as those of the Hongganji, Zen, and Nichiren). There was generally a harmonious relationship between Korean and Japanese Buddhism, but a few conflicts developed. For example, there was a disagreement between the tradition of celibacy in the priesthood in Korea and the tradition of Japanese Buddhism that allowed clergy to marry. Confucian leaders who were neither particularly discouraged nor encouraged by the Japanese colonial government, barely contributed to the independence movement (Kang Wi-jo, 1987). This led to the marginalisation of institutionalised Confucianism.

A church historian, Choo Chai-yonh (quoted in Witvliet, 1985: 163), pays great attention to the part played by Korean Christians in the struggle for national independence against Japanese domination. He argues that from the beginning, Korean Christianity developed amidst an oppressed people, and that Korean Christians played a leading role in the movement towards independence.[7] Of the 33 patriots who signed the Declaration of Independence in March 1919, 16 were Protestant Christians (Cho Yohan, 1984: 11). A classification of imprisoned persons by religion shows that 2,133 were Protestants among a total of 9,456 as of 30 June 1919. Cho Chi-hun (quoted in Hong Kyong-man, 1983: 25) notes that this figure almost doubles the number of imprisoned *Ch'ŏndo-gyo*,[8] the Religion of Heavenly Way (Hong Kyong-man's translation) believers, who amounted to 1,416.[9] Indeed the great, non-violent, March 1st Movement was centred around the schools and churches of Protestant denominations and Christians were the backbone of this movement. Korean Catholics, on the other hand, tended to be uninterested in the movement (Kim Yongbok, 1984: 266). This partly explains why Protestantism has been taken up more readily by Koreans than Catholicism.

In addition, many of the early converts to Christianity became active in social and political affairs and later fought for Korean independence (Dearman, 1982: 168). Sŏ Chaep'il who studied in the United States for ten years to become a physician was deeply inspired by American Protestant principles, such as "freedom of conscience" and other matters like democracy and equality between males and females, which were supported in the thoughts of Jefferson, Locke, Rousseau, and Montesquieu. His interest in these ideas was revealed in the support he gave to political, economic and cultural movements through his newspaper, the first to be published in Korean. Sŏ contributed markedly to the westernisation of Korea and to the national independence movement. When he was exiled by political conservatives in Korea, he returned to the United States and continued to work for independence.

In the years before World War II, Christians bitterly resisted any compromise with Japanese-imposed Shinto worship and, as a consequence, were brutally persecuted. As indicated above, this led to many Koreans identifying with the church more closely as well as with anti-colonialism and Korean nationalism. This helps to explain the popularity of Christianity after the war (Moffett, 1973: 12). Kim Byong-suh (1985: 63) states that the Christian struggle for national independence paved the way for church growth as the non-Christian public respected the church for its supposedly altruistic commitment to national political efforts. In most non-Western countries, Christianity had been seen as pro-imperial and anti-national, whereas in Korea it was a religion supporting nationalism, anti-imperialism, and was pro-minjung (mass or ordinary people) — (Han Wansang, 1983: 124). Historians in Korea generally agree that the role of Christianity was significant in social change and shifting consciousness and that Korean

Christianity never seemed to stand aloof from people in their suffering (An Pyŏngmu, 1983: 345).

Following independence from Japan in 1945, Korean Christianity came to develop different characteristics. Although Christians have continued to form the majority of those who have been involved in the movement for human rights and liberation since national independence, most denominations have disengaged from political and national concerns (An Pyŏngmu, 1983: 346). Han Pyŏngok (1986: 31) assesses the Korean churches, arguing that they had been able to achieve both quantitative and qualitative growth in balance till 1945 or so, but that since then they have been deeply involved in denominationalism, regionalism, and materialism which have resulted in numerous conflicts and schisms. The Korean churches accepted in "The Declaration of Korean Christians, 1973" that since 1945 they had not responded to the expectations of the majority of people in Korea. Of course, there have always been some groups of Korean Christians who have actively expressed their concern about socio-political and economic issues. However, compared to the period prior to 1945, Korean Christianity has subsequently shown only a minor interest in current affairs.

Here, it may be suggested that the rate of church growth is closely related to whether or not a church is deeply involved in social issues and that, in other words, church growth rates in Korea prior to, and subsequent to, 1945 support Kelley's (1972, 1977) contention that conservative churches rather than liberal ones tend to grow. However, whether the Korean church has been conservative since 1945 is an open question. I will argue that although the churches in Korea have not generally been concerned about political matters, a number of non-theological factors have contributed significantly to the process of church growth. This will be discussed in detail in chapter 5.

Development from 1945 to 1960 Affecting Church Growth

Persecution of Christians did not end with Korean independence in 1945. A United Nations conference in Moscow on 28 December 1945 agreed to put the Korean peninsula under a United Nations trusteeship. Consequently, Russian troops occupied the northern part of Korea, the United States the southern. In the north,[10] Cho Mansik, a Christian leader as well as a national leader, along with many Christian youths gathered around him, were active in resisting the UN policy. Revs. Yun Hayŏng and Han Kyŏngjik formed the Christian Socialist Democratic Party which was the first political party in Korea after independence.

The party's main interest was to help the government to set up a stable democracy on the basis of the Christian ethos. Persecutions by Russian troops and some pro-communist Koreans of those activities meant an oppression of Christianity in the northern part of Korea where Christianity was far more alive than the southern part.

When Korea became independent of Japan, there were four major political groups in South Korea, ranging in ideological terms from extreme and moderate rightists to moderate and radical leftists. The right wing groups accommodated a large number of landowners along with some nationalist leaders. They were the most powerful group, with strong backing from the U. S. Military Government (Hahn and Kim, 1963: 306). Christianity in Korea became linked to things regarded as good such as capitalism, democracy and industry, and it was seen as intrinsically opposed to what was seen as bad such as Japanese imperialism and communism. This is what gave Christianity its significance in Korea. Political circumstances at that time and the emergence of the Cold War tended to prevent the development of communism in Korea on the one hand, and encourage capitalism and Christianity on the other. A large number of students went overseas for their higher studies; these numbered 4,800 in January 1962, of whom nearly 4,000 were in the United States. In addition, a large number of political leaders (*e.g.*, 18.2% of 316 top level political leaders in Korea, 1952-1962) spent a large portion of their educational life in the United States. This is partly because the Liberal Government of Syngman Rhee (who was also US educated) sent many people he had recruited to the United States for university education. The religious backgrounds of the 316 top level political leaders in Korea during the Liberal, Democratic, and Military Governments, 1952-1962, are set out below in Table 4.3. About 30-40% in the three categories, Liberal, Democratic, and Military Governments, were Christians, mainly Protestants. Although Korean political activists in the United States occasionally opposed Syngman Rhee's rule in Korea, they were effectively controlled by Rhee's Secret Police, violence, and money (Kim Hyung-chan, 1977c: 73). Rhee's foreign policy over the US has been a significant basis of the close relationship between the two nations that developed quickly from that time on. This has heavily influenced aspects of Korean Christianity in the decades that followed.

The persecution of Christianity again emerged during the Korean War, 1951-1953. Many Christians in the north crossed the 38th parallel. Two hundred and seventy three church buildings were burnt down and 732 destroyed. The remaining churches came to be used as child care centres, sheds, schools, theatres, courts and residential accommodation. The North Korean communist regime put several hundred Christians to death during the war. There was a migration to the south in search of religious and political freedom and this led to the formation of a number of new churches. For those who moved, the church was "a gathering place of the escaped, a site of encouragement for the migrants, a site of thanking God for the freedom of religion, a site of consoling the heart broken by the division of family, an altar to pray for the future re-unification of Korea, a site of pledge to re-establish the destroyed churches" (Song Sŏngch'an,[11] quoted in Kim Yongbok, 1984: 278).

Table 4.3: Religious backgrounds of political leaders and Korean population, 1952-1962

Religion	Total Population	All Leaders	Liberal	Democratic	Military
Buddhism	4.6	13.3	16.2	7.0	19.1[12]
Confucianism	0.7	17.5	17.6	22.1	8.5
Protestantism	2.4	32.5	39.2	19.8	27.7
Catholicism	1.1	8.5	7.4	11.6	4.3
Ch'ŏndo-gyo	0.1	0.3	0.7		
No Affiliation	91.1	27.9	18.9	39.5	40.4
Total	100%	100%	100%	100%	100%

Source: Hahn and Kim, 1963: 316

The migrant Christians soon became the major power in Christianity in the south. It should be also noted that, at the outbreak of the Korean War, the churches in the southern part of Korea took care of the refugees. For example, the Korean branch of the Church World Service received substantial financial support from international church organisations in 1951 and used it for charity; by 19 October in that year, 28,054 refugees had benefited from the service. In the process, the churches worked in close co-operation with the government and the army (Kim Yongbok, 1984: 279, 283). According to a special order of the Christian president, Syngman Rhee, the Korean Army adopted the Army Ministry on 7 February 1952. Theological college graduates served their compulsory army service as priests or ministers and they concerned themselves with the soldiers' church life. The number of such clergy was about 70 in 1952 and it increased to 352 by 1955. This organisation became so significant that Communist advocates often attempted to become members, and to make use, of Christian organisations for political purposes.

On 26 June 1951, the Korean National Council of Churches (KNCC) requested the American President and the UN Secretary to intervene at the diplomatic level in the war. The United Christian Committee, founded by 40 ministers from four major denominations at Pusan Central Church on 9 January 1952, submitted petitions for such intervention to Truman, the UN Secretary General, and MacArthur the UN troop commander, also dispatching Revs. Han Kyŏngjik and Yu Hyŏnggi to the United States to inform the media about the war. Two thousand Christians in the Seoul area held a demonstration to urge re-unification (by the forceful attack to the north) and sent a petition to the Korean and American presidents on 14 June 1953. A similar meeting took place in Pusan on 15 June 1953. Such meetings were also held after the war. About 1,700 Christians who were against communism organised a similar petition on 23 January 1954. Several thousand ministers and 50,000 Christians also had a prayer meeting for re-unification and for the persecuted Christians in the north. These efforts by Christians in the south have continued ever since. Hong Kŭnsu (1991a) argues that such anti-communist movements by Korean Christians have justified in many ways the American penetration into Korea, and that they have hampered the re-unification of Korea in the long run.

Christianity continued to grow after the war. About 2,050 churches were established in the five years following the outbreak of the Korean War. The 70th anniversary of Protestantism was celebrated in 1954, with a drive to establish 500 more churches. The Methodists aimed to establish 100 churches in country areas where there were no churches. The number of churches established during the period by some denominations is given in Table 4.4.

Table 4.4: Number of churches established in the five years following the outbreak of the Korean War

	Presbyterian	Methodist	Evangelical	Others	In Total
No. of Churches Established	About 1,200	About 500	About 250	About 100	About 2,050

Source: Chŏn T'aekpu, 1987: 315

The steady increase in the number of churches as well as church membership after national independence was the result of a number of factors. In particular, the political structure at the time provided favourable conditions for growth. After the liberation from Japan, many Christians were involved in political activities under a Christian president, Syngman Rhee, and his liberal party. Syngman Rhee's pro-

Christian policy led the number of baptised Christians (14,818 in 1948) to increase to 40,781 by 1958. This was a 200 per cent increase in 10 years (cf. Cho Yohan, 1984: 12). Most Korean churches wished to maintain a smooth relationship with Rhee's government because it was favourable to Christianity and they kept quiet even when the government acted corruptly (Cho Yohan, 1984: 84). Kim Byong-suh (1985: 64) notes that "while the image of the Korean church as 'pro-Syngman Rhee' or 'pro-American' was helpful for increasing church membership, many thoughtful people, especially intellectuals and university students, were highly critical of the church's alliance with the dictatorial regime and American capitalism". If churches had reacted to political events as they had done until the independence from Japan, Rhee's government would not probably have been overturned by the military coup in 1961.

Concluding Remarks

Various historical factors were conducive to church growth until 1960. A considerable proportion of the high class of the Chosŏn Dynasty were attracted to Western science and technology, and consequently to Christianity. The high class also organised people against Japanese imperialism. Korean society started to see the coming of Western medicine, education and industry under the impetus of American missionaries. The activities of churches during and after the Korean War also helped Christianity to take a significant part in Korean society. The Korean church grew steadily up to 1960. However, it is in the period since 1960 that the most spectacular growth has occurred.

Most churches in Korea have gained in membership in recent decades as "modernisation" and industrialisation have advanced (see Tables 4.5, 4.6, and 4.7). By contrast, in countries such as Singapore, Taiwan and Hong Kong, churches have not grown as rapidly. At present in Korea, one church is established every four hours — six churches every day. The rate of increase in the number of Christian believers was four times the rate of population growth of Korea during the early 1970s (Moffett, 1973: 11; Moffett, quoted in Vaughan, 1984: 61). In the next chapter I shall argue that factors such as industrialisation and urbanisation, along with other changes in the structure of Korean society as well as factors mentioned before, have all influenced the growth of Christian/Protestant church membership in Korea especially over the last thirty years.

Table 4.5: Number of believers in Confucianism, Buddhism, Catholicism and Protestantism[13]

Year	Confucianism	Buddhism	Catholicism	Protestantism
1950			850,000*	
1962	3,426,120	481,292	559,713	
1969		4,903,110	751,000	3,167,100
1972		7,985,773	790,367	3,463,108
1974		11,767,000	1,012,000	3,720,000
1975		11,973,000	1,012,000	4,019,000
1976	4,723,493	12,154,779	1,052,691	4,658,710
1977**	4,723,000	12,907,000	1,094,000	5,001,000
1978**	4,824,000	13,142,000	1,144,000	5,294,000
1979	4,920,000	13,386,000	1,184,000	5,981,000
1980**	5,177,000	12,324,000	1,315,000	7,175,000
1981	5,201,000	11,130,000	1,440,000	7,637,000

Sources: Ministry of Culture and Information, Seoul
*Chŏn T'aekpu, 1987: 280
** Kim Byong-suh (1985: 65, based on the Ministry of Culture and Information, Seoul)

Table 4.6: Number of clergy in Confucianism, Buddhism, Catholicism and Protestantism

Year	Confucianism	Buddhism	Catholicism	Protestantism
1962		5,800	652	4,110
1969		14,300	3,000	12,600
1972		18,629	3,487	17,562
1974		19,783	3,952	18,281
1975		19,982	3,952	19,066
1976	11,944	21,612	3,921	21,948
1979	9,572	23,480	4,339	27,721
1981	11,950	20,755	4,797	33,851
1983*				40,717
1988**				45,000

Sources: Ministry of Culture and Information, Seoul
* Han Yŏngje (1986: 199)
** Kyomunsa Statistics (quoted in Song Pyŏnggu, 9 Feb. 1991: 11)

Table 4.7: Number of temples and churches of Confucianism, Buddhism, Catholicism and Protestantism

Year	Confucianism	Buddhism	Catholicism	Protestantism
1962		2,161	710	5,793
1969		2,100	400	12,700
1972		1,912	428	13,417
1974		19,783	3,952	18,281
1975		5,692	2,319	16,089
1976	232	6,780	2,265	17,846
1977 *	232	7,416	2,308	19,457
1978 *	232	7,448	2,339	20,019
1979	232	8,086	2,332	21,115
1980 *	232	7,244	2,342	21,243
1981	232	7,253	2,353	23,346
1988**				30,016

Sources : Ministry of Culture and Information, Seoul
　　　　* Kim Byong-suh (1985: 65, based on the Ministry of
Culture and Information, Seoul)
**Kyomunsa Statistics (quoted in Song Pyŏnggu, 9 Feb.
1991: 11)

Notes

[1] For example, Confucius taught that "you should serve your parents as you serve heaven, and serve heaven as you serve your parents." In Confucian teachings, one's civility tends to be extended to the civility of the ancestors who are already dead (cf. Yun Sung-bum, 1973: 18).

[2] The Vatican recently recognised the peculiar way in which Christianity (Catholicism) was introduced to Korea through literature and Koreans themselves rather than through outsiders.

[3] This does not imply that the missionaries either were involved in political activities or encouraged Koreans to be so. In fact, missionaries strongly discouraged it (*e.g.*, independence movement). Rev. Hong Kŭnsu (1991a) argues that especially American missionaries who were mostly fundamentalist in their beliefs did so and led a spiritual revival between 1903 and 1907. According to him, this was the start of forming Korean Christianity without a sense of historical and political concern. On the other hand, the church's non-intervention in politics was advocated by missionaries like George H. James and W. B. Scranton who actually agreed

to be cooperative to the Japanese Governor (Ito) in Korea (Yi Man'yŏl, quoted in Pak Sun'gyŏng, 1985: 36).

4 There were a number of conflicts between the two nations before this treaty, such as the burning in August 1866 of an American schooner, the "General Sherman" with its crew.

5 Missionaries were often contacted by those who were robbed of their land. They were requested to help stop illegal taxing by corrupt government officials. Some requested missionaries to become the nominal owners of houses and land which could otherwise be taken by force. These were often the conditions for some to convert to Christianity (Han'guk Kidokkyosa Yŏn'guhoe, 1989: 235).

6 F. H. Harrington's book is *God, Mammon and the Japanese*. Pak Sun'gyŏng (1985: 31) argues that its proper title should have been *God, Mammon, Japanese, and Americans.*

7 Some American missionaries from a conservative and fundamentalist background advocated that the church distance itself from political issues. For example, A. J. Brown argued, regarding the Korean church's involvement in the independence movement, that

> It is not right for Jesus' disciples to be against the government, but they should simply obey it. ... It is not wise for the young church to join the anti-Japanese movement. ... We are concerned about religious salvation of individuals rather than about social justice. The latter is to be achieved only through the former. The church should be right away from any political movement (A. J. Brown, quoted in Cho Yohan, 1984: 52, 53).

8 This is a combined religion of Taoism, Confucianism and Buddhism. The founder is a Korean, Ch'oe Chaeu. The fundamental purpose of founding the religion was to create consensus among the Koreans following different religions. It was a reaction against Catholicism and the political decadence of the period (cf. Korean Overseas Information Service, 1988: 141).

9 A Japanese governor-general's report (1924, quoted in Palmer, 1967: 65) on the religious affiliation of those arrested for participating in the movement is as follows.

Table 4.2: Religious affiliation of the arrested during the Independence Movement

	Male	Female	Total
Ch'ŏndo-gyo	2,268	15	2,283
Shichon-gyo	14		14
Buddhist	220		220
Confucianist	346		346
Protestant	3065	308	3,373
Catholic	54	1	55
Other Religions	21		21
No religious affiliation	9,255	49	9,304
Unknown	3,809	98	3,907
Total	19,052	471	19,523

10 At the time of Korean independence, there were 300,000-350,000 Christians in a total population of 9,400,000 in northern Korea, *i.e.*, Christians formed about 3% of the population there (Kim Yongbok, 1984: 264).

11 He is an Elder of the Yŏng Nak Presbyterian church, the biggest Presbyterian church in the world, which was formed by such migrants.

12 The sharp increase in the number of the leaders who claimed adherence to Buddhism in the Military government is perhaps because they claimed Buddhism as their religion since they are not Christians, and come from Buddhist families (Hahn and Kim, 1963: 316).

13 Today, about 20% of the national population of Korea are self-confessed believers in Christian doctrines and another 20% are Buddhists (cf. United Nations, 1988: 676). No consistent statistics are available for the period after 1981.

Chapter 5

Church Growth, Industrialisation, Materialism and the Birth of Religio-Economic Entrepreneurship

Confucianism, the Structure of the Korean Society and their Impact on Church Growth

Despite the attention which I have given so far to Confucianism and Christianity, in the history of Korea it is Buddhism which has dominated over the longest period. It had its golden age during the Koryŏ Dynasty (933-1392) which adopted it as a state religion. But the influence of Buddhism started to decrease during the 500 years of the Confucian Chosŏn Dynasty (Yu Tongsik, quoted in Kim Sangho, 1975: 15). Building on the ground of many components of Chinese civilisation that had overflowed into Korea for many centuries, the Yi kings took their political ideology increasingly from the Confucian classics and from the Chinese practices of the T'ang (618-905) and Ming (1368-1628) dynasties. Since then Korean Buddhism has been "mountain Buddhism" or "temple centred Buddhism" rather than "community Buddhism" or "socially relevant Buddhism" throughout (quoted in Korean Overseas Information Service, 1982: 200). Most Buddhist temples are still located in mountains since they were forced to leave residential areas during the Confucian Chosŏn Dynasty. Their religious activities have been "temple oriented" rather than concerned with "everyday life". Christianity in Korea has been different in this respect. What is meant by this is that most of the self-confessing Buddhists visit Buddhist temples only a few times a year and most of them do not read Buddhist scriptures nor do they understand them. Buddhist monks were put into the lowest class, ch'ŏnmin, of the six strata of the Yi court: the royalty, the nobility (*yangban*), the country gentry (*hyangban*), the commoners (*sangmin*), the middle folk (*chungin*), the illegitimate sons of the nobility (*sŏcha*), plus the "humble folk," slaves or *ch'ŏnmin*. Confucian ethics and Confucian attitudes thoroughly permeated Korean society (Yu Sŭngguk, 1983: 77) and have been taken over into Christianity in a very complex way. Grayson (1991) argues that "In a strange way, Confucianism and Christianity entered into a state of dynamic complementarity which provided the right foundation for the social and economic changes which had to be made in order for the transition to an urban-industrial society to have occurred."

The five Confucian virtues of love, uprightness, propriety, knowledge and reliability were seen as essential, especially within the family (Wilson, 1988: 1070). Traditionally Koreans, like many other Asians, consider the family and familial relationships particularly important. Korean historians have often made strong criticisms of the Confucianism of the Chosŏn Dynasty, for the reason that it paid high respect to Confucian scholars but neglected and looked down on others, such as, farmers and those in business. By this means, the former could readily justify their oppression of the latter (Yu Sŭngguk, 1983: 116). In society in general, as in the family, life was hierarchical, dominated both by loyalty to persons and by ritualistic observances. Authoritarianism on the part of the rulers went along with submission on the part of the ruled. Protestant churches, Presbyterian in particular, in the Korean context have come to embody "the Confucian hierarchical order in church community" (Kim Ill-soo, 1985: 231). The Christian clergy tends to be highly authoritarian in relation to their parish members. Juniors are expected to show respect to seniors, children to parents, wives to husbands, and workers to their employers, but it is not expected that seniors need to take care of juniors, husbands to love wives, and parents to show patience to their children (cf. Yu Sŭngguk, 1983: 116). This is of course only one aspect of Korean Confucianism. Nevertheless, this has been pervasive in Korean society. Although Christian values are to some extent contradictory to Confucian values, they are often complemented and strengthened by the latter. Daniels

(1979: 47) describes how influential Confucianism was during the Chosŏn Dynasty as follows:

> The Yi Dynasty [Chosŏn Dynasty] was the golden age of Confucianism in Korea. During the last century of the Koryo [Koryŏ] dynasty there had been a marked increase in interest in Confucianism in Korea, so that by the time Yi Song-kye [Yi Sŏnggye] usurped the throne from the last king of the Koryo dynasty in 1392, Confucianism was already well established. Yi Song-kye adopted the Confucian system of education and government exams. The complete triumph of the Confucian examination system in the government exam system assured them a strong and lasting foothold in Korea. To be a scholar was synonymous with Confucianism. All the boys were anxious for Confucian education and the popularity of these studies caused schools to spring up all over the country. This desire became stronger and stronger century after century, so that Confucianism became even stronger in Korea than it was in Confucius' own country China. Private elementary schools were found in almost every village where the study of Confucian texts began. After these there were the government schools in each district where the Classics were taught. These had their own Confucius shrines and it was here they prepared for, or studied for, the government exams.

This indicates why Confucianism has been more influential in Korea than in most other East Asian countries (Grayson, 1989: 175, 213). Further, it should be noted that "the Confucianism that flourished during the Chosŏn Dynasty is known as Neo-Confucianism, which is a mixture of Confucian, Buddhist and Taoist thought" (Daniels, 1979: 48). It is different from *Ch'ŏndo-gyo* or the Religion of Heavenly Ways. Neo-Confucianism is the Confucianism which has been pervasive in Korea even after the Chosŏn Dynasty. It is still influential in everyday life in Korea today. For example, although many Koreans are not overt followers of Confucianism they still tend to be deeply involved in ancestor worship. Even some Christians have been involved in the activity, which has caused a major dispute among Christian leaders and theologians as to whether or not Christians should do so or be allowed to do so (cf. Yun Sung-bum, 1973). Daniels (1979: 48) argues that the "Confucian tradition is still a very important part of Korean life and likely will be for many years to come. The standard of right living set down by Confucius is as natural to Koreans as eating and drinking and touches every aspect of their lives."

Wilson (1988: 1079) argues that in a society that has gone through rapid industrial change over a short period of time it would be surprising if traditional values were not still pervasive, though perhaps in a modified form. He suggests that modern Korean society remains characterised by many Confucian values (cf. Sun-Ae Chou, 1983: 309). From a questionnaire designed to find sources of dissent among South Korean students, Wilson (1988: 1073) found that there was a very strong belief that a small group of people in Korea control the life chances of the rest in a harmful way and that, even for students, open expression of resentment to authority is not common. According to him, "A Gallup poll of 500 randomly sampled employees of 100 firms found that close intimacy with high ranking persons was deemed the most important factor for success in life (cited by 43.5% of the respondents)". Lee Hyo-chae (1977: 34) maintains that the traditional (especially Confucian) notion of giving men predominance over women is observed not only by non-Christians and non-believers but also among Christians and that there is no significant difference between the two categories. In Korea, over 50% of the population claim that they are not associated with any religion nor with church or temple.[1] *Tonga Ilbo* (11 Nov. 1990) argues that such people are actually leading a "Confucian" life.

Kim Byong-suh (1984) argues that Christianity in Korea has been heavily influenced by an indigenised Confucianism. Kim (1984: 126-128) states that Confucianism has been organised by the idea of "respect for parents" and this has led to Korean life being "family-oriented", with a strong sense of in-group loyalty. This has had implications for Korean Christianity. For example, "churchism" (or *Kaekyohoe chuŭi*), which is a pervasive phenomenon of the Korean church, means that there is little cooperation between churches, whether they belong to the same denomination or not. In other words, the prosperity or otherwise of a congregation is almost entirely its own responsibility, even in denominations which have a conciliar structure beyond the local congregation. This is important in explaining church growth. Kim's explanation does not go any further, although his attempt to make a link between Confucianism and Christianity is important in the context of this book.

To sum up, Confucian teaching has influenced Korean society for a long time. Confucianism has so deeply affected Korean culture and learning (Kim Doo-hun, 1963: 17; Palmer, 1967: 37) that its influence is found even in those individuals who have not made any explicit acceptance of Confucian ideology.

Teaching as an Occupation in Korea

As I have said above, one of the most important aspects of Korean Confucianism is respect paid to teachers or to those seen as learned.[2] According to a survey by the Korean Association of Education (quoted in Chŏng Uhyŏn, 1980: 278), students at one Korean university showed more interest in becoming teachers than in following any other career. A survey conducted in the region centring on Kangwŏn Province showed that the large majority (62%) of all teachers surveyed in the area agreed that, although they were struggling with financial hardship due to a meagre salary, they had "no complaints whatsoever as to their profession". They are mostly content with the social recognition given to teachers (Chung Tai-si, 1966: 15). The reason why many young people and members of Korean society regard teaching as a desirable occupation, despite the low rewards, is deeply rooted in Korean history and culture. As in other Southeast Asian regions, a teacher is perceived as a sacred and august moral entity rather than a mere professional person (Chung Tai-si, 1966: 17). Noting that a significant proportion of the top-level political leaders of the years 1952-1962 had been involved in the teaching profession, Hahn and Kim (1963: 317) argue that this is consistent with "the high social prestige accorded the teaching profession in Korean society". Obtaining a university education or becoming a teacher is a means of upward social mobility for Koreans. In the next section, I will look more closely at the reasons why Koreans have a high regard for education.

The Desire for Education in Korean Society

Living standards in Korea are strongly influenced by higher education. Susan Chira (*New York Times*, 7 April 1987: 6) writes of a man who earns $260 a month in a metals factory working 11-hour shifts, and who says "I think it's unfair — there's such a big difference between office workers and factory workers and I would get double the salary if I had more education." Such discontent has been pervasive over the last 30 years. Under the name of modernisation and national development, a series of educational development plans, especially related to higher education, has been established and enforced since the Five-Year Socio-Economic Development Plan was introduced in 1962. As I indicated earlier, for good or bad, American influence over Korean society in general and in such economic planning is immeasurable. Given this, it is not surprising that Korea has adopted or copied an American system of education ever since the liberation of 1945 (cf. Kim Sung-shik, 1962: 4). The technical assistance given to Korean universities by the US is worth noting. In the few years after 1954, under a contract between the Ministry of Education and the University of Minnesota, 226 university teachers had the opportunity to study in the United States, 121 of them earning higher degrees. In turn 56 Minnesota staff served in Korea. Total funding for this project over eight years amounted to more than $15,000,000. In August 1956, at the request of the Ministry of Education, the George Peabody College for Teachers assisted schools and teachers' colleges in Korea in raising standards, revising programs and procedures to meet societal demands, and helping to upgrade facilities and equipment. Eighty-two Korean educators studied in the United States under this project and 37 American educators served in Korea (Williams, 1962). This gives only a partial picture of American influence over Korean education. This assistance and the other close links between the two nations have heavily influenced Korea over a period of 40 years and remain today[3].

There has been a tremendous increase in higher education institutions and in the number of students enrolled in them over the last thirty years. The increase in enrolments has been 121-fold over a 38-year period (Kim Jongchol, 1983: 7; also see Selth, 1988), something rarely achieved elsewhere. Kim Jongchol notes that "the rapid growth rate in recent years shows a fine contrast with other advanced nations such as USA, UK, France, West Germany and Japan, where the enrolments in recent years show zero or minus growth in general". This view seems to differ from that offered by Kim Sin-bok (1983: 12) who argues that "the quantitative development of higher education is not a Korean phenomenon; it is rather a world-wide phenomenon". However, even Kim Sin-bok (1983: 22), quoting the UNESCO *Statistical Yearbook* (1982), says that compared with 36 per cent growth in the USA, 33 per cent in the UK, 32 per cent in France and 33 per cent in Japan, the four-fold increase in Korea during the seven-year period from 1975 to 1982 looks extraordinary. Such an increase has been possible not only because of government policy, which strongly supports development plans involving education, but also because of "the pressure of public opinion" (Kim Jongchol, 1983: 8). Probably no other parents in the world seem more enthusiastic than Korean parents about ensuring higher education for their children. Not infrequently, parents commit suicide due to the strain and anxiety of getting their children into prestigious schools and into higher education (Paik, 1968: 15). Harman (1990: 4) notes that "a recent survey in Korea revealed that 97% of parents want their sons and daughters to receive a university or college education". The reason is firmly rooted in Korean Confucianism.

In the highly stratified system of the Chosŏn Dynasty, there were six classes as mentioned earlier. They were all determined by birth. Those males who belonged to the *yangban* class were educated with special emphasis on literature. Most of them gained a good understanding of the writings of Confucius, and enjoyed high social status and respect. *Ch'ŏnmin* and *sangmin*, however, had no access to literature and were not respected. Daniels (1979: 47) argues that [during the Chosŏn Dynasty] "Confucian scholars were the moral leaders of the community in the same way the clergy were the moral leaders of the uneducated masses in Europe during the middle ages".

It is interesting to note that while Christian missionaries introduced an educational system which influenced modernisation in Korea, it is the Confucian tradition that has been mainly responsible for the high regard for learning (Kim Chan-hie, 1982: 120). Thus, the work of Christian missionaries who were especially concerned about education found ready support. Eventually, the combination of the practices of both religions has contributed to the development of "high fever" for education.

On the other hand, the staff vs. student ratio in Korean colleges and universities is much lower than in Europe and America (Selth, 1988). This situation has worsened as there has been an enormous growth of enrolments in higher education over the last thirty years. Kim Sin-bok (1983: 26) reports that in 1982, the teacher/undergraduate student ratio was 1:32.8. Table 5.1 presents some basic statistics on the growth of higher education in Korea.

Korea is higher than many advanced countries in the number of college students per 1,000 of the population (cf. Kim Sin-bok, 1983: 23). At present Korea has over one million students enrolled in four different categories of higher educational institutions.[4] In a country with a population of 40 million, a little more than $5,500 per capita GDP, and scarce resources, this figure is very high comparatively speaking. It is similar to a nation with three times Korea's GDP (Adelman and Robinson, 1978: 41). In Korea some feel that too many are enrolled and that there is a possibility of producing an "unemployed intelligentsia". Un- and under-employment have been common among college graduates since the 1970s (Light and Bonacich, 1988: 111). Chung Bom-mo (1966: 8) argued 25 years ago that the number of higher education institutions should be reduced or, at least, no new ones should be allowed. On the other hand, others tend to feel that higher education must be kept open as long as there is a strong demand on the grounds that in the job market "supply tends to create demand" (Kim Jongchol, 1983: 14). However, although "over-supplying" has created demand to a certain extent, Korea has not been able to absorb all the graduates into the workforce. Thus competition for jobs has been high and many educated Koreans have emigrated to find work.

Table 5.1: Growth of higher education (1945-1982)

Year	No. of Institutes	No. of Teaching Staff	Enrolments	Growth Index in Enrolments
1945	19	1,490	7,819	100
1950	55	1,110	11,358	145
1955	74	2,626	84,996	1,087
1960	85	3,803	101,041	1,292
1965	162	6,801	141,636	1,811
1970	168	10,345	201,436	2,576
1975	204	13,981	297,219	3,801
1980	236	19,173	615,452	7,871
1982	235	27,616	954,066	12,202

Sources: Kim Jongchol (1979) and Statistical Yearbook of Education, 1980-1982, quoted in Kim Jongchol (1983: 7)

There is also an unusually wide gap in wages between university graduates and non-graduates. In their discussion about Korean political leaders, Hahn and Kim (1963: 311) argue that "a university education is now for all practical purposes an absolute prerequisite for advancement to a top-level political position in Korea". In Korea, education has been necessary for social mobility (Paik, 1968: 15), unless it is achieved through real-estate speculation and the like. This has driven large numbers of school leavers into higher education even when they are not particularly interested in learning. A relatively well-educated, highly literate labour force has enabled the introduction of new productive methods and technologies, and high wages have been used to ensure that the best students go into industry. This has resulted in great competition to get into universities, colloquially called "university entrance hell". Some who fail the entrance examination, especially those from wealthy family backgrounds, go abroad to pursue a university education (cf. Sin Kipŏm, 15 May 1991: 39; Chang Insŏk, 1990: 448), though most who go abroad usually do so for post-graduate programs. The information centres of foreign universities, not only within Korea but also in countries like the United States and Australia, have profited through this. Some agencies have been involved in fraud such as forging documents (*e.g.*, TOEFL scores, academic records).

Subjects such as Korean, English and Mathematics are most important in preparation for university entrance exams and students often take special lessons. These lessons are called *Kwaoe* or extracurricular study. *Kwaoe* was officially banned by the Korean government in 1980 as it was considered to be providing unequal opportunities, but the banning was reversed in 1989. Many parents are prepared to pay one million Korean won per month (or A$454 per week) for each subject. In addition, some parents mention in the contract that if the student is successful they will pay the teacher a bonus, often around A$10,000.

Failure in university entrance exams has been a major cause of teenage stress and delinquency in recent decades. A few hundred thousand fail each year and a large number of them sit for the exam again in the following year. Those who do this often experience great emotional pressure. Despite an increase in the number of institutions and the number of students admitted to the universities, the competition has become increasingly intense. High school students who are assumed not to be competent enough tend to be neglected by their teachers. The following sentiments expressed by a student in this predicament are typical:

> Only a small proportion of high school students are going to be successful in the entrance exam. But the class is focused on the minority group and this drives me mad. I am very disappointed that I am neglected from the teaching and educational system just because I am not good at studies (*Tonga Ilbo*, 18 Nov. 1991: 23).

As most universities in Korea suffer from a lack of funding and as university education is essential for climbing the socio-economic ladder in Korea, some wealthy parents have been prepared to donate large sums of money to have their children accepted into a university. University teachers have also been involved in taking bribes. Actually, bribery has been a serious problem in Korean society for a long time. The social source of this problem is the authoritarian structure of the society, which, again, has much to do with Korean Confucianism (*Tonga Ilbo*, 11 Feb. 1992).

Rapid Industrialisation and its Consequences

While Korean society has been changing rapidly, partly due to the drive for education, there are a number of resulting problems. According to Western experience, churches generally decline where industrialisation becomes significant and materialism rises. The pace of industrial change in modern Korea, especially since the 1960s, has been so rapid that tensions and dislocations have arisen. Korea's political and economic conditions in the global society have led Korea to become part of the semi-periphery in the world system, to use Wallerstein's terms (Chŏng Sŭngguk, 1986: 79). Because it was under the threat of socialism during the Cold War period, Korea was dependent on American political and military influence in a significant way. Why did churches grow in Korea especially after Korean society had started the process of industrialisation? One part of the answer is that a form of "religio-economic entrepreneurship" came about due to various factors in Korean society. The rest of this chapter is designed to look at these, to show how they are inter-related, and to explore "religio-economic entrepreneurship" and its consequences for church growth.

Rapid capitalist development and Korea's participation in world capitalism since 1960 has been built on an abundant supply of cheap disciplined labour supplied by the exodus from rural areas (Lie, 1992). The rural population formed 58.3% of the population of Korea in 1960 but only 28.9% by 1979 (Cho Yohan, 1984: 13). Such a change has taken place in many so-called Third World countries but the economic growth rate in Korea was extraordinary. It was 41% per annum from 1962 to 1978, *i.e.*, the economy expanded by 250 times in these 16 years. Despite this growth the movement from the rural to the urban areas created unemployment, under-employment, a swollen service sector, and an urban poor (Light and Bonacich, 1988: 111, 112), although not as much as in other so-called developing nations.

South Koreans today are often preoccupied by the question of what people earn. There is a great gap between the "haves" and "have-nots" in both economic and social terms (cf. Cho Yohan, 1984: 13). Material goods are being given priority over human feeling. "People, like Mr. Suh, the 63-year-old technician, are less comfortable with the new prosperity. Although he has done well under the new order — he lives with his wife, a young daughter and his son's family in a spacious three-bedroom apartment — he is suspicious of it as well," says Chira (cited in *New York Times*, 7 April 1987: 6). Chira goes on to quote Mr. Suh: "We've had economic growth without values. ... Out of it came a society with a widespread atmosphere of distrust — between the haves and have-nots, between generations, between neighbours. In the countryside, there were no walls between homes; that's not true in the cities. Our Korean society used to be a society where we gave priority to human beings. Now we give priority to material goods. The result is confusion" (cf. Lie, 1992: 296).

Another aspect of this materialism is the boom in real-estate speculation that has occurred since the 1960s. One report suggests that "Capital gains taxes are in practice almost non-existent, since property speculators are not required to report their dealings to the government, and nominees are used extensively. One result of the speculation is that the gap between those who have property and those who do not is widening. Best estimates are that about 5% of the population own 65% of all non-corporate land" (Clifford, 1990a: 56). Four hundred thousand persons, or one per cent of the population, gained sudden riches from real-estate speculation. Mr. Y. is a typical example of the new Korean. He became a sudden "millionaire" because the block of land his parents bought 15 years ago has turned out to be a "lump of gold". His daily business starts with listening to a schedule prepared by his secretary. It is all about how to consume his money and how to enjoy the day (Chang Insŏk, 1990). Such people tend to go overseas staying in first class hotels, having simple plastic surgery or getting a medical examination which could easily be undertaken in Korea. They usually prefer to go to university hospitals for a five minute talk regarding the flu, whereas those who are injured by car accidents are often turned away by the hospital for they have no money to pay for treatment (*Tonga Ilbo*, 7 Feb. 1992: 12). The industrial sector has prospered with the help of cheap labour and foreign loans which are government guaranteed. But profits are controlled by a few.

An interesting question is why and how socio-economic modernisation in Korea came to have these consequences. If this question can be answered, something can be said about religio-economic entrepreneurship and why Korea is different in this respect from other countries. Korea has pursued a growth-oriented development rather than a stability-oriented one. For example, compared with the development procedures in Japan, Korean "modernisation" has been achieved in a relatively uncontrolled and indiscriminate manner. Japan was able to modernise in a relatively selective and controlled way. Interested in the impact of the unstable process of modernisation in Korea, the political scientist Han Sung-joo (1982: 82) has compared some of the social features that Korea and Japan respectively have experienced. According to Han Sung-joo (1982: 80), during the Japanese colonial period (1910-1945), the Korean traditional elite lost their power and social status, many of their values and practices being discredited or destroyed. While Japan had the Meiji reformation which maintained the emperor system, Korea experienced a disruption of its political institutions and authority structure, due to Japanese control. When Koreans were forming their government after World War II, they had to build their institutions almost from scratch. New mechanisms, such as elections, to generate loyalty to governing structures had to be generated. This has been a long and difficult process.

On top of this, the Korean War (1950-53) brought about massive, often indiscriminate, social change from which Korea is still recovering. Korea, as a newly industrialised society with few intact political and economic traditions, has tended to rush the pace of development in an attempt to catch up with developed countries. In doing this, Koreans have experienced much confusion in respect of their values. Materialism left a moral vacuum within Korean life.[5] Some scholars like Ji Won-yong (1965) argue that a growing number of Koreans sought solace from the experience of anomie by turning to religion. Suh Kwang-sun (1984: 246) argues that the rapidly urbanised and industrialised Korean society has meant that a large proportion of Koreans have come to feel alienated from society and to see churches as refuges. This is one of the reasons given for the growth of Korean churches.

Against this, Han Sung-joo argues that the relatively unstable "Korean modernisation" led to "extreme materialism" deeply penetrating the religious sectors. In this view, the church is not a refuge from materialism but another institutional embodiment of it. Kang Yosep (1983: 385, 386) refers to the tendency for Korean churches to adopt capitalist ideas and practices. Churches tend to be more interested in accommodating the middle class than the *Minjung*, or "mass". They promote the idea that "the bigger the church the better" and also believe in maximising profits. It is not entirely clear what Kang means by the "maximisation of profit", but he clearly considers that materialism and capitalism have deeply penetrated Korean churches (cf. Song Pyŏnggu, 1991: 11). One consequence of Korean rapid development has been the injection of economic entrepreneurialism, that is, capitalistic and materialistic activities, into Korean Christianity. Such activities have been encouraged by the over-supply of the Christian clergy which I have discussed earlier. This is one reason why it is sometimes said that although Korean churches have achieved explosive growth, their ethics and morality have become questionable to Christians elsewhere (Chŏng Chisŏk, 1991: 11). Han Pyŏngok (1986: 31) argues that the sources of many of the problems of Korean churches are to be found among the ministers themselves. A good number of them, according to Han, are more interested in fame and material success than in authentic Christian ministry. He also states that they are "bread-earners" rather than ministers. Even when special meetings for spiritual revivalism are held a few times every year, they are regarded as an opportunity to raise money (Pak Kyejŏm, 1983: 14). Many ministers are most concerned about the economic aspect of the church, particularly the rewards for themselves, tending to neglect the other dimensions of church life including the specifically religious.

Institutionalisation of Religious Organisations: The Role of Church Leaders

How organisations get firmly established depends on various social factors. Complex interactions between the church and the socio-economic conditions in the larger society are involved. Significant in the matter of growth is the role of church leaders. As an organisation struggles to grow, its leaders' roles are significant. The ways in which the clergy are produced not only differ from one religion to another, and from one era to another, but also from society to society. The ways in which religious education centres are organised and the reputation of graduates of the centres (which may be related to the standard of the education or qualification) also vary. In some cases, the priesthood or clergy is an hereditary profession, in other cases it is not; that is, eligibility for the profession varies. The length of the education period also varies for different religions and places.

The introduction of Western education by missionaries coupled with the Korean "high fever" for education has encouraged the output of clergy. I shall show in this section why Buddhism and Confucianism have been unable to establish more than a few educational institutions, resulting in a lower number of clergy being produced. Christianity, on the other hand, has set up a large number of educational institutions which in turn have contributed significantly to the rise of religio-economic entrepreneurship.

The Professional Training of Buddhist Leaders

A four-year educational system for Buddhist monks was adopted during the middle period of the Chosŏn Dynasty. As I have already discussed, this was when Buddhism was politically suppressed and when Confucianism came to be the official state ideology. This traditional Buddhist education system, known as the "teaching temple" system, is still practised at Korean Buddhist temples today. The first stage teaches candidates for the priesthood the required sets of values and patterns of behaviour and knowledge about Buddhist rites. The main content of the curriculum in the second stage consists of Analects on Zen which deal with the high virtue of priests. The third stage concerns four major scriptures and the fourth stage the *Avatamsaka sutra*. This four-stage educational system does not seem to have been consistent across the history of Korean Buddhism partly because there has been no tight control over eligibility for entry into the educational system. There has been no government control or rational-legal administrative control; thus its graduates have received no diploma which enables them to be accepted into the wider society. This is significant because modern Korea has become a "diploma society". Although Buddhism has been in Korea since the sixth century BC, it is argued (Park Sun-young, 1983: 39) that it was only in the latter half of the 19th century that Buddhist leaders came to realise the necessity for institutionalised training to re-establish Buddhism in the face of threats carried by Western civilisation and to preserve national sovereignty. This was, in part, a reaction to the establishment of the educational and medical centres established by Christian missionaries. Buddhists founded schools where they taught Western knowledge and skills. For example, the Myŏngjin School, the predecessor of Tongguk University, was jointly established by many Buddhist temples in 1906.

Although schools and higher education institutions (three) have so far been established by Buddhists, only two universities (Tongguk University and Wŏn'gwang University) offer professional training to produce priests. These two are formal educational institutions under government supervision which maintains academic standards. Students get into these universities through the nation-wide entrance exam and thus they are well recognised in the wider society.

Buddhism has remained a "hermit religion". Most, if not all, Buddhist temples moved into the mountains as a consequence of suppression by the Chosŏn Dynasty (Palmer, 1967: 90), and most of them are still located in mountain areas. In 1456, the Chosŏn Dynasty even decreed that monks were forbidden to enter the capital of Seoul (Ro, 1983). Koreans have come to feel that Buddhist temples should remain in remote locations. In addition, Korean Buddhist temples observe less than 10 services annually (Mok Chong-bae, 1983). For example, one Buddhist sect, "Mirŭk-chŏng of Taehan Buddhism", observes only four major services, one in both January and March and two in June (according to the lunar calendar). Another sect, "Pŏphwa-chŏng of Taehan Buddhism", holds four major Buddhist services and five services of its own each year: the founding day of the sect on 10 May, the anniversary of the recovery of Seoul during the Korean War (*i.e.*, 28 September), the anniversary of the death of the founder, Priest Taegak (4 October), and the regular meetings of 11 May and 19 October, all by the lunar calendar (Mok Chong-bae, 1983: 21, 22). Being located in mountains, Buddhist temples are not easily accessible to believers, although there is a big crowd on the birthday of Buddha in most temples. The following section indicates how the springing up of religio-economic entrepreneurship was hampered in Korean Buddhism.

Korean Buddhism and religio-economic entrepreneurship. Today, Korean Buddhism receives much public criticism as a number of priests have been involved in financial conflicts. Some priests appear to be as keen on worldly fame and assets as they are on striving for a Buddhist way of life. They often regard the properties of their temples as their personal belongings (Mok Chong-bae, 1983). Facing the modern era of "secularisation" with its Korean peculiarities, Buddhism, like Christianity, has not been able to resist involvement in religio-economic entrepreneurship.

However, entrepreneurship in Buddhism has been limited and has not developed to the extent where the majority of Buddhist priests have become involved. Buddhism in Korea also tends to be regarded as an historical heritage of Korean culture, almost as a major piece is in a cultural museum. Mok Chong-bae (1983: 26) points out that it is mainly due to such a notion of Buddhism that the temple property law enforced during the Japanese colonial period still tends to be effective, and many temple resources remain under government control. This seems to have limited the development of entrepreneurship within Korean Buddhism and prevented the "bigness syndrome" which characterises Christianity. Still, some priests are very interested in amassing a fortune and in some cases the conflict over temple property has been extreme.

The Professional Training of Confucian Leaders

After Confucianism was adopted as the state religion during the Chosŏn Dynasty, Korean society came to emphasise "learning". All boys from the upper class were anxious to gain a Confucian education and the popularity of these studies led to schools springing up over the country (Daniels, 1979: 47). Private elementary schools or *Sŏ Tang,* where the basic study of Confucian texts began, were available in almost every village. After elementary school, students could attend government schools where the Confucian Classics were taught. These had their own Confucius shrine and the main task of the students was to prepare for the government exams. The best students were then admitted to Sŏnggyun Kwan University which was a state university. The dominant hope was to gain a high-ranking government post.

As already discussed, Confucianism brought about development in education. However, the educational institutions that came into being existed mainly to teach students to become government officers[6] rather than to produce a Confucian clergy to work for the enhancement or expansion of Confucianism as a religion. Without such a group Confucianism did not prosper as an explicit doctrine, although it penetrated Korean family and social life. This is partly due to the nature of Confucianism, which is often regarded not as a religion but as a set of principles for everyday life.

The Professional Training of Christian Leaders and the Over-Supply of the Clergy

Despite the significant roles that theological training centres have played in the process of church growth in Korea, no study has, as far as I am aware, adequately recognised this point. Chou Sun-Ae (1983: 310) is correct to point out that "the rapid growth of the Korean church today can be traced primarily to Christian education". While her "education" refers to education in general, she also briefly points to seminaries as the source of thousands of graduates each year (Chou, 1983: 316).[7]

Until 1934 there were only two theological training centres established by Korean Protestants, one Presbyterian and one Methodist. This was 50 years after Protestantism had come to Korea (Chŏn T'aekpu, 1987: 238). By 1983, however, there were about 80 theological seminaries in Korea (Kim Chŏngjun, 1983: 27). There had been a review of theological training centres in 1980, many illegal or low standard ones being forced to close down. But this did little to stop the increase in student enrolments. Since 1980, enrolments in theological colleges have increased by about 600 per cent (*Chosŏn Ilbo*, quoted in Song Pyŏnggu, Feb. 1991: 11).

The number of four-year theological college students graduating each year to minister to a church are given in Table 5.2. It appears that these statistics do not include those graduates from various lower-level or unregistered theological seminaries who are also entitled to become ministers. According to *Chosŏn Ilbo* (quoted in Song Pyŏnggu, 26 Feb. 1991: 11), the number of theological department graduates or, in Song's words, "ministers to be" reached about 10,000 by 1985. It appears that this number included the graduates from those theological colleges which are not registered at the Ministry of Education. Hong Pansik (1986: 9), a professor of theology at the Koryŏ Theological Seminary, asserts that the number graduating was about 6,000 in 1986. *Kidokkyo Yŏnhap Sinmun* (quoted in Song Pyŏnggu, 26 Feb. 1991: 11) suggests that there were 15,000 of them by February 1989. Although these numbers are not entirely consistent with one another, they are indicative of the expansion which has occurred.

Table 5.2: Number of people graduating from theology departments in some years

Year	1985	1986	1987	1988	1989
No. of Graduates	1454	1764	1840	2271	3670

Source: The Ministry of Education, Seoul, 1985-1989

Some scholars like Rev. Dr. Mun Minku (interviewed in June 1991) argue that the reason why Korea has come to have over one hundred theological training centres at tertiary level is that the Korean church has grown tremendously, and that more theological training centres had to be established to keep up with demand. However, this only explains part of the matter. Korean Protestantism cannot absorb all those trained to be clergy, whether those from registered theological colleges or from unregistered institutions. The industrial, government and educational sectors do not want to employ theological college graduates, because theological qualifications are not directly relevant to work in these sectors. There are enough other university graduates queuing for such positions. Consequently, there is considerable competition among theological graduates to find a ministerial position. One way to do so is to begin a new congregation and to try to build it up to a size where it can fully support the minister. If the minister succeeds in involving at least some persons who have hitherto not been churchgoers, this very process contributes to overall church growth in Korea. The surplus of theological graduates in Korea also prompts some to migrate overseas, where they contribute to the growth of Korean ethnic churches.

Church Schism, Ecumenism and Church Growth

Church schisms have contributed to overall church growth in Korea. In a religiously pluralistic society, those members who are dissatisfied with church worship and programs in one congregation can easily seek another denomination or perhaps organise a new congregation within the same denominational tradition. Thus, the satisfaction of members is a critically important factor in sustaining the life of a congregation (Roof et al., 1979: 212). Nevertheless, dissatisfaction, leading to schism, has in Korea often been followed by membership increase in both the "parent" church and the churches formed after a split (Yi Sanggyu, 1986: 104). In 1978 there were already 188 denominational bodies, including indigenous churches, within Korean Protestantism, as a result of continuous schisms and sub-schisms within both individual congregations and denominational organisations (Barrett, 1982). Currie *et al.* (1977: 42) argue that church schism may result in a decline of churches, but this does not seem to be the case with churches in Korea.

Why have there been so many church schisms in Korea? Ji Won-yong (1965) states that "an American theologian ... after teaching and lecturing in Korea for several months during 1964, commented that as far as he could see there is very little theological basis for church splits in Korea [cf. Kim Ill-soo, 1985: 234]. He felt that strong personality factors exist". From a sociological point of view, if personality factors are involved, these need to be understood in relation to the particular social settings of Korean society. In the Korean church such personal factors often have something to do with money, power and prestige, even if theological reasons for the schism are given (Yi Sanggyu, 1986: 112). Why have such factors been involved in church splits in Korea, especially since the 1960s?

The schisms of contemporary Korean churches are firstly related to the ways in which Protestantism has been brought there since 1885 (Yi Sanggyu, 1986: 106). The most influential group of missionaries in Korea came from the United States. Presbyterian and Methodist churches in the United States were already split due to the Civil War and each denomination pursued its own mission policy in Korea (Han'guk Kidokkyosa Yŏn'guhoe, 1989: 193). Some of the early Presbyterian and Methodist missionaries from the United States attempted to unite to form a single Protestant church in Korea. Largely because their head offices in the United States were against it, nothing came of this attempt. As a consequence, Korean Christianity was divided from the outset. This helped to create an environment more conducive to competitive denominationalism than to ecumenism.

Nevertheless, during the period of Japanese imperialism, Presbyterians and Methodists agreed to amalgamate their newspapers but the Japanese suppressed it (Chŏn T'aekpu, 1987: 194). Mergers of Methodist and Presbyterian churches, educational, medical and publishing institutions were also advocated by some missionaries and Korean Christians after 1905. However, the proposals for church union failed, due mainly to opposition from Presbyterian missionaries. The possibility of merger was again raised after 1919, but, again, nothing came of this because of the opposition of Presbyterian leaders (Chŏn T'aekpu, 1987: 218). Although there had been some ecumenical initiatives in the area of magazines, schools, and hospitals, no attempt at uniting was made in the area of theological seminaries. Each denomination maintained its own theological college (Han'guk Kidokkyosa Yŏn'guhoe, 1989: 212). These separate institutions became a major long-lasting source of denominationalism. Theological debates between Methodists and Presbyterians about divorce and "women's teaching in church" were raised during the 1930s and this caused conflict (Chŏn T'aekpu, 1987: 240).

In order to avoid unnecessary conflict and competition, major groups of missionaries from different nations had in 1892 adopted an "Agreement on Division of Territory". A few big cities remained the concern of every mission group, but the different provinces of the Korean peninsula were distributed to six groups of Methodists and Presbyterians. This policy lasted for thirty years. It did not stop all competition, but it led to the formation of separate forms of Christianity in the different regions. This regionalism became another source of conflicts in Korean Christianity during the 1930s and in the period following independence.

A. J. Brown (quoted in Yi Sanggyu, 1986: 112), a former director of the Board of Foreign Missions of the Presbyterian Church in the USA, suggested that for the first 25 years the American missionaries in Korea were typically Puritan in their beliefs and practices. Thus "conservative Christianity" strengthened over that period. However, since the 1930s, different theologies arrived in Korea, not only through the missionaries, but also through the return of overseas-trained Korean theologians. These differences contributed to the propensity for division in Korean churches.

Church splits continued after Japanese colonialism ended in 1945. The diverse relationships that had developed between Korean Christians and the Japanese, some supporting imperialism, others opposing it, provided another cause of schism in Korean Christianity. One of the most urgent problems Korean Christianity faced after independence was related to Christian involvement in Shinto worship during the colonial period (Oosthuizen, 1972: 227, 231). For example, from the Kyŏng Nam Synod many ministers were killed or imprisoned due to their resistance to the Japanese even when a large proportion of Christian leaders at the time were involved in Shinto worship. This caused conflict and led to splits in many churches after independence. A successful merger had occurred when the two Methodist denominations introduced by the Southern and Northern Methodist Churches of the United States united in 1930. However, this united Methodist Church split into two in 1946 over the issue of Shinto practices and collaboration with the Japanese (Grayson, 1985: 122). As most Methodist churches were financially dependent upon foreign support, they were keen to have close relationships with missionaries. Whenever new missionaries arrived in Korea, Methodist churches did their best to "seize" them. This caused bitterness between the different Methodist denominations. Nevertheless, the Methodist churches united again in 1949, but this denomination split in two a year later. This division was not healed until 1958 (Chŏn T'aekpu, 1987: 286-288).

The Presbyterian churches have also experienced many schisms, ostensibly because of doctrinal differences, although sometimes other factors, such as regionalism, have also contributed. Those who broke away to form new branches of Presbyterianism have, at various times, accused the denomination from which they were separating of being too liberal, too ecumenical, too closely related with Shinto collaborationism, anti-ecumenical, or pro-communist (Oosthuizen, 1972: 223-236). Presbyterianism in Korea is still divided into various competing denominations.

When examining church schisms in Korea it should be noted that church schisms before 1960 tended to be denominational splits, bringing about the establishment of more denominations. After 1960 schisms were mostly within congregations, although this often led to the formation of new denominations. Moreover, the reasons for denominational splits and church schisms in the two different periods are not always the same. In the latter period, splits were caused more by secularisation and materialism, and theological disputes were about different matters (Ji Won-yong, 1965: 7). Yi Sanggyu (1986: 103) argues that church schisms in Korean Christianity in recent decades have had to do with "trivial matters such as factionalism, regionalism, and power struggles between the leaders, rather than differences of theology or faith" (cf. Pak Sun'gyŏng, 1985). As indicated by Yi (1986), these causes of schisms may be trivial from a theological point of view. However, they are significant from a sociological perspective, and they are generated by the social context of Korean society.

Especially since the 1960s, conflicts within individual churches are closely related to the over-supply of *Chŏndosa* or ministers-to-be. While thousands of them are graduating from a large number of seminaries every year, not all of them are sufficiently qualified to serve a church (Hong Pansik, 1986: 10), and most graduates struggle to find employment. In addition, many of the church leaders, such as elders who are serving the church on a voluntary basis, tend to think that they are the employers or owners and that the ministers are the employees. The voluntary service of elders and the fact that there are more than enough ministerial candidates to serve the church has led the elders to be "hard-nosed" in their general attitudes towards ministers. If a conflict develops between a minister and some or all of the elders, or between subgroups within the eldership, this can sometimes result in a split within a congregation, leading to the formation of a new congregation or denomination in competition with those remaining in the previous congregation. Such competition acts as a spur to growth in both the old congregation and the new one.

Related Demographic Factors and Unemployment

The population of Korea, which is increasing at a rate of about 2.7% per annum, was reported to have reached a total of 29,194,379 by 1965, a five-year increase of 4,205,138 persons. This gave South Korea a population density of 280 persons per square kilometre, a little higher than that of Japan, and one of the world's highest. The Economic Planning Board reported that 8.7% of the 7.5 million labour force were unemployed at the end of 1965. It was also reported in August that 97.6% of the spring 1966 graduates of technical schools had found jobs, but only 60% of the spring 1966 liberal arts graduates of colleges and universities had gained employment (quoted in Paige, 1967: 28). *Tonga Ilbo* (19 Oct. 1990) reported that 300,000 university graduates, including those unemployed from previous years, were competing to find jobs but that only a third of them could expect to be employed in 1991. These figures give some indication of the general economic environment in which theological graduates find themselves, of the difficulties they would face in finding employment in a non-church occupation.

Religio-Economic Entrepreneurship in Korean Christianity

When a minister establishes a church with a few members, one of their first actions is to rent a meeting place. Then their top priority is to have their own building. In some ways, pastors/ministers may be seen as investors in their church. A church planning to build at an estimated cost of 1,200 million won (A$24 million) benefited from the pastor of the church who willingly contributed 70 million won (A$140,000) from his own pocket (Kang Chŏnggyu, 1983).

The dimensions of the church building, its extravagant decoration, and the size of the annual budget have been used as measures of a successful ministry (Chŏn T'aekpu, 1987: 331). Korean churches have been experiencing what Kim Byong-suh (1985: 71) calls the "bigness syndrome" and many have been greatly interested in expanding their congregations. Kim Byong-suh (1985: 72) was also able to see the problems of materialism and of the "secular" age which have deeply penetrated churches in Korea, when he argued that "personality structure and lifestyles developed by human interaction based on the money economy and calculability of 'cold cash' have spread among the people in the church". Most churches in urban areas are actively involved in fund-raising to extend their church buildings. The prime interest seems to be gathering more and more people in the church for financial and status reasons as much as for purely religious reasons (Pak Kyejŏm, 1983: 30). Hong Pansik (1986: 11) accuses the Korean churches of maintaining their "nobility" by being on the side of the "haves" and of those with power while neglecting the "have-nots" and the oppressed. Dr. Harvie Conn, professor of theology, who has taught in Korea for twelve years observes that "Korean churches seem to be concerned about the rich rather than the poor. ... They should be careful not to fall into materialism" (quoted in *K'ŭrisch'yan Ribyu*, Sept. 1991: 12; also cf. Yi Sam'yŏl, 1984: 182). Son Bong-ho (1983: 337-338), with respect to the "bigness syndrome", points out that "a fatal lack of critical attitude toward the materialism of contemporary culture" is pervasive within Korean Christianity. Some church leaders over-stress "God's material blessings in the present life" in their sermons (Clark, 1986: 25).

The bigness syndrome and the materialism of Korean churches have attracted a great deal of attention which is directed at the budgets and assets of the churches in Korea. The Research Institute of Christianity in Korea (quoted in Kim Byong-suh, 1984: 151) notes that the average annual budget of churches in the metropolitan cities (16,028,000 Won or A$29,141) is four times that of country areas (4,630,000 Won or A$8,418). The former is over twice the average of all the churches in Korea (7,033,000 Won or A$12,787). No Ch'ijun (1983, quoted in Kim Byong-suh, 1984) notes the enormous imbalance between the budget of the churches in the Seoul area and that of the country areas: the average annual budget of the very large churches (over 1,501 membership) is 60 times that of the small churches (less than 100 membership). The property of the churches has increased due to the offerings of the million extra people who become churchgoers each year. However, purchasing property (building and real estate) has not been the only means to accommodate the increasing membership. Other investments are also significant. "Block busting" has been a typical way of occupying an area and expanding property for many churches (Kim Byong-suh, 1984: 155, 156). When a church is built in a block the price of houses and land in the area drops, then the church purchases them for the purpose of expanding property. In a newly developing area, the Korean government distributed blocks of land for church use at a special price similar to that charged for buildings for public use. However, since the late 1980s churches are no longer included in this special category. Ninety churches throughout the country formed an association to overturn this policy. On the other hand, some think that "the coming of such a policy is quite proper because the church has been deeply involved in expansionism and materialism, instead of taking the roles of the light and salt of the earth" (*Saenuri Shinmun*, 20 July 1991). Kim Byong-suh (1984: 156) goes on to argue that the enormous size of church budgets is not the core of the problem: the question is the way in which the budget is used and for whom it is used.

It is well known in Korea that some ministers actually sell and buy churches: a practice which is perhaps the epitome of religio-economic entrepreneurship. The price of a church depends upon the size of membership, which largely determines the minister's income. Yi Sŏngnŭng, a Korean migrant in Sydney, who attended a theological college for a couple of years, observed such a case. He told me that one of his friends bought a church. After the purchase, the membership of the church grew, allowing it to be resold at a much higher price. Rev. Pak Ch'ŏlsu (quoted in *Saenuri Shinmun*, 1 June 1991: 10), in a conference with the theme "The Problems of Korean Churches and their Future", described Korean churches as a group of selfish organisations which should now try to free themselves from their obsession with money, factionalism and power. Whether or not one agrees with that assessment, it is clear that religio-economic entrepreneurship has been an important contributor to church growth in Korea.

Concluding Remarks

The impression given in this chapter as well as in this book as a whole may be that I tend to downplay the religious aspects of the Korean church. Of course, without a religious aspect, religio-economic entrepreneurship could not have come about. However, as Moffett[8] (23 Nov. 1973: 10) argues, "Not all the factors contributing to church growth in Korea were spiritual and theological or the consequence of sound mission practice".

In a church growth seminar conducted for missionaries working in Korea held on 16 October 1980, a leader of a well-known inter-denominational mission listed the following as defects in many Korean churches:

> Pride of bigness; preoccupation with money; ... mishandling of money by leadership; hedonism; ... authoritarianism of pastors; high rating of finances for qualifications of elders; salvation by

church attendance; excessive stress on tithing that produces burdens; lack of social concern; ... mixed motivation for missions; denominationalism; regionalism; ... Confucian structures; ... Shamanistic view of ministry; materialistic view of the kingdom; and humanism (Nelson, 1983a: 193).

Nevertheless, it is clear that at least some of the features have contributed to church growth in Korea.

This book focuses mainly on quantitative growth rather than qualitative growth. Rev. Kwak Chŏnt'ae (*Yŏnhap Kidok Sinbo*, 17 Sept. 1991), the president of the Methodist Church in Korea mentions that

The number of Christians in Korea is over ten million. So-called quantitative growth has been achieved over the last few decades. Thus, qualitative growth is likely to follow sooner or later. The symptoms are already there. For example, some Christians are deeply involved in Bible study and Korean churches are active in overseas missionary activities. ... I tend to find a similarity between Korean Christianity and the bamboo tree which grows in height first for a while and fattens and fills inside later.

Kwak's comment seems to indicate there has been insufficient qualitative growth in Korean Christianity. Only time will tell us whether or not the few promising signs which have been actually observed in Korean Christianity as it has been growing quantitatively are the start of a qualitative growth.

Notes

[1] The Korean Economic Planning Board in its census report notes that such people make up about 57% of the population and the Korea Gallup Survey reports that 51.0% are in this category (cited in *Tonga Ilbo*, 11 Nov. 1990).

[2] Korean churches run a variety of Bible study courses which may take several months to a year or so to complete. The graduates are permitted to wear a square college cap (*Tŭlsori Sinmun*, 24 Nov. 1991). This reflects the

fact that Korean society based on Confucianism tends to show respect to the learned.

[3] It should not be overlooked that if it were not for the US, the socio-economic development or the "dependent development" of Korea would be markedly less. However, from the United States' point of view, any help that has been provided was mostly for its own benefit. In this respect, many argue that Korea has been exploited. This has been a major cause of student demonstrations. A few American Cultural Information Centers have been often used as sites of student demonstrations to resist American influence and at least one of the centers was burnt down. The Korean government has forcefully suppressed the activities.

[4] They are four-year Colleges and Universities, two or three-year Junior Vocational Colleges, four-year Teacher Training Colleges and four-year Miscellaneous Collegiate Schools. In 1983, the number of these institutions was 97; 128; 11; and 19 respectively (Kim Jongchol, 1983: 6).

[5] What E. Durkheim called "anomie" has been a significant feature of Korean society.

[6] Palmer (1967) terms this group or class "the scholar-official bureaucratic".

[7] It is not clear whether she has included those seminary graduates who are not from theology departments. Considering the statistics from the *Ministry of Education*, Seoul, 1985-1989, the number appears to refer to those graduates from theology departments only.

[8] He was a United Presbyterian missionary and associate president of the Presbyterian Theological Seminary in Seoul.

PART III: THE GROWTH OF KOREAN ETHNIC CHURCHES IN SYDNEY

Introduction

In the previous two chapters I examined the growth of churches in
Korea. This provides an important part of the background to the growth
of Korean churches in other countries such as Australia. Now I turn to
the question of what factors have influenced the growth of Korean
churches in the Sydney area. Various dimensions of the Korean
immigrant churches will be explored in the light of the theoretical
perspective proposed earlier in this book. The data come from
participant observation, interviews, and from Korean ethnic
publications over the last ten years (see methodology in chapter 3).

Chapter 6

Overview of the Life of Koreans and Korean Churches in Sydney

Australian Immigration Policy and Korean Immigration to Australia

The historical link between Korea and Australia was made when Australian missionaries first started working in Korea in 1885. This led some Koreans to come to Australia for short periods of study, and some Koreans to settle in Australia as housekeepers to assist Australian families between 1921 and 1941. Before 1970, there were a few Korean students under the Colombo Plan, some government officials undertaking various technical courses in Australia, and students in English language institutions. Migration of more Koreans to Australia started in the early 1970s. When the South Korean government was withdrawing Korean troops from the Vietnam War between 1972 and 1975, about 500 Korean civilians and technicians who were in Vietnam at that time came to Australia as tourists (*Hoju Sosik*, Sept. 1984: 8) with the help of the Easy Visa Scheme introduced by the Whitlam government. Most of them were single men who stayed on and obtained permanent residency at the time of the amnesty in 1975. Many of them had the chance to bring out family members from Korea under the Family Reunion Scheme set up in 1978. According to Korean government statistics (quoted in *Hoju Sosik*, Nov. 1982: 12), there were 6,500 Koreans in Australia by late 1982, while the Korean Society of Sydney estimates that there were 8,000 Korean migrants in the Sydney area around the same time. This figure rose to 10,000[1] by early 1986 (*Hoju Sosik*, Jan. 1986: 12), 20,000 by early 1990, 25,000 by mid-1990, and 30,000 by early 1991.[2] Since the start of significant Korean migration to Australia in 1972, 85-90 per cent of Koreans have settled in the Sydney area (cf. *Hoju Sosik*, Jan.-Feb. 1983: 2)[3].

Various Organisations of Koreans in Sydney

There are many kinds of organisation within the Korean community in Sydney. These include: the Korean Yudo (Judo) Association of Australia, the Korean Navy and Marine Corps Association of Australia, the Korean Chamber of Commerce and Industry in Australia, the Korean Association of Cleaning Contractors of Australia, the Korean Chamber of Commerce in Campsie and Canterbury, Australia (established in 1987), the Christian Business Men's Committee of Sydney, the Ch'ung Ch'ŏng Association in Australia (organised by a group of people born in Ch'ung Ch'ŏng Province), the Korean Vietnam Veterans' Association in Australia, the Korean Business Migrant Association Inc., the Australia-Korean Welfare Association Limited, alumni associations, and various churches and temples. All these organisations tend to consist exclusively of Koreans. These organisations encourage members to maintain their "Koreanness" and may even create "ethnic islands" in Australia. Of these organisations, churches are the most notable. The way in which the Korean churches in Sydney have been influential in the life of Koreans and the consequent growth of these churches is the focus of this study.

There were over seventy Korean churches in Sydney by early 1994. According to a Korean community newspaper (quoted in Im Tonggyu, 1989: 10), 82.5 per cent of the Koreans in Sydney are self-confessed Christians of which 70.2 per cent are Protestants and 12.3 per cent Catholics. Rev. Im Tonggyu (1989), who was a Korean missionary to Australia and who served the Galilli Yŏnhap Kyohoe (the Galilee Uniting Church) for several years, says that "whenever I, during my early days in Sydney, tried to introduce the gospel to Koreans, I was told in most cases that they were already churchgoers". A survey of the Korean community in Sydney (reported in *Hanho T'aimjŭ*, 26 Jan. 1990) finds that, of the 405 respondents, Protestants numbered 208 (51.1%); Catholics 91 (22.5%); Buddhists 17 (4.2%); atheists 68 (16.8%); the remaining 19 (4.6%) having not answered the question.

Koreans in Sydney agree that the ethnic churches are their most popular and important centres. Rev. Kim T'aein (*Taeyangju Nyusŭ*, 15 Dec. 1990) points to the significance of the churches in the Korean community in Sydney, saying that if Koreans want to build a co-operative Korean community in Sydney, the first and most important thing is for the Korean churches to be friendly and co-operative to each other.

Compared to the history of Korean migration to the USA, the history in Australia is relatively short. The significance of the brief examination of the experiences of Korean ethnic church ministries in the USA in an earlier chapter, in addition to the review of relevant studies, lies in the fact that the Korean experiences in the USA have encouraged a great number of theological graduates in Korea to seek a church ministry in other countries such as Canada, New Zealand and Australia. Australia is often called a "heaven in the twentieth century" by Koreans who plan to migrate overseas. There is even an information booklet called *The Way to Australia: a Heaven on Earth in the Twentieth Century* (Chŏn, 1985).

The first Korean church was established in Melbourne in 1973. In 1974, another church was begun in Sydney. There were already 30 Korean churches in Sydney by April 1987 (Lee Sang-taek, 1989a: 42), seventy established churches, and about 20 or 30 home churches in the Sydney area by early 1994. Such growth in numbers is extraordinary. All churches maintain at least one ordained minister, or a theological graduate who will be working to become ordained later. Further, there are about 100 or 150 ordained ministers or theological graduates who were born in Korea and who are planning to minister to churches (*Hanho T'aimjŭ*, 13 July 1990: 31). While both Buddhism and Christianity are major religions in Korea, the former is not as influential in the life of Koreans in Sydney. The reason for this was partly explored in earlier chapters.

Korean Buddhist Temples in Sydney

Before I look in greater depth at Sydney churches, I will briefly look at Korean Buddhist temples in Sydney. Each Korean Buddhist temple in Sydney maintains a professionally trained priest. Only about two hundred members are registered in the temples (*Hoju Tonga*, 17 May 1991: 7), and an average of about one hundred Koreans regularly attend. Analysis of the Korean ethnic newspapers published in the Sydney area since 1982 shows that the Korean Buddhist temples have never been a significant centre of Korean ethnic activities, nor have Buddhist masters been important social leaders in the Korean community. Buddhist temples are rarely mentioned in the ethnic newspapers, whereas churches provide them with abundant news. Furthermore, Christian ministers form a major group of people contributing articles to Korean ethnic newspapers in Sydney (Yun Yŏmun, 1991). It was not until 1986 that the Korean community came to have its first Korean Buddhist temple, the Hong Pŏp Sa Temple. This was twelve years after the first Korean church was established in Sydney. In 1988, the Hong Pŏp Sa Temple experienced a split out of which came the Pulgwang Sa Temple at Summer Hill (served by Master Chang San). The Hong Pŏp Sa Temple changed its name to the Talma Sa Temple and invited Master Sŏk Sŏngu who was working in Hong Kong at that time. In 1989, some members of the Korean community founded another temple, the Kwanŭm Sa Temple. There were three Korean Buddhist temples until October 1991, but the number decreased to two following the amalgamation of the Pulgwang Sa Temple and the Talma Sa Temple as of 3 November 1991, the new temple being named Chŏng Pŏp Sa.

According to the Sydney Buddhist Society (quoted in *Hoju Tonga*, 17 May 1991: 7), there were 80,387[4] Buddhist believers in Australia in early 1991 of which 14,439 of them are Asian migrants and their descendants. Buddhism in Australia is a minor religion in terms of the number of believers. According to Master Sŏk Chayŏng of Talma Sa Temple (interviewed in March 1991) and Master Chŏngo of Kwanŭm Sa Temple (interviewed on 28 Nov. 1989), it is extremely hard for Buddhists to set up a temple in Australia as they have to rent a house, modify it and fill it with necessary decorations and tools which they have to bring from Korea. Master Sŏk Chayŏng (*Hoju Tonga*, 17 May 1991: 7) of Talma Sa Temple says that

> Proselytising "Australians" or maintaining a temple in Australia is not easy because Australian society is not much aware of Korean Buddhism, whose priests wear grey coloured robes. But Australians are quite used to South East Asian Buddhism whose priests wear orange coloured ones. ... I often get over-conscious of the way people look at me downtown.

Moreover, it is generally much harder for Korean Buddhist masters to migrate to Australia than for Korean Christian ministers. Master Chang San of the Pulgwang Sa Temple is the first Korean Buddhist master to be awarded permanent residency in Australia. He returned to Korea about four months after the establishment of the Pulgwang Sa Temple, so that he could apply for immigration. The temple then invited him back. According to the Pulgwang Sa Temple (cited in *Hoju Sosik*, Jan. 1988:

22), because Australia is a Christian dominant country and does not have much understanding about Buddhism, there have been many obstacles in the process of the master's migrating to Australia. The process was delayed, as there was no category of "inviting a Buddhist master" in the Australian immigration regulations. According to the Pulgwang Sa Temple (cited in *Hoju Sosik*, Jan. 1988: 22), the case of Master Chang San pioneered a route for Korean Buddhist masters migrating to Australia. However, only a few Korean Buddhist masters have come to Australia to replace the masters who have left. This is partly because, unlike in Protestantism, there has been no over-supply of the clergy in Korean Buddhism and because Buddhist priests are under the strict control of Buddhist authorities. In other words, religio-economic entrepreneurship has not developed within Korean Buddhism and this left overseas Koreans without a large number of the clergy.

This contrasts to these Korean churches in Sydney that are connected to parent churches in Korea but which are virtually independent of them. When a parent church in Korea establishes a church overseas, it provides the new one with a minister and supports it financially. However, as the new church grows in church membership, only a nominal relationship remains between the two churches. All the Korean Buddhist temples are quite strictly dependent upon their parent temples in Korea, particularly in terms of the supply of clergy (masters). This has major ramifications for institutional growth.

Reasons for Attending Buddhist Temples

According to the priest of Talma Sa Temple (interviewed in March 1991), an average of thirty Koreans attend every Sunday service in the temple. Most of the registered members were not Buddhists before coming to Australia, even though Buddhism is a major religion in Korea in terms of the number of believers. However, Buddhist templegoers in Sydney certainly form a minority group of Koreans, compared to the number of Korean Christians in Sydney. It is interesting to note that the Buddhist temple is sometimes visited by some of the Christian churchgoers when they are depressed.

Some of those Koreans in Sydney who were Buddhists prior to migration have become churchgoers since their arrival in Australia. However, they are not always satisfied, or are even unhappy, with various aspects of the churches, and hence become temple attenders. Buddhist masters, interacting with such a group of members, seem to have some understandings about why they have switched back to Buddhist temples. The masters avoid making comments in detail, simply saying that it is because of various types of conflicts which have been pervasive in the Korean churches right from their beginnings in the 1970s. In this respect, a significant reason for attending Korean Buddhist temples is not for what the Buddhist temple provides but because of Korean church practices and conflicts. Despite this, it is the churches which grow and not the temples.

A Brief Picture of Korean Churches in Sydney

The following information is based on a survey by the *K'ŭrisch'yan Ribyu* (Jan. 1991), a Korean ethnic monthly Christian magazine. The survey was undertaken by mail, phone and interviews. Although the report carries the title, "The Korean Immigrant Churches Today", it notes that "five Christian sect groups such as Jehovah's Witness and the Catholic churches were excluded in the survey" (Jan. 1991: 23). No reason was given for this exclusion. The review tends to be too dismissive of the few Korean ethnic Christian churches in Sydney and religious bodies which may be generally categorised as cults or sects by some sociologists and to orient itself towards Protestantism. Despite these limitations, this is the first survey of Korean churches in Australia. While excluding some sect groups and the Catholic churches, the report surveyed 90 per cent of the Korean churches in Australia (94 per cent of the churches in the Sydney area and 80 per cent in the rest of Australia) in existence during the survey period (12 Nov.- 23 Dec. 1990). This survey report is sufficient for the purposes of this section and I will extensively cite its contents.

According to the report, there were 73 Korean churches in Australia during the survey period, of which 52 were in the Sydney area (see Table 6.2). Twenty seven churches in Sydney (*i.e.*, 51.9 per cent of these 52) were established during 1988, 1989 or 1990 (see Table 6.3). The number of Korean ethnic churches has been steadily growing for the period of the 1970s and 1980s. This is in parallel with a general growth in ethnic churches in Australia (cf. Black, 1991).

Table 6.2: Number of Korean churches in different parts of Australia

Names of the areas	Number of churches
the Sydney area	52
Wollongong	1
Tasmania	1
Melbourne	4
Canberra	1
Newcastle	2
Adelaide	3
Perth	4
Brisbane	4
Gold Coast	1
In total	73

Source: *K'ŭrisch'yan Ribyu*, Jan. 1991: 22-27

Table 6.3: Number of churches established each year in Sydney

Year	Number of churches	Per cent
1974	1	1.9
1977	2	3.8
1979	1	1.9
1980	1	1.9
1981	2	3.8
1982	2	3.8
1983	1	1.9
1985	4	7.8
1986	7	13.5
1987	4	7.8
1988	9	17.3
1989	9	17.3
1990	9	17.3
In total	52	100

Source: *K'ŭrisch'yan Ribyu*, Jan. 1991: 23

Table 6.4: Number and per cent of churches with their own building and the amount Korean churches pay per week for the use of church buildings

Rent fee	Number of churches	Per cent
Own building	5	10
Free of charge	14	27
Less than $30	12	23
$31 - 50	9	17
$51 - 70	4	7.5
$71 - 80	4	7.5
$81 - 100	1	2
$101 - 150	2	4
More than $200	1	2
In total	52	100

Source: *K'ŭrisch'yan Ribyu*, Jan. 1991: 24

   Although there are over seventy Korean churches in Sydney, only a few of them have so far been able to obtain their own church buildings (see Table 6.4). In Korea it is not possible to use or rent an existing church building to establish another church, regardless of whether or not the renter or the rentee belong to the same denomination. This is because of the competition between churches. However, in Australia it is easy for an ethnic church to rent part or the whole of an existing Australian or other ethnic church building because of decline in churches. Most Korean ethnic churches pay only a maintenance fee to use another church building. The Uniting Church in Australia (UCA) rules that no member church of the UCA should charge another one for the use of church buildings. Korean immigrant churches that are members of the UCA usually offer a maintenance fee on a voluntary basis (*K'ŭrisch'yan Ribyu*, Jan. 1991: 24).

The Religious Dimension of Korean Churches in Sydney

It goes without saying that the religious dimension of the Korean churches should neither be over-emphasised nor underestimated. There are different estimates of the importance of religiosity in explaining church attendance. Some of the interviewees who hold critical attitudes towards the Korean churches argue that the reason Koreans go to church has little to do with religion. Kim (interviewed on 15 March 1991), who was reluctant to state his name, and who was about to return to Korea after four years illegally staying in Australia, asked: "How many of us Korean immigrants go to church for religious reasons? There must be only a few like that." He particularly mentioned that "a lot of them go to church to have lunch" by which, I take it, he meant that Korean immigrant churches are little more than sites of general social gathering.

However, it seems that many Koreans do go to church to worship what they see as their God, to listen to the sermon, and to feel saved. Many of them say that such religious reasons are more important than, say, economic reasons in motivating their attendance at church. Rev. Kim Mun'gil (interviewed in Nov. 1989), the pastor of the Sidŭni Sunbogŭm Kyohoe (Sydney Full Gospel Church) with a membership of 3,000, observes that while some join the church for reasons other than religious ones, most of them come to believe in God. Otherwise, they tend to leave the church". I visited Mr. Kim Mun'gil's church on Nov. 1989. Many of the registered members of the church were staying out of the worship service, although plenty of seats were available inside. Some were chatting and some were even moving in and out of the church building. While interviewing Mr. Kim Mun'gil, I realised that he tended to be theologically conservative in his views on the Korean churches in Sydney, probably reflecting the denomination with which he is associated, and that he tended to regard the church as a purely religious institution. According to my fieldwork, religiosity is a significant part of Korean church activities, but it does not fully represent the motivation of Korean church involvement. However, it appears to me that the majority of Korean churchgoers think that the Korean church is a religious organisation and that the various activities which take place there are different ways in which the church expresses its religious concerns.

Many Korean churches in Sydney hold prayer meetings at 5 o'clock in the morning (Monday to Friday) as do most churches in Korea. Unlike services on Sundays, most of this time is spent in prayer and it seems that the most important reason to attend the meeting is to pray. Generally speaking, the Korean churches in Sydney tend to be conservative in terms of their theological positions (Yang Myŏngdŭk, 9 Aug. 1991: 13), and Korean Christians tend to give a high priority to blessings from God. Theologically conservative Christians are not necessarily more religious than liberal ones. What I am pointing out here is that although Korean churchgoers are involved in different dimensions of the church, they tend to see their activities as religious, and this itself indicates a degree of religiosity. The purpose of praying may have to do with material blessing for some people and with evangelical work for others. When a Korean moves around the Central Railway Station with some Biblical messages written on a placard, the activity is probably more religious than economic, ethnic or political. The point I am making here again is that religious reasons cannot be discarded from the factors that bring Koreans to the church, but they are only one factor.

Some elders of the Sidŭni Hanin Yŏnhap Kyohoe (Sydney Korean Parish of the UCA), the first Korean church in Sydney, demonstrate a religious aspect of the Korean Christians in Sydney, although other dimensions could well be involved. An elder of the church, Yu Chaekyŏng (quoted in *K'ŭrisch'yan Ribyu*, Sept. 1991: 33) states, "We, the first group of Koreans in Sydney, arrived in Sydney with no money at all. All we each had was a suit case. Most of us were working in factories. Our wage was about A\$120 per week. Owning our own church building was only a dream for us. However, we all said, 'Let us purchase one of our own'." Another elder of the church, Kim Chunyŏng (quoted in *K'ŭrisch'yan Ribyu*, Sept. 1991: 33) recalls that "In those days, we did not own our own house, our cars were old second-hand ones. But we brought our offerings to the church. Our priority was given to purchasing our own church building." It is clearly noticeable that religious enthusiasm among Koreans in Sydney has influenced the growth of Korean churches.

Missionary Zeal as an Expression of Religiosity

Some Korean immigrant churches have a missionary zeal which reaches overseas. For example, the Sydney Korean Parish of the UCA has been financially supporting a student at a theological college in Peking. The church also supported a Chinese student in the United Theological College, Sydney, who was ordained at the end of 1992. After the Gulf War in 1991, the church hosted a joint assembly of 18 Korean churches in the middle East (*Yŏnhap Kidok Sinbo*, 17 Sept. 1991).

The Tong San Uniting Church has been supporting two missionary couples: one family in the Philippines and another in Paraguay. Both families were members of the church. Rev. Son Tongsik (July 1991: 25), after his visit to the mission field in Paraguay, comments as follows:

> Why is this young and promising couple taking all the trouble to go to the remote mission field in which neglected Indians live? Can they undertake it by their own will or with the help of God? Are they doing it for fame? Not at all. ...

The religious aspects of the Korean immigrant life sometimes act as a form of catharsis of the hardship involved. For example, some Korean churchgoers believe that, although they have come to live in Australia for many different reasons, there is a clear-cut plan made for them by God; therefore their Christian mission should never stop but continue throughout their pilgrimage (Ch'oe Chŏngbok, 1991; Lee Sang-taek, 1988). There is clearly a religious element here.

Migrant Theology

There is a theological perspective developed in overseas Korean churches which claims to explain the life of migrants and which offers encouragement. This perspective is termed "Imin Sinhak (Migrant Theology)". Rev. Hong Kilbok (1988: 124) is a minister who promotes this theology. He states that the church is a community of faith, hope and love, and that in addition to this, the Korean immigrant church is a community of fellow Korean immigrants (*K'ŭrisch'yan Ribyu*, Aug. 1991: 22). According to him, Jesus was a migrant himself, moving from heaven to earth, and again to other foreign lands. Abraham, Moses and Jesus all had to leave their home and live in foreign countries, coping with various problems and difficulties.

Some Koreans come to Australia through circumstances not of their own choosing. They might have come to Australia because they were not successful in Korea or because they were not admitted to the USA. Some Koreans who fought in the Vietnam War had to move around the world after the war and they came to Australia because they had no hope of working in their occupation of choice in Korea. The difficulties, whether psychological or physical, faced by Koreans in Sydney are soothed by messages in the Korean immigrant churches. Rev. Lee Sang-taek (1988: 22-24) emphasises that "wealth should not be our only goal as migrants. We are here to influence and improve every part of the Australian society: Christianity, education, politics, economy, culture. ... We should realise that God has sent us to Australia to carry out such missions."

Migrant theology also encourages migrants not to give up achieving in non-religious areas and encourages Koreans in Sydney to achieve material well-being (Lee Sang-taek, 1988). This tends to make up for the deprived situation of many Korean migrants in Sydney. Rev. Lee Sang-taek (quoted in *K'ŭrisch'yan Ribyu*, Sept. 1991) who has ministered to a Korean church in Sydney for over ten years, says that one of the long term goals of his ministry is to develop a guidebook for Bible study especially suitable for the immigrant life.

Concluding Remarks

Some activities of Korean churches in Sydney tend to be purely religious or ethnic or economic or political in their characteristics, whereas some others tend to be mixture of two or more of these. Throughout their history, Christian churches in various countries have not only been concerned with religious matters but also with many other aspects of social life (Brown, 1982: 8). Likewise, Korean churches in Sydney have been involved in many aspects of the life of Koreans. In the next three chapters, I shall consider the extent to which ethnic, political and economic aspects of these churches have contributed to their rapid growth.

Notes

[1] The Korean Society of Sydney (cited in Kim Man-souk, 1988) estimated the number of Koreans in Australia at 12,000 in the middle of 1986.

[2] These numbers include those Australian-born children under Korean parents.

[3] Table 6.1: Number of Koreans (by the place of birth) residing in different states of Australia

NSW	VIC	QLD	SA	WA	TAS	NT	ACT	AUST.
16,137	1,572	1,244	543	926	158	60	357	20,997
76.9%	7.5%	5.9%	2.6%	4.4%	0.8%	0.3%	1.7%	100%

Source: 1991 Census (Australian Bureau of Statistics, 1991)

[4] According to the 1991 Census, 139,795 people in Australia claimed to be Buddhists (Australian Bureau of Statistics, quoted in *The Australian*, 9 June 1993: 10).

Chapter 7

The Ethnic Dimension of Korean Churches in Sydney

Introduction

As soon as Koreans arrive in Sydney, most make a visit to a church irrespective of whether or not they are Christians. This is because they are already well informed that the church is a place where they can meet other Koreans and where they can obtain the information they need in order to establish themselves. They have often been informed by travel agents in Korea that the churches in the Korean community in Sydney are the main site of Korean gatherings and that they help newcomers in various ways. In his congratulatory message on the fifteenth anniversary of the Sydney Korean Parish of the Uniting Church in Australia, Rev. Pak Chongch'an, the president of the Association of Korean Ministers in Sydney, stated that the (first) Korean church in Sydney was the place of fellowship for "fellow Koreans" (Ŏ Yun'gak, 1989: 2; Yang Myŏngdŭk, 1989a: 2). The church is still the most significant gathering place for Koreans in Sydney.

As the most significant centre of ethnic activities for Korean immigrants in Sydney, the Korean church has been involved in many types of activities (*Hoju Sosik*, Aug. 1983: 26; cf. Cho Insuk, 1982: 6). For example, a Korean who is running a Korean food store may be associated with a Korean organisation like a Korean church in Sydney as s/he is interested in having more Korean customers for the business. Within the church, something "Korean" or something that has to do with "Koreanness" is maintained or is encouraged to continue. Koreanness in this book refers to the "sense of being Korean" or "the subjective feeling of being Korean."

The Korean churches in Sydney have often hosted many activities like Korean folk games or sports games (*e.g.*, *Hoju Tonga*, 1 Nov. 1991: 15) or have been involved in such meetings in one way or another (cf. *Hoju Sosik*, Nov. 1987: 17). *Hoju Sosik* (July 1983: 2) accuses the Korean Cheil Church of co-hosting and being unnecessarily involved in such a meeting as "A Musical Night for Koreans in Sydney". This is because *Hoju Sosik* thinks that the church should have nothing to do with such a gathering. However, *Hoju Sosik* realises simultaneously that there is no other organisation that can handle such an event and goes on to suggest that various organisations be founded so that they can be responsible for each part of the diversity of immigrant life. *Hoju Sosik* (Oct. 1983: 10) states that "After ten years' history of migration the Korean community came to have thirteen churches. What about business associations? There is only one as such: The Korean Chamber of Commerce and Industry in Sydney which is two years old".

What is clear is that the church had the significant role in the Korean community at the time of the above report; in fact, it has always taken such a role since the start of Korean migration to Sydney in the early 1970s. Han Sangdae (in *Hoju Tonga*, 17 May 1991: 2), a lecturer in Korean studies in the University of Sydney, observes that the Korean ethnic churches in Sydney form not only a community of Christians but also a community of fellow Koreans. Thus, they have contributed to hosting social meetings, music concerts, sports activities, and running Korean language schools. Why has the Korean church developed and sustained this significance? What are the things that distinguish Koreans in Sydney from other ethnic groups in Australia which help to explain this?

I will begin by looking at ethnicity. Koreans in Sydney generally speak Korean among themselves, wear national dress on some occasions and maintain many aspects of their culture. They generally want to marry Koreans rather than people from other ethnic groups. The Korean immigrant church is where a Korean can meet others and also look for a marriage partner. Advertising about its counselling service, the Sidŭni Sunbogŭm Kyohoe claims that one can come and talk to the counsellors of the church not only about religious matters but also about general problems in immigrant life. In this church a special counsellor is to be appointed to deal with marriage. An information network, connected to Korea, will be established to facilitate the search for potential marriage partners (*Hoju Sosik*, Dec. 1987: 16). This is to be set up by a Korean church in Parramatta which contains a group of people who are looking for marriage partners (*Hoju Sosik*, March 1985: 14). The group is well known to the Korean community as it has helped many Koreans to find partners. The report of *Hoju Sosik* jokingly recommends that those who want to marry soon should join the group. This suggests not only that Koreans in Sydney tend to prefer to marry other Koreans but also that Korean churches encourage this. One consequence is that the churches eventually gain a membership increase.

Other aspects of Korean ethnicity are often expressed directly or indirectly in the Korean churches. Koreans are highly supportive of vertically structured hierarchies (Chŏn Kyut'ae, 1983: 13). White-collar occupations are considered more admirable and respectable, and manual work is generally looked down upon. A university education significantly influences social status and respect. It may be argued that this is not peculiar to Koreans, however, as was shown in the section on the desire for education in Korea, there is a difference between Koreans and others in this respect (*Hoju Tonga*, 9 Aug. 1991: 2). Confucian culture remains significant whether or not Koreans migrate to other countries. *Hoju Sosik* (Sept. 1982: 9) reports that the prime concern of Korean parents about their children is their education, and at least the first generation of overseas Koreans tend to impose university education on their children. As in Korea, those parents whose children attend the university are proud of them. This is especially so when children study medicine or law. Those parents whose children have failed to enter the university feel ashamed, regardless of their children's interest or ability. Korean parents in Sydney try to send their children to private schools rather than public ones although some of them can barely afford it. For the sake of their children's study, they often give them the bigger and better rooms in their homes (Ch'oe Chŏngbok, 1991: 8). Korean students in schools in Sydney, especially high schools, often undertake extra-curricular studies through private study agencies. There are several such agencies which are run by Koreans.

This longing for education is often expressed in ways inappropriate to mainstream Australian education culture. The editor of *Hoju Sosik*, Sin Kipŏm (1991b: 10), tells us of his conversation with the principal of a school in St. Ives area.

> According to the principal, the school has about ten Korean children and their mothers visit the school too frequently. Whenever one of the mothers comes to the school, they bring

some "presents" for the teachers. The value of the presents has
been steadily going up. Teachers take it as an expression of
gratitude to them in the first place. However, when they are given
a sum of money, they become confused. Classes are disturbed and
the teachers do not know what to do when those Korean mothers
turn up.

The high expectation for children's performance often causes
negative consequences. In late 1990, a Korean university student in
Sydney committed suicide, throwing herself under an oncoming train.
The editorial of *Yŏnhap Kidok Sinbo* (17 Sept. 1991), avoiding
disclosing the details of the incident but pointed out that having
unnecessarily high expectations for their children's education is not the
way for Korean parents to fulfil themselves in their new country.

Maintaining these characteristics is a way of expressing what they
see as important facets of Koreanness in the context of a plural society
like Australia. These characteristics or lifestyles are also explicitly
readily observable in the area of language. A survey of the Korean
community in Sydney (reported in *Sosu Minjok* or Minority, Aug.
1990: 9) finds that 48.1% of the respondents say that the language
barrier is the most difficult problem in their immigrant life. According
to the 1981 Census, 51% of Korean-born people aged 5 years or older
assessed their English speaking ability as "nil" or "not good". This is
the seventh highest percentage among the 83 non-English speaking
birthplace groups included in the Census. Those Koreans who do not
have a reasonable English proficiency tend to maintain relations almost
exclusively with other Koreans. Most Koreans in Sydney speak Korean
at home. This is not only because the first generation of Koreans can
speak Korean better than English, but also because they want to
encourage 1.5[1] and the second generation to maintain the Korean
language. The speakers at the "Cultural Seminar for Korean Immigrants
in Sydney" (reported in *Hoju Sosik*, May 1984: 13) who were
exclusively Korean-born emphasised that the Korean language should be
maintained not only to communicate freely among Koreans but also to
remain as "Koreans".

Here is a typical example of a family of five members: husband and
wife with their three children, the eldest of whom was born in Korea
and came to Australia when she was very young and the other two of
whom were born in Australia. The eldest was a third year university
medical student in 1991. The husband and wife talk to each other in
Korean at home. They have a rule that everybody should speak Korean
on Sundays. The eldest child used to think that the Korean language
was of no use in Australia as she had fluent English, and the youngest
still thinks so. However, the eldest has tended to put considerable effort

into learning the Korean language since she became a university student. A married couple among her relatives think that the girl is often faced with a barrier between herself and the larger Australian society which she finds difficult to get over so that she is trying to "recover her identity" and maintain it.

In the Korean community it is commonly acknowledged that Koreans in Sydney watch five or six videos per week imported from Korea. There were eight video shops which provide Korean video-tapes in 1991 (*Sidŭni Hanin Chusorok*, 1991-92) and this increased to thirteen as of June 1993 (*Chugan Saenghwal Chŏngbo*, 18 June 1993). Standing near the video shops, a large number of Koreans can be seen moving in and out of the shops with often two plastic bags of tapes. The tapes contain movies, documentary, children's programs, and Korean news. Some Korean television programs are regularly taped and get supplied to the Korean video shops in Sydney. Many Korean parents believe that providing their children with children's programs from Korea is one way to encourage them to learn Korean.

Those Korean children adopted by Australian families, and the old people in the Korean community, were invited to a specially prepared party on 3-4 August 1991. The party presented Korean folk songs and plays. The president of the *Saek Tong* (or Rainbow) Mothers' Association which was the main contributor to the party stated that it was especially important that the adopted children were introduced to something "Korean" (*Hoju Tonga*, 9 Aug. 1991: 17).

Singing and listening to Korean songs also help Koreans to maintain an ethnic identity, though ideas about what this is differ. In Korea, there is a kind of song which reflects the general social and historical contexts of the last 80-90 years of Korean society. These songs describe Korean sufferings under Japanese colonisation, the poverty they experienced for centuries, the sufferings during and after the Korean War, doing good for their parents, and the nostalgia experienced during the process of urbanisation/industrialisation of Korea. These sufferings are often known as "*han*". *Han* songs are broadcast once a week through a Korean television show. The leader of the program usually starts by saying something like this:

> Beloved Koreans and fellow Koreans in many parts of the world. ... Despite your wish to see your parents, old friends, teachers, neighbours, ... you may not be able to come home for various reasons. ... I wish your nostalgia or "*han*" may be dissolved by the songs to be presented now which are also the songs that you and I have been singing for many decades.

About 30,000 Koreans are scattered all over the Sydney area, although the density of the Korean population is higher in the suburbs of Campsie and Canterbury. Social solidarity remains high in spite of this geographic spread. Koreans in Sydney usually answer the phone with "*Yŏposeyo?*" meaning hello. This partially indicates that those who are ringing Korean families are mostly Koreans.

Another aspect of life-style which is explicitly observed among Koreans in Sydney is eating habit. In the *Chugan Saenghwal Chŏngbo* (18 June 1993), thirty nine Korean food stores are advertised. These stores import Korean foods and have some vegetables planted in Sydney suburbs for Korean customers. Most tables of Korean households in Sydney are not much different from those in Korea. In fact, the tables I have shared with many Korean families are more Korean, and better than the average table in Korea in the sense that they are more nutritious and have a greater variety of typically Korean foods than the middle class in Korea. Seventy seven Korean restaurants are also advertised in the review. Describing the general picture of the life-styles of Koreans in Sydney, Kim Ŭn'gyŏng (*Hoju Sosik,* Jan. 1987: 11) says that one can live a more "Korean" life than one could in Korea. A Korean church elder, Ch'oe Chŏngbok (*Yŏnhap Kidok Sinbo,* 17 Sept. 1991), used to enjoy Western food during his stays in foreign countries until he reached the age of forty. Now he prefers Korean traditional foods like *Toenjang* and *Kimch'i.* It often seems to be that the longer Koreans stay as immigrants the more they tend to maintain their Koreanness, though the extent varies from one to the other.

He also says that while studying in an Australian theological college and getting involved in ministering to churches he has come to learn about, and to appreciate, some characteristics of Korean Christianity, although what they are is not clearly stated. Bearing in mind the characteristics of Korean Christianity which have been discussed by a number of scholars, the characteristics may only refer to spending a great deal of time in meditation and Bible reading and the practice of a fundamentalist belief, despite the fact that the characteristics also include that churches in Korea, as discussed in Part II, are often imbued with rather materialistic values. He goes on to argue that the Korean immigrant churches in Australia which are part of the Uniting Church in Australia (UCA) should, on the one hand, learn from, and be challenged by, what the UCA does, and that they are simultaneously responsible for preserving their cultures and traditions on the other.

Probably like other ethnic minorities, Koreans are emotionally touched by seeing the national flag. When the Pusan Elders Choir from Korea made a visit to Sydney and presented Korean hymns at the

Bankstown Town Hall in April 1991 over a thousand people came to the presentation, though some were non-Koreans. A Korean traditional hand-fan with a symbol on it from the Korean national flag (the sign of *ying* and *yang*) was given to each person in the audience. According to *Hoju Tonga* (26 April 1991: 17), the fan emotionally stirred the Koreans and made them nostalgic. The subtitle of the report in the paper was "A storm of applause from the fellow Koreans; foreigners too were deeply touched and had tears in their eyes".

These sorts of Korean ethnicity are expressed through, and are explicitly observed among, the Korean immigrant churches in Sydney. I was observing an evening service of Sidŭni Sunbogŭm Kyohoe, one of the three days of special services for spiritual revival with sermons by Rev. Yi John Songgi of the Yŏŭido Sunbogŭm Chungang Kyohoe (the Central Full Gospel Church, Seoul), which is the parent church of the church in Sydney. Many women members were standing in two lines, facing each other, in the entrance to welcome the visitors and also to collect freewill offerings. The significant thing about the women members was that they were all dressed in Korean traditional costumes, Hanbok (white jacket and sky blue long skirt). For those women, the church was amongst other things a place to demonstrate what they saw as their Koreanness. It was also a place where other Koreans would be reminded of their ethnic origin.

During fieldwork in Sydney I also observed another example of the way in which the Korean immigrant church serves an ethnic function. While a worship service was taking place in the Korean Catholic Community, Auburn, about one hundred members stayed out of the church building (24 March 1991). The first reason they stayed out was because the church building is too small to accommodate all the members who come to the church every Sunday. However, some members who arrived after all the seats were occupied stood near the entrance doors and took part in the service, whereas others formed groups here and there and got involved in sharing what had happened to each other during the previous week. I approached a group of grandmothers who were involved in chatting. I learned that those who have young grandchildren are often engaged in baby-sitting on week-days and they look forward to attending the church, which they often call "the school for the elderly", on the weekend where they can see other elderly persons and speak Korean. They have mostly come to Australia to join their sons or daughters, often to look after their grandchildren. The school for the elderly or *Kyŏngnodaehak* is held in many churches on Saturdays or Sundays. Those churches that hold school on Saturdays provide the elderly with transport. Mostly, they do not speak English and cannot drive so the church becomes an important focal point in their lives.

Towards the end of the service, I observed that three new members of the church who were also newcomers to Australia were being introduced to the congregation, and people were welcoming them by clapping. I could not see the newcomers for a couple of minutes and everyone was looking back and forth, trying to find where the new members were. Then finally, the newcomers, who were dressed in Korean national costumes, walked into the church building and received another clap. The Catholic community also had a group of members selling cool drinks at the corner of the church yard on the day of my visit there. They told me that it was basically for fund-raising for various purposes. If Koreans go to church primarily for religious purposes, it is less likely that such an act of fund-raising would take place during the time of the worship service. This indicates the multi-dimensionality of the church. Apart from attending the service, some Koreans spend several hours in the church before and after it, chatting and discussing various matters. This aspect of the church as an ethnic organisation is observed not only in cities like Sydney or Melbourne, in which a good number of Koreans have settled, but also in Hobart, Tasmania, where 43 Koreans live. The minister of the Agape Mission Church in Hobart, Rev. Son Sehwan (1991), states that the church serves as the "Korean Society (Association) in Tasmania" because there is no other organisation which fulfils this role.

The Church as an Ethnic Shelter for Koreans

The Korean church has taken care of some groups of people who are in need of help, but who may be often neglected by other Koreans. The minister of the Gallili (Galilee) Korean Church of the UCA, Rev. Im Tonggyu (*Hanho T'aimjŭ*, 20 Oct. 1989), thinks that the Korean community in Sydney is faced with four problems: the future of illegal migrants; aging Koreans; youth (*e.g.*, juvenile delinquency); and a Korean identity crisis which is linked to defining Korean values in the new nation. The Galilli Yŏnhap Kyohoe has especially been active in helping these groups. The church fully supported "the Conference to call for amnesty" made on 24 September 1987. In the same year, the Galilli Yŏnhap Kyohoe established the Tŭngdae-ŭi Chip (Light House) to provide new Korean immigrants with temporary accommodation, English conversation classes and job information. Recent arrivals can stay in the Tŭngdae-ŭi Chip for up to two weeks, during which they may find out more about where to go and what to do. The Galilli

Yŏnhap Kyohoe, and many other churches, have established meeting places for elderly Koreans which have made their immigrant life more meaningful than it might otherwise have been. One group of elderly people has even achieved the feat of performing an English play.

The Tŭngdae-ŭi Chip has recently changed and has been re-organised as the Sosu Minjok Sŏn'gyowŏn (Society for Ethnic Mission or SEM), a combined project of ten Korean and Anglo-Australian Uniting Church parishes in the Campsie-Earlwood area. Its services are open to people of any national origin, but with few exceptions it is only Koreans who look to it for help. Most other immigrant groups in Australia have their own organisations like the SEM. The SEM still maintains the Tŭngdae-ŭi Chip with similar functions to those mentioned above. In addition, the SEM helps newcomers with opening bank accounts, obtaining driver's licences, choosing schools for their children, job information, and finding accommodation. The Tŭngdae-ŭi Chip has also become a refuge for overseas students and for those who are involved in family break-ups and evictions. There are ten beds in two dormitories, with cooking facilities available (*Ethnic Link*, Nov. 1990: 6).

The SEM offers a counselling service in cases of racial discrimination. When such cases have been serious enough, Rev. Yang Myŏngdŭk (1989b), director of the SEM, has had to work in collaboration with Australian human rights lawyers. Other kinds of counselling services deal with domestic violence, juvenile delinquency, immigration of illegal migrants or of those who want to stay on after temporary visa has expired. The SEM runs a Korean ethnic school to encourage 1.5 and second generation Koreans to maintain their "Koreanness". The school offers lectures on Korean history, language, culture and arts. It actively interacts with other immigrant organisations, whose roles are similar to that of the SEM. These organisations share information on ways to help immigrants settle in Australia. The SEM once invited a group of Aborigines for four weeks to learn about their culture and religion. This was meaningful because, as the director of the SEM, Rev. Yang Myŏngdŭk (1989b) argues, the Aboriginal experience since European settlement explains much of what ethnic minorities are experiencing today.

The SEM has also been influential in promoting church growth and has tried to assist Anglo-Australian churches to grow. It has been co-ordinating a multi-cultural worship service every Sunday evening. About 15-20 people with different ethnic backgrounds gather in the Galilli Yŏnhap Kyohoe. They seek to understand each other's culture in the hope that it may enhance multi-culturalism in Australia. I participated in the service a number of times. On one occasion in June

1991, an Anglo-Australian minister delivered a talk about the "World Capitalist System" with reference to the many ways in which the first world has exploited the third world. He quoted many ideas from Karl Marx and suggested that the first world should regret what has happened to the world system and that Christians should work for international reconciliation. I have since learned that the message was delivered as a means of achieving reconciliation between ethnic and Anglo-Australian Christians after a heated discussion about similar issues in the previous week which had stirred up ethnic differences.

Many non-immigrant Australian Christians still seem to think that they are the hosts and hostesses and that immigrant Christians including even those who have been in Australia for a long time, are the outsiders or visitors within the church organisations (Yang Myŏngdŭk, 1989b). So Rev. Yang Myŏngdŭk makes visits to Anglo-Australian churches and delivers sermons and lectures, trying to help his hearers realise that both Anglo-Australians and immigrants are hosts and hostesses and that they are equal in many ways. The SEM also encourages ethnic churches to be open and to develop fellowship with Anglo-Australian churches and other ethnic churches, especially if they are not already doing so, or if they tend to be alienated from the larger society.

Korean Language School

Korean language is an important part of Koreanness. Attempts to sustain it have been achieved through church participation. About a decade ago, *Hoju Sosik* (Sept. 1983: 3) and Yang Myŏngdŭk (1983: 16, 23) argued that Korean immigrant churches in Sydney should pay a great deal of attention to Korean language teaching for young Koreans. Ch'oe Chŏngbok (1983: 7) maintains that the Korean language is the core of "Koreanness". Koreans in Sydney (particularly the first generation) like to speak in Korean and read books and magazines written in Korean. Since the start of their migration to Australia in the early 1970s, Koreans have put much effort into establishing the Korean Library in Sydney (cf. *Hoju Sosik*, Nov. 1987: 9 and Dec. 1987: 16, 29). Most of the relatively well-established Korean churches (judged by the size of their membership in the Korean community in Sydney), run their own Korean language school for 1.5 and the second generation Koreans (cf. *K'ŭrisch'yan Ribyu*, June 1991: 49). Some Korean language schools established within Korean churches are also involved in teaching Korean history, music and dancing, for example, the Sydney Korean Parish of the UCA (*Hoju Sosik*, Sept. 1984: 3) and the Hoju

Sunbogŭm Kyohoe (Australian Full Gospel Church) — (*Hoju Sosik*, Jan. 1988: 24). The Korean language school usually runs every Saturday (cf. *Hoju Sosik*, Jan.-Feb. 1984: 9 and April 1987: 9 and Nov. 1987: 19 and 20 March 1989: 3). The school (established in Oct. 1983) of the Sydney Korean Parish of the UCA published a volume of teaching material in collaboration with the Australian Department of Education in 1991. A second volume is to be published. Because it takes up to an hour of driving to reach the church they regularly attended, the parents of the young people or the church usually provide transport. As the educational achievements of Korean migrants are relatively high, it is not too hard to find a qualified teacher to teach Korean. The Sidŭni Sunbogŭm Kyohoe advertises its Korean language school, which is held every Saturday, saying that the school sustains several former school teachers and related professionals (*Hoju Sosik*, April 1987: 9).

There is a tendency for newly arrived Korean immigrants to join a church which already has a reasonable Korean language school where children are encouraged to speak Korean rather than English. Essay writing competitions take place a few times a year. A Korean church of the Full Gospel Church, which has an adult membership of more than 3,000, runs several such language schools in different parts of metropolitan Sydney, so saving on travel times. This appears to be a way of attracting a large number of people into the congregation. The children may attend various branches of the language school, but they come to the church with their parents on Sundays. It is interesting to compare this with the Central Full Gospel Church, Seoul, which maintains several hundred district churches, but all the members come to the central church for the Sunday worship service. Many members of the district churches in Seoul seem to be happy to hear sermons by head pastor in the central church, but others wonder whether it is necessary for a large number of people to gather in one building.

Language school seems to be only one of two places where the children are encouraged to speak Korean, the other being the home (although some parents find it hard to communicate with their children in Korean, and thus use English at home). I have noticed that most young children playing in the church grounds of the Sydney Yŏngnak Church after Sunday School speak English. I have attempted to talk to 1.5 and the second generation Koreans in English because I noticed they spoke English well. But their parents tend to encourage children to speak in Korean when talking to Koreans. Such advice to their children in the presence of me was a polite way of admonishing me not to speak in English to their children.

The Sidŭni Sunbogŭm Kyohoe runs a few hours radio broadcasting each week. It consists of sermons, counselling and broadcasting hymns. *Hoju Sosik* (Sept. 1983: 12) reports that

> According to Sidŭni Sunbogŭm Kyohoe, the broadcasting helps Korean Christians to grow spiritually. In addition, it is very significant to broadcast in Korean language in Sydney where Korean immigrants are completely under "foreign" language and customs.

The opening ceremony of the language school is often attended by the Korean consul in Sydney and leaders of the Korean community (*Hoju Sosik*, Nov. 1982: 5). The Yŏngnak School of Korean Culture (of The Sydney Yŏngnak Church) was established to encourage Koreans to maintain their sense of being Korean. The school teaches Korean language, traditions, culture, dancing, drama, and *Taekwŏndo* (a Korean martial art).

In 1980 the Sydney Korean Parish of the UCA used to publish *Saenghwal Chŏngbo* (or *the Weekly Life Review*) because the church was concerned about some Koreans trying to adjust to their immigrant life. The Review brought out a summary of important news and reports published by the various newspapers, television and radio stations each week. The church also used to report news of the Korean community and deliver the gospel from the Bible through an F.M. educational radio channel. But it could not continue due to the lack of finance and professional knowledge needed for broadcasting (Lee Sang-taek, 1989b: 2). This has partly influenced the participation in church activities.

Caring for the Elderly

The church more than any other organisation has been active in encouraging the elderly. This helps more Korean families to be involved in church activities. Paying great attention to the elderly is a feature of traditional Korean culture, and this is reflected in the activities of the churches. The eldest son and his wife usually take care of his parents from the time of his marriage, although more recently because of social pressures the number of nuclear families has increased. Most elderly Koreans in Sydney have come to Australia after the age of fifty. They tend to be less capable of adjusting compared to the rest of the Koreans in Sydney, and they also suffer more from the loneliness of immigrant life. The Sydney Korean Parish of the UCA, for example, opened a Saturday college for the elderly in 1990 and a year later established a welfare centre for senior Koreans from the church as well as from the Korean community. A few other Saturday schools and welfare organisations for senior Koreans, run by other Korean churches and voluntary organisations, have merged with those in the Sydney Korean Parish of the UCA.

When the Korean Peace Church purchased a prayer house in Berry, NSW, it also bought a medium-sized bus. Rev. Im Yŏngsun (cited in *K'ŭrisch'yan Ribyu*, Feb. 1991: 29), the minister of the church, says that the bus will be used to run regular trips to different places for the elderly so as to provide activities in their immigrant life.

Traditional Korean Festivals and Celebrations

Most Korean churches in Sydney, one way or the other, observe Korean festivals or celebration days such as New Year's Day (Sŏl Nal), Independence Day, August Full Moon (Ch'usŏk or Korean Thanksgiving Day), the Foundation Day of the Korean Constitution (Chehŏnjŏl), the Day of Foundation of Korea (Kaech'ŏnjŏl) and Remembrance Day (Hyŏnch'ungil) — (*Hoju Sosik*, Feb. 1985: 8 and Aug.-Sept. 1987: 51 and June 1987: 4, 17 and 7 July 1989). They are attended by many Koreans who see these celebrations as very significant. The Sydney Korean Parish of the UCA celebrated the forty-sixth anniversary of Independence Day (Kwangbokchŏl) on 18th August 1991. A well-known professor from Korea delivered a message on "Eternal Liberation". The church sang the Korean national anthem in the worship service. In Korean churches, a special speech is made on each of these occasions.

Most Korean churches in Sydney offer their members lunch after every Sunday worship. The Korean churches in the USA might have offered lunch (Korean food) after the worship service up to the 1970s, but they now offer only drinks and light foods such as biscuits or snacks. The Korean churches in Sydney are likely to take this same step. The Galilli Yŏnhap Kyohoe offers a reasonably heavy lunch one week and a light snack the next week. On the above special occasions and on their church anniversaries, Korean festival foods such as rice cakes, *Chapch'ae* and *Pulgogi* are provided for lunch. As time goes, Korean church members in Sydney may prefer a light snack on usual Sundays, but on Korean festivals some Korean dish which could be easily prepared. This may not necessarily mean the decline of Korean ethnicity because there are various ways in which they try to maintain their ethnic identity. It is likely that Korean festivals or celebrations will be remembered by the church at least for the next few decades.

Drifting Churchgoers

A pervasive phenomenon of Korean churches in Sydney is that members change their church. This is partly related to Korean culture based on Confucianism. The change of church affiliation normally takes place during December and January each year, which is the time when Korean churches appoint new staff such as deacons and elders. Those who feel that they deserve to be appointed as one of "the servants", but who were disappointed tend to leave their church and join another. The Rev. Chi Suyong (interviewed in March 1991) observes that such members attempt to establish close relationships with others, depending on the size of the membership of the church. This is a process of "fighting for supremacy in the church" (Lee Sang-taek, 1989a: 40). According to Rev. Chi Suyong, those Koreans who have been in Australia for less than ten months or so tend to try to adapt themselves to the ways of the churches they attend. However, once they pass this period and their life gets reasonably well established, they tend to develop their own ideas about Korean immigrant churches and come to think that it is not they who should adjust to the church, but that it is the church that has to be modified to support immigrants like themselves. The wife of an assistant minister of the Galilli Church (interviewed on 19 June 1991), informed me that a deacon she knew changed his church association seventeen times as a result of such a process. Rev. Ch'oe Pyŏnghak (*Hoju Tonga*, 8 Nov. 1991), who was a visiting minister to the Korean Presbyterian Church in Sydney, stated, after his year-long ministry, that some Koreans drift from one church to another and that one Korean family is still not settled in a church even after thirteen such changes.

Church affiliation changes for various reasons. A significant reason for change is that Koreans are looking for what could loosely be called ethnic satisfaction they are hoping to achieve from interaction with their fellow Koreans. The occupation of those who attempt to move from one church to another, sometimes by themselves, sometimes with others, varies. It is not only particularly marginalised Koreans who search for ethnic satisfaction from the Korean church; those who are active in the larger Australian society also seek this. This matter of ethnic satisfaction is related to "status inconsistency", as suggested by Hurh and Kim (1984a) in their study of Korean-Americans. Lee Sang-taek (1989a: 38) has similarly discussed "status incongruity" with reference to Koreans in Sydney. Although status inconsistency is not a central concept for the purposes of the present study, it is useful. 15.3 per cent of both overseas and Australian born persons of the whole population of Australia are university graduates (1986 Census of

Population and Housing: Overseas Born and Other Ethnic Population: p.18), whereas 51.9 per cent of adult Koreans are in this category (*Sosu Minjok*, Aug. 1990). However, most Koreans in Sydney find it difficult to enter relatively high status occupations in Australia. Many are employed in the business sector of the Korean community. The rest are mostly production or process workers and labourers such as welders, plasterers, cleaners, and trolley collectors. It is well known that more than half of the working Koreans in Sydney are cleaners (Yun Yŏmun, in *Hoju Tonga*, 9 Aug. 1991: 10).

This indicates that the majority of Koreans in Sydney do not have the social status they would have expected to have had in the home country (cf. Jo, 1992: 405). Of course, it is by no means certain that had they not emigrated, they, especially university graduates, would have held the occupation of their preference in Korea. This point does not seem to be considered among those frustrated university graduates who currently have working class occupations in Sydney. On the other hand, they are reasonably satisfied with the monetary reward they receive, which is high compared to what they could get in Korea. Korean Confucianism emphasises the level of education attained, and Korean society is organised in an authoritarian way and this is often connected with whether or not people have attended university. This Korean culture is still an important part of the life of Koreans in Sydney. The first generation Koreans, whether they are university graduates or not, suffer most from status inconsistency. They have been involved in their own ethnic organisations such as religious groups, alumni associations and trade associations as a way of improving their status. In the case of the Sydney Korean Parish of the UCA, in which 900 members are registered, there are the head minister, one associate minister, two assistant ministers, seven elders and 142 deacons (*K'ŭrisch'yan Ribyu*, Sept. 1991: 34; *Yŏnhap Kidok Sinbo*, 17 Sept. 1991: 5). Many Koreans who are not able to get into mainstream jobs or who think that they deserve better jobs than what they have want to hold "respectable" positions in the community. This often leads them to try to become elders or deacons in the church. This is how every Korean church has come to offer those positions to a large proportion of their church membership.

In the Korean community in Sydney, church elders are more powerful than deacons. People are appointed as deacons, and then they are "promoted" to elders later, depending on their religious practice as well as on other factors such as their reputation in the wider society or the Korean community. It is well known that the other factors tend to dominate in the process of appointing church elders. As in Korea, those Koreans serving a church as minister, assistant minister, elder or deacon, are named according to their surname and their position — *e.g.*, *Kim Chipsanim* (deacon), *Yi Chŏndosanim* (assistant minister), — not only within the church but also in the Korean community, unless they hold a high status position such as company director, doctor, lawyer, or professor. Not surprisingly, the ceremony of appointing elders and deacons is one of the most important events during each year. The ceremony of each church is advertised in most of the Korean ethnic papers in Sydney (*e.g.*, *K'ürisch'yan Ribyu*, April 1992: 4; cf. *Hoju Sosik*, 1 Feb. 1989: 7). It is not only a ceremony to provide the candidates with a special status in the Korean community but also one which helps to strengthen the foundations of the church. The day is a turning point after which they devote themselves more seriously to church activities and also contribute more to the church financially. This has also been observed among Korean churches in the United States and Canada (Kim Ill-soo, 1981).

Some businessmen also drift from church to church. As the population of Koreans in Sydney has been increasing since 1972, the number of Korean travellers between Korea and Australia has been also growing. Those who run travel agencies often go to a church in order to establish a link to customers. Once this is done, they tend to move out of that church and join another. One man with a travel agency has changed his church association over fourteen times (*Hoju Sosik*, March 1984: 18 and Sept. 1984: 5 and Nov. 1985: 7 and Aug.-Sept. 1986: 28 and March 1988: 1 and 14 Sept. 1989: 15; *K'ürisch'yan Ribyu*, July 1991: 23, 50).

Generational Change

The first generation of Korean immigrants in Sydney tend to think that the 1.5 and second generations do not have much to worry about, as they have fluent English and are getting educated. However, later generations also suffer from a kind of cultural deprivation in a way not appreciated by the first generation. Ch'oe Chŏngbok (1991: 8) contends that the ethnic church should be a warm and encouraging site for young people, as the future of the church and of the Korean community relies heavily on them.

I have argued that many Korean activities are centred around the church and that this is often beneficial for church members. However, the ethnic focus may serve as a barrier to integration into mainstream economic processes. Koreans recognise this but also worry about losing their ethnic identity. This is a dilemma for the Korean churches in Sydney. Rev. Lee Sang-taek, the president of Korean Churches Council in Sydney (*Taeyangju Nyusŭ*, Nov. 1988) argues that it is now time to pay more attention to second generation Koreans and to encourage some of them to think about clergy as their future career. The first generation is, however, still dominant in every facet of the Korean community, and the Korean churches in Sydney are still responding to their needs, thereby tending to neglect the needs of the second generation. The Korean churches help Koreans in Sydney sustain an ethnic identity and this is one of the main reasons why churches grow. However, the ethnic dimension only partially explains this growth.

In an earlier part of this book, I noted two kinds of ethnicity: first, that based on the country of origin and the immigration process; second, that which develops after the immigration process as a consequence of living in the country of destination. The second kind of ethnicity can be markedly different from the first. My data reveal that the sources of the growth of the Korean churches in Sydney are more related to the first generation of Koreans rather than to 1.5 or the second generation and that the first generation tend to observe the first kind of ethnicity. It will take some time before it is clear how the second kind of ethnicity relates to the Korean ethnic churches in Sydney.

Concluding Remarks

The social life of Koreans is centred around a church more than other ethnic groups. Koreans in Sydney maintain an ethnic identity through church activities and the church encourages them to do so.

Notes

[1]This refers to those persons who were born in Korea but who, as young people, emigrated with their parents.

Chapter 8

The Political Dimension of Korean Churches in Sydney

The Church Polity of the UCA and its Relation to Korean Churches in Sydney

This chapter focuses mainly on those churches in Sydney which are part of the Uniting Church in Australia. This is because the UCA's polity and its concern about wider social issues have been important in the growth of the Korean church. This makes it different from other denominations. The UCA came into existence after the Methodist Church of Australia and a large proportion of the Presbyterian Church of Australia, along with Congregational Union of Australia, agreed to form one denomination on 22 June 1977 (Black, 1983: 86). One reason for its being called the *Uniting* Church in Australia could be that it is in the process of uniting Anglo-celtic and migrant ethnic churches, since the UCA advocates multi-culturalism as a church policy. This is argued by Rev. Yang Myŏngdŭk (interviewed in June 1991), who is a member of the New South Wales Synod of the UCA. Compared to other denominations, the UCA's concerns about Aborigines and migrant groups is stronger, and it has been taking issues of social justice or equality seriously as part of its church polity. Such concerns were specially taken up in the 6th Assembly of the UCA, held in

Brisbane from 13-20 July 1991. It is not difficult for Anglo-Australian member churches of the UCA to put into practice some aspects of the so-called "multi-cultural church". For example, it is a principle that "(w)here two Uniting Church congregations or parishes are involved on a continuing basis, it is inappropriate for the sharing of property to be based on a rental or tenancy agreement" (*The Uniting Church in Australia: Property Policy*, a monograph). But there is still discrimination in this "the multi-cultural church". For example, most, though not all, overseas trained ministers are called by the less important terms "ministers-in-association" or "ministers-on-loan" rather than "ministers of the Word of the UCA" (*Report of Working Group Meeting on the Calling and Settlement of Ministers from Overseas*, a monograph).

Reflecting what they see as multi-culturalism in Australia, those Korean churches which are members of the UCA are discussing the possibility of forming a nationwide Korean ethnic Synod within the UCA. It would be similar to the special synod of Aborigines. Up until now, the Korean churches which are members of the UCA have not been able to influence the church policy. It is hard to discuss any agenda in the synod meeting because the synod includes many other ethnic churches and their interests are considerably diverse. Doctrines, rituals, church polity, disciplining, clergy training, reception of clergy from other denominational backgrounds, and church property management, may be more relevantly handled by the Korean churches, which understand each other. The dominant group does not understand the Korean churches. The difference is closely related to different social and historical contexts which have been influential in the ways in which the church as an institution has come into being. Forming a Korean ethnic Synod would largely solve these problems.

There are also disadvantages in forming a Korean ethnic synod of the UCA. The Korean churches might become isolated, not only from other member churches of the UCA, but also from the larger society (Brown, 1991: 10). However, the attempt to form it went ahead, and the special constitution and rules that were proposed on February 1988 and that would apply to Korean immigrant congregations were officially recognised in the nationwide Assembly of the Uniting Church in Australia, in July 1991. The constitution and the rules give the impression that the characteristics of the church described there are not significantly different from those of the churches in Korea and that they are for temporary use while the first generation is the dominant group in the Korean immigrant churches in Australia and that they may be revised in the future, depending on how internal church politics develops. However, those who are concerned about the rules of the constitution are generally satisfied with them as they provide the Korean churches with their sought after autonomy (*Yŏnhap Kidok Sinbo*, 17 Sept. 1991: 8).

The UCA and its Korean Member Churches and their Concern about Political Oppression in Korea

Some churches are actively involved in political matters outside the church. The UCA, for example, has been very concerned about political oppression in Korea. It has helped some politically persecuted Koreans to settle in Australia. Rev. Han Tŏksu (*Hoju Sosik*, Oct. 1984: 6) who worked as Director of Yŏngdŭngp'o Urban Mission (a mission group much concerned about the urban poor) and who was persecuted by the Korean government, was invited by the UCA and appointed as an associate minister of an Anglo-Australian UCA Parish in Pitt Street, Sydney. It was Rev. Dr. John P. Brown, Director of the UCA's Commission for World Mission, who was influential in inviting Rev. Han Tŏksu to Australia (*Hoju Sosik*, April 1986: 1). Dr. Brown spent eleven years (1960-1970) in Korea and taught in a theological college in Seoul. Rev. Han Tŏksu has also been concerned about the human rights movement and political oppression in Korea. However, he ended up establishing a Korean church, the Galilli Yŏnhap Kyohoe, in November 1985 (*Hoju Sosik*, Jan. 1986: 8). Upon the Rev. Han Tŏksu's return to Korea, Rev. Im Tonggyu arrived in Sydney to serve the church. He has also been actively involved in various political affairs in Korean society. This has led to the Galilli Yŏnhap Kyohoe being known not only as a site for religious pursuits but also as a place for political discussion.

Churches, being the centre of many activities, are often used as a place where the Korean community can meet with influential people, such as mainstream politicians. Undoubtedly, the politicians also make use of the church for political campaigns. For example, the Sydney Korean Parish of the UCA, Strathfield, came to have its own church building in November 1982, *i.e.*, eight years after its establishment. The parish invited the Korean Ambassador to Australia, the Korean consul in Sydney, the president of the Sydney Korean community, the New South Wales Premier, N. Wran, the president of the UCA. (*Hoju Sosik*, Sept. 1982: 11). The premier and the consul delivered congratulatory addresses (*Hoju Sosik*, Nov. 1982: 1 and Dec. 1982: 11). *Hoju Sosik* reports that according to the church, nine hundred people came to the ceremony where Korean traditional dancing was demonstrated and other entertainment was offered. *Hoju Sosik* also mentions that the Premier, Mr. Wran is a well-known politician who takes care of voters and that it is important to keep such (big) politicians close to the Korean community in Sydney.

Korean churches have helped some Korean illegal migrants who have a variety of problems and this has contributed to the growth of Korean churches. This also indicates the significance of the Korean church as an organisation in the Korean community in Sydney. The Korean community in Sydney has always included a number of illegal migrants. There was an amnesty for them in 1975, and new illegal migrants want to know if there will be another one. They rush into church every Sunday, not only to attend the worship service, but also to enquire about this political matter. This practice was also observed after the amnesty in 1980 (Lee Sang-taek, 10 Sept. 1989b: 2). The interest in gaining permanent residency still explains why some Koreans go to church, even when there are about ten Korean newspapers and magazines which provide information about migration (cf. Yang Myŏngdŭk, 1989a: 2). The Korean churches in Sydney which are members of the Uniting Church in Australia have unsuccessfully called for another amnesty.

The Association of the Korean Community in Sydney, and the Korean churches in Sydney, in co-operation with the Australian Council of Churches and the Immigration Reform Council, jointly opened the Conference to Call for Amnesty on 24 September 1987 in the hope that the Australian government would offer permanent residency to illegal migrants in the year of the bicentennial of European settlement in 1988. A minister from the Australian Council of Churches delivered a talk on the churches in Australia and immigration, a representative of the Immigration Reform Council talked on the legal status of illegal migrants and Rev. Yi Sangjin spoke about the illegal migrants (*Hoju Sosik*, Oct. 1987: 3).

In 1989 the Australian government offered a special period during which illegal migrants could apply for permanent residency. The Sidŭni Sunbogŭm Kyohoe (led by Rev. Kim Mun'gil) arranged an adviser for such applications. Rev. Jim J. Smith, the minister of the International Full Gospel Church, encouraged illegal migrants among the members of the Sidŭni Sunbogŭm Kyohoe to consult him. Those who did not go to church at all, and members of other churches, also came to the church and took the opportunity to see the minister. This whole issue of obtaining permanent residency through the help by *Jim Moksa* or Rev. Jim caused a series of disputes which were aired in the various Korean ethnic newspapers. Some of the Korean applicants who were rejected, or who had not heard from the Department of Immigration, had a fight in the office of the Sidŭni Sunbogŭm Kyohoe, blaming the church and the Rev. Smith for acting improperly. *Hoju Tonga* (26

April 1991: 4) reports that Rev. Smith held a prayer meeting for those who had put in an application. Around 250 Koreans had applied for permanent residency through the help of the minister before 19 December 1990. One hundred and forty of them were told to attend a medical check-up, which was "a good sign", according to Rev. Smith. He also put an advertisement in an ethnic newspaper saying that "If you have not heard from the government after lodging the application for permanent residency with the help from Rev. Jim in December 1989, please let me know" (*Hoju Tonga*, 9 Aug. 1991: 17). This advertisement was placed for the following reasons. First, those who apply for permanent residency do not, for obvious reasons, use their own residential address and this causes a mail delay. Second, the Rev. Smith put the applications of hundreds of Koreans into the Parramatta office of the Department of Immigration. When the office moved, most of the Korean applications were left in the basement of the old building. This further delayed the processing of the applications. In the meantime, especially during 1991, a large proportion of illegal Korean migrants returned to Korea because they thought there would be no chance of becoming permanent residents in Australia.

Recognising the Qualifications of Migrant Ministers with Overseas Education Background

Recognising ethnic ministers' overseas qualifications and welcoming their involvement in decision-making at the Anglo-Australian presbytery could be influential in the growth of the ethnic church. Reverend is the official title of ministers in the UCA whether they are ethnic or Anglo-Australian. There are a number of categories of ministers: supply ministers, ministers of the Word of the UCA, ministers-on-loan, ministers-in-association, and pastors (*Discussions and Recommendations of Ten Workshops*, a monograph, May 1991). There are two major kinds of ministers within the UCA Korean churches. These are ministers of the Word of the UCA and ministers-on-loan. They have almost all been educated in Korea and are ministers-on-loan. One of the exceptional cases is Rev. Yang Myŏngdŭk who graduated from a theological college in Korea and also undertook the course of Bachelor of Divinity in the United Theological College and came to be ordained by the authority of the UCA. Rev. Lee Sang-taek who was ordained in Korea after his theological course also undertook further study in the United Theological College and came to receive the title of Minister of the Word of the UCA. Whether Korean ministers-on-loan are keen to receive the title of Minister of the Word is not at issue here, although they sometimes do not aspire to it because of their lack of proficiency in English. It is recognition by the authority of the UCA which is at stake.

Here is an example of the ordination of an overseas trained evangelist. Mrs Pae Sunyŏng is the wife of a minister of the Korean Methodist Church who is undertaking his Ph.D. in theology in a university. Mrs. Pae has been in Australia since her husband came on a student visa. Mrs. Pae was a graduate of the Korean Methodist Seminary in Seoul, served for fourteen years as an evangelist in the Korean Methodist Church, was qualified to become a minister of the Korean Methodist Church, and was enrolled for the Master of Theology program of the United Theological College (Rev. Dr. J. Brown, Director of the UCA's Commission for World Mission, 1988). Mrs. Pae wished to be ordained, but was refused by an Australian male minister in the UCA board. As she regarded him discriminating against her on the grounds of sex, this developed as a court case and as a dispute between Mrs. Pae, the Korean churches in Sydney, the UCA, and the Methodist Church in Korea. She was not ordained.

Although Australian church authorities are reluctant to fully recognise the overseas qualifications of ministers, migrant ministers are never discouraged from establishing a congregation. So far, the UCA has maintained a relatively close relationship with ethnic churches compared to, for example, the Australian Baptist and Presbyterian churches. Having a voice for the Korean ethnic churches in such other denominations may become possible shortly (Yang Myŏngdŭk, interviewed in April 1992). This could further help the growth of the Korean churches.

Ministering to the Korean Church and the Immigration of Korean Ministers

The Korean ethnic churches, in addition to their helping illegal migrants, as discussed earlier, also try to gain permanent residency for Korean ministers (the Association of the Lay Members of the Korean Churches in Australia, in *Hoju Sosik*, Jan. 1986: 18). Some Korean ministers or theological college graduates may not have been successful in securing a position in Korea, so they go abroad to serve an ethnic Korean church or to pursue a higher degree. It was the practice in the United States, at least up to the 1970s, that where a minister gathered a group of 30 ethnic members and formed a church, the minister then could apply for permanent residency. Since the 1980s, the United States government has virtually stopped issuing visas to Korean ministers or theological graduates no matter what their reason for wanting to stay in the United States. Australia has turned out to be a more obliging country in this respect.

Involvement in Economic Disputes

Although the church is not exclusively a political organisation, it does exercise some political power in society. Korean ministers are sometimes involved in disputes not merely as religious leaders of an ethnic minority but as ministers of the Uniting Church in Australia and as a pressure group. When an industrial dispute occurred in the Seoul branch of Westpac (an Australian banking company), which almost led to the closure of the branch, the ministers of the Korean churches in Sydney, who were concerned about the employees, requested that the Uniting Church in Australia be allowed to help resolve the problem. Their intervention was successful (*Tonga Ilbo*, 15 April 1991). One reason why the Korean churches in Sydney deliberately involved themselves in this dispute is economic. They did not want those Koreans working in the Seoul branch of Westpac to lose their jobs. In addition, Westpac's presence in Seoul might assist the development of trade relations between Australia and Korea. Another reason is political. A few Anglo-Australian ministers of the UCA, along with Korean ministers, sat at the negotiating table. The Rev. Yang Myŏngdŭk (interviewed in March 1991), who was one of the Korean representatives, suggests that the UCA was instrumental in encouraging Westpac to come to the negotiating table in the first place.

The Korean Youth movement in Australia

The Korean Youth Movement in Australia is another part of the political dimension of the Korean church. It is a group of young Koreans who try to overcome their problems as children of migrants. During the second half of the 1970s there were only a few Korean churches and these were the centre of the activities of the youth movement. When church schism became pervasive in the Korean community in Sydney during the same period, those young people felt that they should not split up. They formally organised an inter-denominational association called the Korean Christian Youth Fellowship (KCYF). The advisers of the fellowship were leading ministers such as Rev. Lee Sang-taek and Rev. Han Tŏksu. As mentioned earlier, the latter was deeply involved in Christian and human rights movements in Korea. This put him at risk of political persecution, so the UCA invited him to Australia. The main activities of the fellowship between 1982 and 1984 were centred around bible study. From 1985, this focused on Minjung Theology and political issues, and gradually turned to criticism of under-development in Korea. The fellowship incurred much protest from the Korean community, which was centred around the churches and which tended to be conservative in their attitudes to social issues. Some of the members of the fellowship whose beliefs tended to be conservative and who could not cope left. During the second half of 1986, the KCYF felt that it could not be progressive as long as the fellowship stayed within the limit of the church, so the fellowship decided to move out in June 1987. After preparing for six months, the fellowship was reformed as the Korean Resource Centre (KRC). Since then the centre has become a purely political organisation, though it still maintains a few ministers as advisers and the majority of the members are self-professed Christians. It is too early to say that the change which happened to the KCYF is a sign of church decline, considering the importance of the church in the community.

The activities that the KRC has been involved in are: disclosing details of the Kwang Chu Incident in 1980 where hundreds of civilians were killed; calling for an amnesty for illegal migrants; running a Korean language school and a history class. Another important concern of the KRC is to work for the re-unification of the two Koreas (cf. *Hoju Sosik*, 15 Feb. 1989: 16). The centre helped Im Sukyŏng, the president of the Association of University Students in Korea, attend the International Committee for the Peace and Reunification of Korea, held in P'yŏng Yang, North Korea, from 20-27 July 1989, where 650 representatives from 30 nations participated. Although Im Sukyŏng planned to attend the committee, she did not know how to evade the legal restrictions of the South Korean Government. A key member of the Korean Resource Centre in Australia, Dr. Kim Chinyŏp, was working as head of the dental department in the Il Sin General Hospital, Pusan. He is an Australian citizen and a missionary dentist sent by the UCA. He is also the elder son of Rev. Kim Sangu, the first Korean minister in Sydney. He was partly responsible for helping Im Sukyŏng reach P'yŏng Yang (*Chosŏn Ilbo*, 5 Sept. 1989, cited in *Hoju Sosik*, 14 Sept. 1989: 28) in that he helped her to contact the North Korean Embassy in East Germany where she obtained her visa to North Korea. Im Sukyŏng reached P'yŏng Yang via East Germany. Dr. Kim Chinyŏp served 18 months in a Korean prison for his action. Four members of the Korean Resource Centre in Sydney also attended the committee in P'yŏng Yang and reported what they had observed to the Korean community in Sydney (Yang, 1991).

The KRC went through a slight reformation in mid-1989 in order to be ready for the 1990s; it was re-established in early 1990 and named itself the "Korean Youth Movement in Australia" (The Korean Youth Movement in Australia, 1990: 6; Sin Chunsik, 1991). Sin Chunsik is the president of the centre at present. He was actively involved in the student movement in Korea prior to coming to Australia. He is not a Christian. The Korean Youth Movement tends to stay remote from the Korean churches as well as from the Korean community in Sydney, today. Members of the movement accuse the Korean church of staying away from the issue of human rights especially in Korea and of being more involved in church expansion, whereas the church blames the movement for being too radical.

The Korean Churches in Sydney and their Concern about the Re-Unification of the Two Koreas

The Korean churches in Sydney always remember the Korean anniversaries such as the Independence Movement in March and Independence Day on 15 August, and they hold special worship services and prayer meetings for the peaceful re-unification of Korea. On the occasion of the Seventh Assembly of the World Council of Churches, held in Canberra, on 7-20 February, 1991, Christian leaders from both South and North Korea gathered together. During the conference, the Commission for Mission of the UCA and the Korean Council of Churches of the UCA in Sydney organised a weekend of special events. On Saturday 16th February 1991, a Harbour cruise offered Korean Christians in Sydney and delegates from both North and South Korea the opportunity to share their concern about re-unification. They danced and sang songs together during the cruise, and held hands. According to the report, the delegates from North Korea were touched by the love of their fellow Koreans. Rev. Ko Kichun from the North mentioned that "blood is certainly thicker than water", meaning, on this occasion, that they have the same ancestors, thus they are all brothers and sisters whose relationships last forever wherever they are (*K'ŭrisch'yan Ribyu*, March 1991: 26-29).

On Sunday 17th February, two combined worship services of the eight Korean congregations of the UCA in Sydney were held, including the visiting delegates from the two Koreas: one in the Korean Parish of the UCA and another in the Cheil Church of the UCA. Rev. Dr. Ko Kichun of the North Korean Christian delegates was the preacher at both services. There was also a seminar on the re-unification of the two Koreas in the United Theological College (3:00pm 17th February,

1991). Rev. Ko delivered a talk on "Christianity in North Korea, Today and Tomorrow" and Dr. Yi Sam'yŏl from the South Korean delegates spoke on "The Role of Christianity in the Re-unification Movement". Without the support of the Korean churches in Sydney and their concern about the re-unification of the two Koreas, such a meeting would not have been possible. As Rev. Ko says, Korean immigrant churches in many other countries have also shown much interest in the re-unification of the two Koreas (*K'ŭrisch'yan Ribyu*, March 1991: 32). According to *Ethnic Link* (May 1991: 9), "the fellowship between the delegates from the South and the North is a lesson in the reconciling power of Christ's love which the politicians do not easily learn".

Rev. Yang Myŏngdŭk (*Hoju Tonga*, 9 Aug. 1991: 13) makes it clear that the Korean community in Sydney is still like a Christian community or church community as "most" of the Koreans in Sydney go to church. Thus it is the Korean churches in Sydney that tend to be responsible for active involvement in the re-unification movement. However, South Koreans tend to be careful in becoming involved in any active movement for re-unification, as they are generally very anti-communist, and the South Korean government has discouraged any private organisation from being involved in the matter. This is the reason why the Korean churches in Sydney tend to lead the movement (*K'ŭrisch'yan Ribyu*, Oct. 1991: 24-27).

It is notable that the UCA's Commission for World Mission plans to set up a Committee for the Peaceful Re-unification of Korea. Every member of the UCA in Australia prayed for the matter on Sunday August 15th, Korean Independence Day, 1991. This was a symbol of the UCA's concern about peace in Korea as well as that of the world (Yang, in *Hoju Tonga*, 9 Aug. 1991: 13). This is also a way of encouraging Korean churches to be part of the Australian society and to grow further.

Why are there Over Seventy Protestant Congregations but Only One Catholic Congregation?

The church polity in Protestantism is different from that in Catholicism. Because of its polity, Catholicism in Korea has only a few theological colleges. However, as I discussed in Part II, Protestantism has over one hundred. When there is any conflict between the members and the clergy within a Catholic church and the members want the clergy to be replaced or the clergy wants to quit, it needs the consent of a higher authority. Conflict can be institutionally resolved step by step.

Power struggles within the Korean churches in Sydney have often led to schism. When conflicts occur in a church, a number of things can happen: some members may leave the church and join another; some members may try to replace their minister; and some members may invite another Korean minister, often one who is temporarily staying in Australia for higher studies or for a tour, to establish another church. In this process, a Korean Protestant church does not have to report anything to a higher authority.

I have discussed, in this section, some of the political reasons why the Protestant church outnumbers the Catholic. Other reasons will be given in the next chapter.

Concluding Remarks

The political dimension of the Korean church appears not to be as significant as its other dimensions in understanding church growth. As Korean migrants stay for a longer period of time in Australia and increase their population, the political aspects of the Korean church in Sydney are likely to become more critical in understanding the organisation of the Korean church. The Korean church may become more influential not only within Anglo-Australian denominations, but also in mainstream political matters. These will, no doubt, affect the future growth of the Korean church.

Chapter 9

The Economic Dimension of Korean Churches in Sydney

Introduction

The Korean church in Sydney is also a site within which economic activities are pursued. First, there is the internal part of the church economy. Basic expenses need to be met, for example, building and motor vehicle maintenance and wages. Second, churches are concerned about their members' finances, although this affects the internal arrangement of the church's economy to a degree. Third, there is a concern about economic matters in the larger society. This is rather limited at present. The fact that Korean churches are most concerned about their internal economy and that most of the churches are relatively small seems to have limited their concern about economic matters in the wider society. This is also closely linked to the way in which the church in Korea uses its budget, which was discussed earlier. All of the various aspects of the economy of the Korean churches are inter-related to a degree.

When each dimension of the church interacts with another, a combined activity is produced. For instance, when a minister is involved in earning his income through his religious service, his action is neither purely religious nor purely economic, but religio-economic.

The Over-Supply of Theological Graduates in Korea

As mentioned earlier, a conspicuous feature of Protestantism in Korea is that it has an over-supply of theological graduates (*i.e.*, *Chŏndosa* or clergyperson-to-be). This has influenced the economic dimension of the Korean churches in Sydney to a great extent. One aspect of the dimension is the salary for the clergy. Clergy are paid full-time workers engaged in church activities. The income of the clergy differs from one religion to another and from one denomination to another. Even within Buddhism there are differential incomes which may, for example, be decided on whether or not a monk can marry.

The economic dimension of the church also reflects the employment market in the larger society. How generously church members will contribute monetarily to the church depends not only on the emphasis put on this by the church, and on the members' attitudes toward money, but also on the financial condition of each member.

Just as the churches in Korea suffer from the "bigness syndrome", most Korean churches in Sydney, though small in their membership, actively pursue growth. This is because ministers of churches with a large membership are considered more successful in their careers. One way in which they show that they admire churches with a large membership is that the Korean immigrant churches in Sydney often invite speakers from Korea to hold special meetings which are always said to be about religious renewal or revivalism. When such a meeting is to be held, Korean ethnic newspapers advertise it to tell which church the speakers serve in Korea and how many members that church has (cf. *Hoju Sosik*, 23 Aug. 1989). One example of such an advertisement is as follows.

> Speaker: Rev. Kim Chosun, serving Sungŭi Methodist church in Inch'ŏn city, Korea (30,000 members) ... (*Hoju Sosik*, Dec. 1983: 1).

Another advertisement:

> The Sidŭni Sunbogŭm Kyohoe (ministered by Rev. Kim Mun'gil) is going to hold a revival meeting on the occasion of its 10th anniversary: from 13-15 January 1989. The guest preacher is Rev. Min Daesik who is the president of the Full Gospel Association in Korea. He is the head minister of the Southern Full Gospel Church with a 50,000 membership.[1]

Those ministers serving "big churches" in Sydney are relatively comfortable financially. Such ministers are provided with more expensive houses and better cars. Their churches usually practise a division of labour in their various activities, for example, on their planning board, and in worship, evangelism, education, budget management, fellowship, publishing, cultural activities, sports, and induction of new members. This practice takes a burden off the minister. However, those ministers who minister to the church with a small membership need to be involved in all dimensions of the church, but their income barely meets basic needs. The reasons for the difference of Korean clergy's income between "big ministers" and "small ministers" are again related to the church growth in Korea and its impact on overseas Korean churches.

Some parts of the surplus of Korean theological graduates have been absorbed into countries such as Canada, the USA, and Argentina. Since 1972, Australia has become another destination for Korean ministers and theological graduates in search of a position.

There have been a number of ways for them to get into the ministry. There are differences in the social status of ministers at the time they established churches in Sydney. Some churches in the 1970s were set up by theological students who came to Australia for advanced studies or, in a few cases, by ministers invited from Korea. During the first half of the 1980s, churches were often established by ministers from Korea. Since then, ministers in Sydney have established churches simply because they are ordained as, or trained to be, ministers (Nam Kiyŏng, 1990: 15). In this respect, Catholicism is different from Protestantism. As mentioned earlier, Korea has maintained only a few tertiary education centres to produce Catholic clergy, hence there is not an over-supply of Catholic theological graduates. This, together with the more centralised structure of Catholicism, and its preference for integrating members of various ethnic groups into Anglo-Australian parishes, helps to explain why there is only one Korean ethnic Catholic community (church) in the Sydney area. Moreover, because the patterns of authority within Catholicism are different from those in Protestantism (Bouma, 1991), there is less scope for schism within the Catholic church.

As in Protestant churches, there are various conflicts between the clergy and the members of the Catholic church. However, as there is no excess of priests, no segment of a break-away church would be guaranteed that another priest would serve it. In response to the question about whether there is any possibility for the church to have a Korean priest, Father Frank Ferrie, former priest of the Korean Catholic church in Sydney, who lived in Korea for 25 years and speaks fluent Korean, said that "he hoped so, but the decision is up to the higher authorities of Catholicism" (quoted in *Hoju Sosik,* April 1983: 10). A group of Korean Catholics who worshipped in the parish of Auburn planned to build their own church building and were ready to start in 1989. The Sydney archdiocese would not allow them to go ahead. In fact, this group is still not a fully-fledged church, for the Catholic church recognises it only as a "community." During the late 1980s, the Sydney Korean Catholic Community was served by an Australian priest who was considered unfavourably by Koreans because he strongly advised them to integrate into Anglo-Australian churches. Perhaps the Australian Catholic authority will recognise it as a Catholic congregation sooner or later, reflecting the process that other ethnic Catholic churches have gone through in Australia and elsewhere (cf. Lewins, 1978a). Most Korean ethnic Catholic churches in the United States have achieved full recognition by the American Catholic authorities (Kim Ill-soo, 1981: 196).

Eventually the Korean Catholic Community ended up buying a church building at Auburn and in April 1991 the Sydney Korean Catholic Community also came to have a Korean priest. This priest, Father Thomas Chang Yŏngsik, applied for an entry visa to Australia, but he had to wait for a long time to persuade the Australian Immigration Department that his intention to come to Australia was "not like many other Protestant clergy" whose primary intention is to migrate or to establish a church from which to make a living. It is commonly known in the Korean community in Sydney that Korean Protestant ministers apply for entry visas to Australia and tend to stay on after establishing a church. Rev. Kim Sŏnil (in *Taeyangju Nyusŭ,* 15 Dec. 1990) accuses some Korean ministers of "establishing churches as a backdoor to settling in Australia". He considers it undesirable and even sinful. He also observes that competition between the churches is a problem and that, from God's point of view every Korean church in Sydney should grow and become strong, but in reality each of them wants to grow at the expense of others. This causes unnecessary competition and conflict in the Korean community.

Korean ethnic newspapers and magazines carry advertisements looking for ordained ministers or assistant ministers (*Hoju Sosik,* Nov.-Dec. 1984: 4). Two examples follow.

Minister Wanted
Over 10 years experience of ministering necessary.
Fluent in both Korean and English.
40-55 years old with permanent residency.
Please ring (045) 77 5978.
Worship: 1:30pm on Sundays.

Address: Cnr. Sackvill Rd. & Harold St., Blacktown 2148.

(*K'ŭrisch'yan Ribyu*, Jan. 1991: 75)

Minister Wanted
Qualifications: A theological college graduate.
Permanent resident or Citizen of Australia.
Fluent English.
Location of the church: Pymble, St. Ives area.
Application period: 20-27 January 1991.
Interview will take place after the examination of each application.
If you wish to be involved in the ministry in the above area, please fax your application through to number 449-5958. (*Hoju Tonga*, 18 Jan. 1991: 15)[2]

My inquiries about such advertisements led to the following points. First, a group of people who are not happy with their church can move out of the church and advertise, knowing that there will be enough Korean applicants. This can happen to any church regardless of whether the church is affiliated to a well-established denomination or denominationally independent. Second, Koreans have experienced and observed many kinds of troubles and schisms within their churches. They would like to have someone with enough experience in the ministry so that it is less likely that their church will experience conflicts and so that the minister may be better able to resolve any problems which occur. Third, Korean Christians expect ministers to be able to help them in a number of ways, not just in religious matters. For example, English ability is crucial because it helps the church to raise its voice in the various domains of the larger society. Fourth, instead of making the church a route for obtaining permanent residency, the Korean churches in Sydney usually want somebody who already has this because such people are likely to be more stable.

As a participant observer for this study I visited the Korean Galilli Yŏnhap Kyohoe in Campsie in December 1989. A Korean minister (Rev. Yang Myŏngdŭk) was invited to preach at a particular Sunday morning service because Rev. Im Tonggyu who had been ministering to the church on a fixed term had left. He returned to Korea to a big and well-established church he had worked in before he came to Australia. Members of the church were recovering from the loss of his services. I was informed that Rev. Im had been very much loved and respected by all the members of the church and his loss caused them to weep. However, I observed that members of the church were obviously satisfied with, and proud of, the fact that the Rev. Im had not abused his fixed-term contract by trying to stay on. The members of the Galilli

Yŏnhap Kyohoe were full of hope that their church would firmly establish this tradition that the immigrant church is never to be used as a step for the migration of ministers.

If Rev. Im had nowhere to go in Korea, things could have been different. That is, even if Rev. Im had left the Galilli Yŏnhap Kyohoe he would possibly not have left Australia, but established another Korean ethnic church. Since Rev. Im has left the church, the church has had to cope with an assistant minister whom only a few members of the church seem to admire. In the meantime, the church happened to find an ordained Korean minister on a temporary visa, whose trial sermon was satisfactory to the members of the church. He soon left for Korea and returned to Sydney with a work visa. The church again made sure that the church would not be used as a backdoor for migration. The minister had to apply for a work visa rather than permanent residency. According to Yi Hongchun (interviewed in March 1991), a key founding member of the church, the church could not continue to perform many activities during the absence of an ordained minister. Therefore he thinks that the present regulation of a short term contract should be extended so that members of the church do not have to be without a minister for a lengthy period.

According to Rev. Dr. Lee Sang-taek, Koreans in general perceive the church as a building as well as a gathering of the saints. Thus Korean clergy borrow a church building to start a church as soon as they can afford to pay the rent. While it is both rather hard and expensive to find a hall to start a church in Korea, it is relatively easy and inexpensive to do so in Australia. This facilitates church growth.

Many Korean immigrant churches in Sydney seem to prefer remaining independent to joining existing Anglo-Australian denominations (see Table 9.1). Korean ministers in Sydney appear to be willing to serve a church even though there would be a slight theological difference between the church being served and their own theological backgrounds (see Table 9.2). However, as happened in Korea and in the Korean churches of the United States, when any economic interest is involved in the conflict, the slight theological difference becomes exaggerated and is used as an excuse for the church to split. This is how one minister, whose theological education is from Presbyterian background and who has served a Korean congregation of the UCA for several years, and some of his followers from the church, have left the congregation and established a church of the Assembly of God (*K'ŭrisch'yan Ribyu*, May 1992: 49).

Table 9.1: Denominational affiliation of the Korean immigrant churches in Sydney

Denominations	Number of churches	Per cent ratio (%)
Independent	17	29
Australian Presbyterian	12	21
Uniting Church in Australia	10	17
Australian Baptist	8	14
Assemblies of God	3	5
Church of Christ	2	3
Catholic	1	2
Other sect groups	5	9
In total	58	100

Source: *K'ŭrisch'yan Ribyu*, Jan. 1991: 23

Table 9.2: The theological background of fifty two church minsters in Sydney

Theological backgrounds	Numbers	Per cent ratio (%)
Church of Christ	1	2
Evangelical	2	4
Presbyterian	30	58
Pentecostal	2	4
Baptist	10	19
Methodist	3	5
Uniting Church in Australia	1	2
Australian Presbyterian	1	2
Not found	2	4
In total	52	100

Source: *K'ŭrisch'yan Ribyu*, Jan. 1991: 24

Recruitment

The Korean church takes care of not only its members but also new arrivals irrespective of their religion. This is related to the economic dimension of the church. Sydney Airport is a place where economic activity on the part of churches is observed, although religious concern is also involved. Korean Airlines has been landing in Sydney on Tuesday since April 1990. Some Korean ministers go to the Airport to meet newcomers from Korea (*Hanho T'aimjŭ*, 13 July 1990: 31). As soon as the new Korean immigrants exit from the customs hall, their luggage is taken by porters who are volunteers from Korean churches.

These churches usually provide accommodation for a period and find jobs for the newcomers. In the meantime, as they are settling into their new life as members of a Korean church, it is politely suggested to them that they contribute tithes to the church. It is understandable that Korean church ministers or their aides go to the airport and welcome potential members, if it is borne in mind that some newcomers have already been directed to Korean churches in Sydney by travel agencies or brokers of higher education overseas. These agencies in Korea "fax" Korean churches in Sydney with brief information and details of forthcoming arrivals. According to Rev. Kim Yongsŏn (interviewed in June 1991), most, if not all, of the Korean churches in Sydney are connected to travel agencies in Korea. Often Koreans who used to be associated with Buddhist temples in Korea are welcomed by churchgoers at the airport and generally come to be associated with Christian churches in Sydney.

Schisms

Church schism is one of the central characteristics of Korean churches in Sydney. Understanding it helps explain much about church growth. However, finding out about it is difficult because the Korean community in Sydney, and especially the clergy, do not want to discuss it. This is because they have experienced severe trauma as a result of schism experiences (Chi T'aeyŏng, 1983: 12). Pyŏn Hyosŏp wrote a few articles on how the Korean churches in Sydney started and experienced numerous splits. However, he could not continue his writing as he was blamed for disturbing the Korean community. He wrote an apology to the readers of his articles, saying that,

> ... Many people in the Korean community seem to think that it rather hurts the community to think back on what happened to the Korean churches in Sydney and to analyse the related problems. They are not aware that it is in fact harmful to put the analysis completely aside. The mistakes made in the past will only be repeated. ...
>
> Pyŏn Hyosŏp
> Hornsby, 19 September 1991.
> (*K'ŭrisch'yan Ribyu*, Oct. 1991: 50)

Pyŏn Hyosŏp (interviewed in April 1992) also mentioned that there was a particular Korean minister, whose name was often mentioned in Pyŏn's articles. This minister had influence at the *K'ŭrisch'yan Ribyu*, and he advised it to stop publishing Pyŏn's articles.

The schisms have been with the community since its inception in Sydney and are likely to be with it in the future. There are social forces at work here not well understood by Koreans. Koreans in Australia are generally aware that Korean immigrant churches are self-absorbed. Friendly relations between them are rare whether they belong to the same or different denomination. They are involved in tough competition to gain membership and they split over theologically trivial matters. *Hoju Sosik* (Nov. 1982: 5) presented a brief account of schisms affecting some Korean immigrant churches in Sydney. Diagram 9.1 is a chart of main events.

Diagram 9.1: A brief picture of church schisms among some Korean immigrant churches in Sydney till the early 1980s

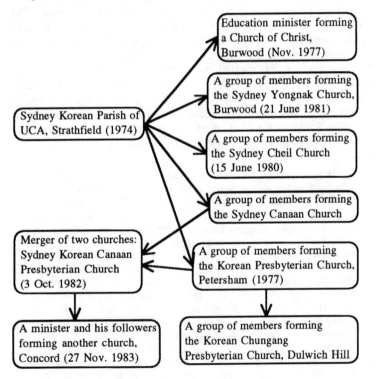

Source: Based on *Hoju Sosik* (Nov. 1982: 4 and Aug.-Sept. 1983: 17)

The earlier form of the Sydney Korean Parish of the UCA, Strathfield, was the first Korean church in Sydney established in 1974. Twelve Korean immigrants and Rev. Dr. John Brown who had worked in Korea for over ten years had their first meeting in the Inner City Parish at Redfern on 8 September 1974. Rev. Kim Sangu who served as a missionary in Vietnam during the war period was called by his fellow Christians who had also worked in Vietnam, and he came to Australia when the war ended. Rev. Kim Sangu started to serve the church from September 1976. Part of the Presbyterian and Congregational churches and the whole of the Methodist Church in Australia merged and formed the Uniting Church in Australia in June 1977. The Korean church joined the UCA on 25 September 1977 and came to call the church the Sydney Korean Parish of the UCA. Rev. Kim Sangu resigned from his ministry in the church in August 1980 and left for the United States. A joint meeting of the Korean Parish of the UCA and an Anglo-Australian group of the UCA elected Rev. Lee Sang-taek the chief minister of the church on 12 July 1981. The induction service was carried out under the auspices of the Sydney Synod of the UCA on 11 October 1981 (*Yŏnhap Kidok Sinbo*, 17 Sept. 1991: 5). *Hoju Sosik* (Sept. 1984: 8) was the first issue of Korean ethnic newspapers in Sydney to bring out an article about the Rev. Kim Sangu at the time he was invited to the 10th anniversary of the Sydney Korean Parish of the UCA[3]. According to that article:

> ... He is welcomed by some Koreans in Sydney who have been missing him for several years. It has been four years since he had to leave Australia and go to the USA due to a schism of the church he was involved in four years ago. ... If one thinks that the minister of an immigrant church should be not only religious in his/her service but also be engaged in meeting the social needs of the immigrants, Rev. Kim Sangu is such a person. His character was one reason for the schism four years ago. He established a church in Orange County near Los Angeles and put much effort into studying, which led him to obtain the degree of Doctor of Ministry. ... Apart from serving the church, this first Korean minister in Sydney used to run around, day and night, to help organise the immigration of Korean illegal migrants and to help Koreans in hospitals as they did not have English proficiency. According to Rev. Kim, one of the reasons he left for the USA is that anyone living in one place too long is likely to miss something important and new in life[4].

Rev. Pak Chongch'an, who was undertaking further study in an Australian seminary, joined the Sydney Korean Parish of the UCA in

1975 as education minister, and served the Sunday School. Then in November 1977 he suddenly left the parish and established a church in Burwood. Pyŏn Hyosŏp (Feb. 1991: 32), and others, assumed that it had to do with his different theological background as he was from a theological college of the Church of Christ. Pyŏn Hyosŏp regrets the departure of Rev. Pak Chongch'an, saying that it "was due to the church's poor reward for the education minister. The church's financial arrangements in those days were not good enough, and suggest that Rev. Pak Chongch'an did not leave for a theological reason" (Feb. 1991: 32).

The Korean Presbyterian Church at Petersham came to be established in the following way. When Kim T'aein, who was a Presbyterian theological graduate, and also the choir conductor of the Sydney Korean Parish of the UCA, along with all the members of the choir, left the church just before Christmas 1977. According to Pyŏn Hyosŏp (Feb. 1991: 32-33), the split had four causes.

(1) The church joining the UCA.
(2) Conflict between the head minister, Rev. Kim Sangu, and those who left the church.
(3) Dissatisfaction with newly confirmed elders.
(4) Conflicts between the early Korean immigrants and the newly arrived ones from Vietnam at the end of the Vietnam War.

Rev. Kim T'aein who was from a Presbyterian background now says that his action in 1977 had simply to do with the shift to the UCA (quoted in Pyŏn Hyosŏp, Feb. 1991: 33). A woman deacon (quoted in Pyŏn Hyosŏp, Feb. 1991) who was one of those who left the church at that time says that "We left the church because Rev. Kim Sangu had Kim T'aein stopped from conducting the choir without any reason. Moreover, we felt Rev. Kim Sangu had certain shortcomings as a minister." The former seems to be the cause of his sudden departure.

Around the year 1977, church schisms in the Korean community in Sydney became even more pervasive than before. Pyŏn Hyosŏp (Feb. 1991: 34) argues that these rarely had to do with theological differences, but in fact mostly concerned conflicts between the clergy and the laity, or the personal frustrations of the clergy. He goes on to say that such schisms disappointed many Koreans in Sydney, as the churches had been offering meeting places to lonely Koreans in a new country whether they were Christians or not. Pak Semyŏng of the Sydney Korean Parish of the UCA, and sixty six fellow believers close to him, moved out of the church and had their first worship service in a park on 21 June 1981. This group established the Sydney Yŏngnak Church at

St. James Church, Burwood (*K'ŭrisch'yan Ribyu*, July 1991: 21). The church later invited a minister from Korea.

Hoju Sosik (Nov. 1983: 9) reported that the merger of the Sydney Canaan Church and the Korean Presbyterian Church at Petersham in October 1982 was a celebration involving the whole Korean community. It goes on to say that

> It is well known that there have always been conflicts between the clergy and churchgoers in the Korean community. It is not surprising to know that the merged church has split. ... According to some churchgoers, the shepherd should not leave the sheep in any case. ... Sixty Korean Christians who followed Rev. Yi Tuchong when he left the merged church (*i.e.*, Sydney Canaan Presbyterian Church) have been worshipping in a park until they found a church building to rent.

The following issue of *Hoju Sosik* (Dec. 1983: 14) reports that Rev. Yi Tuchong and his followers established another church in Concord and that the Sydney Korean Canaan Presbyterian Church appointed Rev. Ko T'aesun from Melbourne. Rev. Ko T'aesun later left the church and established the Sydney Seoul Church (*K'ŭrisch'yan Ribyu*, Feb. 1991: 24).

The article, "Sydney Yŏngnak Church's Conflict Continuing", in *Hoju Sosik* (Aug.-Sept. 1985: 14), gives us a brief picture of the conflicts between the clergy and the lay members. The article writes that "It is well known that there are often conflicts between the laity and the clergy of the Korean churches in Sydney. This time, Sydney Yŏngnak Church is in trouble again due to conflicts between the minister and the lay people."

The Association of the Lay Members of the Korean Churches in Australia (*Hoju Sosik*, Jan. 1986: 19) argues that the schisms in Korean churches and the continuous conflicts between the clergy and the laity have been the main obstacle to achieving the unity of the Korean community in Sydney.

A Trial Merger of Pentecostal Churches in Sydney

Until 1984, there were two Full Gospel churches in Sydney: the Sidŭni Sunbogŭm Kyohoe at Punchbowl served by Rev. Kim Mun'gil, and the Sydney Central Full Gospel Church at Campsie, ministered by Rev. Yi Siyong. Both are branch churches of the Yŏŭido Central Full Gospel Church in Seoul. The church in Seoul and its head minister, Yi John Songgi, were not happy with two branches in Sydney being separate. *Hoju Sosik* (Feb. 1985: 1) carried an advertisement on its front page saying that

> Dear fellow Koreans and fellow Christians, we thank you for your concern and prayer that the two Full Gospel churches in Sydney be united. ... In accordance with the final decision of the World Mission of the Full Gospel of the Yŏŭido Central Full Gospel Church in Seoul (president: Yi John Songgi), the one in Campsie will merge with the other in Punchbowl. There will be a special service to celebrate this special occasion. We invite all fellow Koreans and fellow Christians. Your attendance at the service will be appreciated and be a great encouragement for us. ...

The merger lasted only a few months. By 1988, there were three Full Gospel churches in Sydney, all related to the Central church in Seoul. They receive sermon tapes by Yi John Songgi, and the weekly news of the Central church which they distributed to Koreans in Sydney. The Sidŭni Sunbogŭm Kyohoe sells a monthly Christian magazine and a less religious daily newspaper both of which are published by the Central church in Seoul on its behalf. Yi John Songgi mentioned in a combined revival meeting of the three Full Gospel churches in Sydney in 1989 that he had tried to help the three to merge, but had failed. Although Yi John Songgi is an important figure for the three Full Gospel churches in Sydney, in terms of the ways in which the Full Gospel churches are organised, they are financially independent from the parent church in Seoul. Due to the polity of the Central Full Gospel Church (its branch churches are somewhat under the control of the parent church in Seoul), many assistant ministers of its branches in Sydney do not have the same reasons to establish their own churches. This contrasts with what has happened in many other, especially independent Protestant, churches.

During the early 1970s, the Korean churches in Sydney were established mostly by lay persons, who then invited ministers from Korea. The population of the Korean community in Sydney sharply increased during the latter half of the 1970s, during which time various types of problems, especially schisms, occurred, and many new churches were established. This increase due to schism continued till the early 1980s. Korean ethnic publications often announce the "foundation of another church," although not often with much enthusiasm. For example, *Hoju Sosik* (Sept. 1983: 17) mentioned that the Korean community does not welcome the establishment of any more churches. It reported that there were, apart from the Sydney Korean Catholic Community, twelve churches in the Korean community of about ten thousand. It went on to say that some Koreans in the North Shore suburbs requested Rev. J. Brown to help found a Korean church in the area. He had maintained close relations with the Korean community in Sydney throughout the 1970s and 1980s. Although he had been approached by these Koreans he had been hesitant to encourage them to go ahead because he was worried about the possibility of the community thinking that establishing another Korean church would mean that another schism occurred.

According to Nam Kiyŏng (1990: 14, 15), until the early 1980s the schisms were caused by conflicts between the clergy and the laity, or conflicts among the laity within the church. This led both groups to establish more churches. As mentioned already, when it came to the middle of 1980s, however, churches were mostly established by ministers or theological graduates. They began with a Bible study group and then established a church later. An assistant minister of a Korean congregation of the Presbyterian Church of Australia organised a Bible study group for some members of the church who lived close to each other. The meetings went on for several weeks in 1989. When a deacon of the church came to know about them, he persuaded the assistant minister to stop, and the meetings soon came to an end. One family (Yi Sungbae and Yu Chŏngok interviewed in 1990) in the group informed me that

> According to the deacon, there was a situation where an assistant minister of the church used to run a Bible study group. After some time, the group established their own church. Thus, no assistant minister is supposed to hold meetings independently unless they are regular meetings held with the permission of the parish committee.

Since the second half of the 1980s, ministers have often put an advertisement in Korean ethnic newspapers to inform the readers that there is going to be an inaugural meeting of a church. This happened when the following churches formed: the Sydney Somang Church of the UCA and the Sydney Yŏng Kwang Church (*Hoju Sosik*, Aug.-Sept. 1987: 26: cf. *Hoju Sosik*, July 1987: 4 and April 1987: 23 and 9 June 1989: 32 and 10 Nov. 1989: 18); the Summer Hill Miral Presbyterian Church (*Hoju Sosik*, Aug. 1988: 26 and July 1988: 43); the Sydney Evangelical Holiness Church (*Hoju Sosik*, June 1988: 12, 40); the Sydney Chung Ang Baptist Church (*Hoju Sosik*, May 1988: 21 and cf. p.31); the Strathfield Siloam Presbyterian Church (*Hoju Tonga*, 9 Aug. 1991: 2); the Sae Sun Presbyterian Church (*K'ŭrisch'yan Ribyu*, April 1992); and the Bethel Church (*Hoju Tonga*, 29 April 1992).

The Sydney Somang Church, UCA, advertised under the names of the church members to announce its establishment. Other churches do this in the name of the head minister. There might have already been an agreement that the Rev. Kim Myŏngch'ol would minister to the church. The advertisement was as follows:

> May the peace of God be with all of our fellow Koreans in Sydney. We regret that our deeds have not been appropriate to fellow Koreans or to God and we beg your forgiveness. Reflecting our mis-deeds in the past, we will be dedicated to grow as mature Christians and to make a better community of Koreans in Sydney. Thus, with the support of the UCA and its Korean member churches, we are about to establish the Sydney Somang Church and appoint Rev. Kim Myŏngch'ol as head minister. Your prayer and loving care for us would be much appreciated. We inform you that the foundation meeting and appointment of the minister will take place as follows.
>
> 2:00pm, 29 June 1986
> Venue: Central Uniting Church
> Cnr. Haldons St., & The Boulevard,
> Lakemba (near the railway station)
> Advertised by the members of the Sydney Somang Church, the
> UCA.   (*Hoju Sosik*, June 1986: 3, 4)

Rev. Min Konghun, in establishing the Sydney Kwang Lim Church, considered that the church is going to grow by proselytising non-Christians rather than by taking believers from existing Korean churches (quoted in *Hoju Sosik*, Aug. 1988: 26). Rev. Kim Sŏnil (*Taeyangju Nyusŭ*, 15 Dec. 1990) suggested that all Korean churches should develop friendly relationships among themselves instead of snatching church members from other Korean churches.

According to Rev. Yang Myŏngdŭk (interviewed in Nov. 1989), most ministers involved in church schisms tend to provide theological reasons for the split and to ignore the fact that they occur irrespective of whether there are theological differences or not. It seems that theological reasons have not much to do with the schisms and that other social forces are at work. Rev. Yang (1989a: 2) contends that the problems are mainly due to a power struggle or competition between ministers or an unhappy personal relationship prior to the schism. Elder Pyŏn Hyosŏp (in *K'ŭrisch'yan Ribyu*, May 1991: 38-40) argues that the establishment of the Sidŭni Cheil Kyohoe (the Sydney Cheil Church) which resulted from a split of the Sydney Korean Parish of the UCA illustrates conflicts between the clergy and the laity, and between the laity, but he points to theological trends as major causes of the schism. However, again, Rev. Kim Sŏnil (*Taeyangju Nyusŭ*, 15 Dec. 1990), in a symposium celebrating the third anniversary of *Taeyangju Nyusŭ*, argues that one reason why there are 60-70 Korean churches in Sydney is the personal conflicts between the ministers, or between the minister and the elders or the laity, thus a minister or a lay person establishes a church to be as they would like.

Being critical of "too many churches" in the Korean community in Sydney, Jay Won (*Taeyangju Nyusŭ*, 1 Oct. 1990) argues that "Korean ministers who tend to judge each other because of their different ideas and doctrines are only proving that they are fighting for a bowl of rice or a piece of pie".

Finally, I argue that schisms are the result of not only of power struggles or competition within Korean churches in Sydney but of a particular social environment which includes factors related to church growth in Korea, such as, Confucian culture, rapid industrialisation, and the boom in higher education as well as some factors more often found in Sydney, such as status anxiety.

Stipends of the Clergy

Neither minimum nor maximum stipends are set for Korean clergy in Sydney and in Korea. In contrast to this stipends are generally set for the Anglo-Australian clergy. The stipend system for the clergy of the Korean churches in Sydney varies from one church to another. If a church maintains a large group of people, a certain minimum stipend is usually set, but not a maximum. The more successful ministers from five Korean churches in Sydney which have a membership of 300 or more receive, in addition to their stipend, a variety of fringe benefits such as provision and maintenance of accommodation, a motor car, and overseas mission trips (Kim Yŏngsŏk, 1991: 18-19). Nam Kiyŏng (1990: 15) regrets that most Korean churches in Sydney seem to focus on looking after their ministers financially when they should be performing more religious duties and showing their concern about social problems in the Korean community.

In Korea, even if a minister establishes a church, his livelihood is not secure until there are about a hundred regular members in his church. Similarly, in Sydney, even if a Korean minister establishes a church, he is not necessarily guaranteed his basic financial needs. As in Korea, whether he succeeds as a minister and secures his economic and spiritual power largely depends upon his overall ministerial capacity in the significant dimensions of the church. Competition and hard work among Korean ministers are often observed more than in other ethnic groups.

About two thirds of the ministers of the Korean churches in Sydney are involved in earning income from activities other than their church ministries only because the church budget is not able to provide them with enough income. They hope to drop second jobs and be involved only in the church. Forty one of the fifty two Korean churches in Sydney maintain a membership of less than one hundred, and twenty nine of them less than fifty (*K'ŭrisch'yan Ribyu*, Jan. 1991: 24). The Sydney Han-Maum Baptist Church had ninety members by late June 1991, and the church maintained one head minister and one assistant minister. When I interviewed the head minister, Rev. Kim Yongsŏn (interviewed on 21 June 1991), the assistant minister, Kim Yunkŭn was visiting him, so I conducted a double interview.

The head minister is living in a rented unit. He is married with one young child. To my question about his income, he said that it was just enough for their everyday life, but he could not save anything. He mentioned that he is fortunate enough not to have to look for another job to supplement his basic financial needs. According to his observation, at least two thirds of Korean head ministers in Sydney have to take a second job and many of them are in cleaning work. As the assistant minister of the Baptist church does not receive enough income from the church to live on, he holds a second job. According to these interviewees, Korean assistant ministers have to get a second job to supplement their income from the church. I assume that most ministers of the twenty to thirty home churches[5] are involved in such jobs as cleaning. An assistant minister (interviewed in June 1991) of the Sidŭni Cheil Kyohoe with 1,000 members, receives $130.00 per week. His wife takes in Korean boarders to supplement their income. $130.00 per week for an assistant minister in the Korean community is a relatively good salary. They are generally paid $80.00 per week. A former assistant minister of a congregation of the UCA used to get paid $80.00 per week while he filled in as head minister of the church. Soon after the minister arrived from Korea, his wage was cut in half. In addition to this cut, he did not want to endure the new minister's way of working, so he left the church and joined another where he has been better rewarded financially.

The Church Budget

The church would not be able to carry out its activities without financial resources. The contributions of church members are the most significant way of forming the church budget. In this matter, Korean churches are not much different from others. However, the Korean church is different in the ways in which members are encouraged to contribute to the church. The Association of the Lay Members of Korean Christians in Australia accused some ministers of ministering to the church just to make a living out of it (*Hoju Sosik*, Jan. 1986: 18). Like many churches in Korea, most Korean churches in Sydney emphasise the importance of offerings in the "Christian's pilgrimage". The weekly news sheets of churches usually name those who have given a tithe and those who have made a special offering of thanksgiving in the previous week (Kim Yŏngsŏk, 1991). Professor Pak Tongik, a political refugee who formerly taught in a North Korean university, made many visits to Korean churches in Sydney without introducing him to them in detail. He states that most churches list the names of those who have pledged a tithe, or brought a special or thanksgiving offering, on the back wall of the worship hall. He said he felt uncomfortable as he wondered whether the churches are begging for money (*Taeyangju Nyusŭ*, 15 Dec. 1990).

The practices of Korean churches in Sydney have made an impact on Korean Buddhists. Many members of the Talma Buddhist Temple who formerly attended Christian churches, but who now attend the Temple, tend to put their names on the offering envelope. The leader of the temple says that such does not happen in the temples in Korea and she is ashamed of such thing taking place among Buddhists in Sydney. She argues that many Korean churches in Sydney tend to be very materialistic.

Social Services Provided by the Clergy

Another aspect of the economic dimension of the church is observed in the various ways in which the clergy support church members. What is at work here is a mutual economic exchange. The clergy are involved not only in religious matters, but also in providing services such as finding information about housing, jobs and even many trivial everyday problems like buying a washing machine (*K'ŭrisch'yan Ribyu*, Aug. 1991: 20). The clergy even take care of those lay people who are in the process of obtaining a driver's licence and they often help as interpreters. Ministers attend the opening ceremonies of businesses and offer blessings (*Hoju Sosik*, Nov. 1988: 37; cf. *K'ŭrisch'yan Ribyu*, May 1992). Because of such activities, Koreans in Sydney tend to be very dependent upon the clergy. A typical example is of a minister being phoned by one of his church members reporting that her kitchen sink was blocked and that she did not know what to do. The minister arranged a plumber to fix the problem. Another minister was even asked to buy a bunch of sprouts, and a refrigerator for particular church members.

Especially during the early settlement of Koreans in Australia, Korean ministers were deeply involved in most parts of the lives of Korean immigrants. Following the amnesty for illegal migrants in 1975, a great number of Koreans rushed into Australia in the hope that there would be another amnesty. This led Korean ministers to carry out a considerable amount of additional social work. The involvement of Rev. Kim Sangu, the head minister of the Sydney Korean Parish of the UCA, in such matters caused conflict between the laity and himself. Pyŏn Hyosŏp, an elder of the church, suggested that Rev. Kim should:

(1) establish organisations within the church to deal with the immigrants' non-religious needs.
(2) not help those who are not Christians.
(3) pay close attention to the church members' spiritual needs (*e.g.*, sermons, visiting the church members' homes, Bible study)
(4) pursue a conservative ministry.
(5) stop interaction with organisations not related to Christianity.
(6) not officiate at the weddings or the funerals of those who are not registered members of the church.
(7) not be concerned about financial matters, which should be left with the church treasurer (in *K'ŭrisch'yan Ribyu*, April 1991).

According to Pyŏn Hyosŏp (April 1991: 39), the members of the church are split on the basis of their attitudes towards these points. There were those who supported the minister, those who were against the minister, those who supported elder Pyŏn and those who were against the elder. Eventually the elders Pyŏn Hyosŏp and Yu Chunhak left with a group of people to establish the Sidŭni Cheil Kyohoe. As Pyŏn demonstrates in his writings about the schism of the Korean Parish of the UCA, those who were involved still maintain different views about its causes. However, it is clear that the schisms had mainly to do with deep cultural and organisational matters rather than with theological reasons.

Those ministers with fewer members in their church tend to be more involved in non-religious activities than those with a larger membership, for the former tend to be responsible for most aspects of their church. However, as the membership grows, churches establish various sections which are in charge of different aspects of immigrant life. As a consequence, the ministers come to be involved more in the religious dimension and less in other kinds of church activities. A minister (interviewed on 27 March 1991) who is now the minister of a church with a membership of about 1,000 used to help Korean children enrol in school when the English of their parents was not good enough for this purpose. He also helped his church members apply for family allowances and find accommodation.

A small proportion of social services are provided by the Australia-Korean Welfare Association. This association was organised in 1979 by Koreans in Sydney who were concerned about the difficulties faced by new Korean immigrants. Voluntary workers provided most of the services for those Koreans in need. The association was able to employ a full-time worker in 1983 with funding from the Federal government. It provided counselling services on immigration on the grounds of family re-unification, social security benefits, domestic problems like divorce and violence, and information about English classes, and motor car accidents (Dr. Yu Ŭikyu, the president of the association, in *Taeyangju Nyusŭ*, 1 Nov. 1988). Although Rev. Lee Sang-taek says that the Korean churches are grateful to the association for taking over some of the services which used to be provided by the churches (Lee Sang-taek, *Taeyangju Nyusŭ*, Nov. 1988), the level of services provided by the association is still minimal when compared with what over sixty churches can do. I feel that it will take a while before the church loses its significance in providing welfare services for the community.

Here is another example to indicate ministers' involvement in social services. Rev. Chi Suyong started a church in 1988. Three families, including his, attended its foundation meeting. The membership was less than fifty by March 1991. He spends 30 per cent of his work hours as a clergyman and 70 per cent as a social worker. According to him, he has warned his church members that no one should complain of the quality of his sermons as he is not able to spend enough time to read and pray.

The Korean churches sometimes offer English language classes. Both the Bethel Church and the Zion Baptist Church run classes which are open to church members as well as to other Koreans (*Hoju Sosik*, Aug.-Sept. 1985: 5; *K'ŭrisch'yan Ribyu*, Oct. 1991: 46). The Hallelujah Presbyterian Church advertises an English Bible Class as follows,

> **You are invited to an English Bible Class.**
> 1) Time: 7:30-9:30pm. every Thursday
> 2) Venue: Cnr. Knox St. & Liverpool Rd., Ashfield
> 3) Characteristics of the Class
>> (1) Australian students are coming along.
>> (2) It will be interesting as the class is focused on various topics each week.

(3) It will improve your pronunciation and vocabulary.
(4) You also have a chance to get used to Australian expressions and cultures.
(5) We can share Christ's love in the class.

Hallelujah Evangelical Church Tel: 582-4576.
(*Taeyangju Nyusŭ*, 6 Dec. 1991)

This advertisement places heavy emphasis on learning English rather than studying the Bible. This may help the church to recruit some young Koreans or encourage young people to become active.

In 1989, a survey of the Korean community in Sydney by the Korean Resource Centre and the Society for Ethnic Mission with the support of the Korean Society of Sydney finds that most Koreans think that Korean churches should regard their social services as equally important as their religious services (see Table 9.3).

Table 9.3: Service priorities of churches

religious	both religious/social	social	un-answered
27.3%	43.8%	22.0%	6.9%

Source: A Survey of the Korean Community (1989) by the Korean Resource Centre and the Society for Ethnic Mission (quoted in *Hanho T'aimjŭ*, 26 Jan. 1990)

These statistics indicate that the Korean churches in Sydney are expected to provide both religious and other services to their community. These other aspects of the Korean church in Sydney will certainly be a significant feature of Korean churches in Sydney for many years, and are strongly implicated in their growth.

The Korean churches look after the financial needs of the clergy, although the clergy often take care of their own needs, as discussed earlier. The churches are also interested in helping the economic well-being of the members. Advertising about its counselling service, the Sidŭni Sunbogŭm Kyohoe notes that "If any Korean business person needs to employ workers, please let us know. We will introduce appropriate persons for your business. If you want to sell your business contract,[6] contact us" (*Hoju Sosik*, Dec. 1987: 16).

Some of the economic activities run by Koreans are particularly directed at Koreans. Food stores and restaurants are the main examples. It is often suggested that those who run such business sometimes attend church to know more people for the sake of their business. Rev. Dr. Lee Sang-taek says that many of the Koreans in Sydney are illegal migrants who also have the problem of English proficiency. Thus, Korean lawyers and interpreters have been in high demand in Sydney. It is the Korean church where these services can most easily be found. The Sidŭni Cheil Kyohoe, in the brief booklet (*Kyou Such'ŏp* or fellowship diary, 1990, 1992) which is published every year and distributed to members, lists the names of all members, and specifically of those who are running various kinds of businesses.

A subgroup of the Sidŭni Cheil Kyohoe donated twenty bags of rice to *K'ŭrisch'yan Ribyu* to be given to the needy in the Korean community. Members of the group think that if anyone looks around the community carefully enough, they will find quite a few fellow Koreans in need and that Christian faith needs to be expressed through action (Kim Myŏngdong, Feb. 1991: 28). Ch'oe Chŏngbok (1991: 8) argues that the Korean immigrant churches should be concerned not only about spiritual salvation but also about social justice and welfare in the larger society. His view is that most Korean immigrants in Sydney are marginalised people without social roots, and, therefore, that Korean churches should allocate more money for those in need.

Some Koreans form a self-help group of people centred around a key organiser and contribute an amount of money every month. Each month one member of the group receives all the money and then pays it off so others can have their share. This *kye* has been a Korean traditional way of making a large sum of money which may be in need for a particular purpose, and it cannot be carried out without total trust by all other members. Often church members are involved in the *kye*. When they belong to the same church, the degree to which they trust each other tends to be greater. A member of a *kye* group, who was a businessman and a Christian, committed suicide in July 1991, and those who had not taken their share suffered a financial loss. This consequently led to a severe quarrel in the church grounds, while a worship service was in progress, between deacons and other members of the church who were involved in the *kye* (*K'ŭrisch'yan Ribyu*, Nov. 1991: 9).

Concluding Remarks

I have mentioned that both the clergy and the laity seek economic benefit through church activities. The Korean immigrant church fulfils various economic needs which are necessary or helpful while immigrants settle into Australia or cope with exigencies of life here. Ministering to a church is also a paid job. Given the over-supply of Koreans with ministerial training, success in the ministry depends heavily on providing what churchgoers demand. Although this situation sometimes creates conflicts and schisms in Korean churches, it also contributes significantly to overall church growth.

Notes

[1] Other recent advertisements are as follows

> Revival Meeting at the Sydney Full Gospel Church
> Hallelujah! We are glad to inform you that we are going to hold a revival meeting. The speaker is Pastor Son Dŏkhwan (the head minister of Taeku Full Gospel Church where over 10,000 people gather every Sunday). You are all welcome to come along and to share the grace of God. Time: ... (*K'ŭrisch'yan Ribyu*, Aug. 1991: 31)

> Revival Meeting at the Sydney Korean Parish, the UCA.
> Speaker: Rev. Kim Pongjo. He is a Korean produced revivalist and minister working internationally. A large number of Christians have experienced change in their life thanks to his powerful message. He established the Kŭm Ran Church and his spiritual leadership has led the church to a membership of 40,000. Time: 7:00pm 26-29 September 1991. (*K'ŭrisch'yan Ribyu*, Sept. 1991: 15)

[2] Another advertisement reads:

> **Minister Wanted**
> The successful applicant should be prepared to minister to a church in the North Ryde area.
> 1) Qualification: an ordained minister from Pentecostal theological background.
> 2) Fluent in Korean.
> 3) Salary: $450 per week.
> If you are interested in the above position, please send application and certificates in both Korean and English to this address: P. O. Box 779, Liverpool, NSW 2170. (*Taeyangju Nyusŭ*, 30 Aug. 1991:18)

[3] It is not easy to contact any Korean ministers who once ministered to a Korean church in Sydney but who do not live in Sydney any more. I knew that Rev. Kim Sangu was the first Korean minister in Sydney. However, I did

not know much about him till I came across the September issue of *Hoju Sosik* (1984). The newspaper was in print from 1982.

[4] Generally speaking, Koreans are not likely to disclose what happens to them, especially if it was not a good event and if it still bothers them.

[5] A minister or an assistant minister leads services usually for a few or several families. Their meeting place is home.

[6] This is often a cleaning contract or a supermarket trolley collecting contract.

PART IV

PART IV

Chapter 10

Summary and Conclusion

The primary concern of this study has been to explore social sources of church growth among Korean immigrants in Sydney. In order to do this, I have adopted the supply/demand congruence theory of church growth. That is, church growth is most likely to occur when there is a high degree of both demand for, and supply of, what the church has to offer. In this study I have used the term "supply" from the viewpoints of those who provide what church members require from the church. The term "demand" is used from the viewpoints of church members as they attempt to obtain diverse services through the church or as they attend church for many reasons. I have set this analysis within the context of Korean culture as it has developed over the centuries.

The expansion of the church in Korea, especially in the last few decades, has been a significant factor in the growth of Korean ethnic churches in countries such as Australia. Korean Christians have a greater propensity to migrate than followers of other religions or the non-religious. As Christianity has expanded in Korea in recent decades, now constituting about 20% of the population, there has been a gradual increase of the proportion of Christians among Koreans who migrate. The migration of Korean Christians into Australia has been the basic cause of the demand for Korean ethnic churches. This demand has been met by an abundant stream of clergy from Korea, where an over-supply of theological college graduates has resulted from a number of social factors in Korean society. While there is a close parallel between the supply/demand factors causing the growth of the Korean church in Australia and churches in the homeland, this study has also dealt with the ways in which the growth of the church in Korea and the growth of the Korean church in Australia are distinct. In doing this, the church is viewed as a multi-dimensional organisation closely linked to the wider society.

Some of the historical background of Christianity in Korea before 1960 has also contributed significantly to the explosive expansion of the church in Korea during the last few decades. When Catholicism was introduced to Korea in 1784, it was regarded as something that is closely related to Western science and technology, especially by some Confucian scholars who formed the high social stratum of the Chosŏn Dynasty. The interest of the higher classes in Christianity led to more interaction between the various classes. It also led to a revival of the Korean alphabet, which had been invented in the 15th century but largely neglected during the Chosŏn Dynasty. The use of the alphabet made it possible for most churchgoers to read the Bible.

Fortuitous circumstances, such as the gaining of recognition by royalty, due to missionaries helping the queen's injured nephew to recover during the conflict between the conservatives and progressives in 1884, also helped Christianity to take its foothold in Korea. In the following years, this was followed by the start of Western medicine and hospitals, and of Western-style education. It was particularly American missionaries who helped to develop these institutions in Korea. All this was associated with American expansionism in the late 19th century. This American influence led not only to the development of railways, waterworks, power stations and telephone facilities in Korea, but also to the close relations between the two nations prior to, and after, the Japanese colonial period.

Most of the American industries were taken over by the Japanese when they started to annexe Korea in 1902. During the period of Japanese colonialism, the national independence movement in Korea was closely connected to churches in the homeland and abroad, Christians providing much of the core of this movement. Although Western missionaries in Korea tended to encourage Christians to focus on religion rather than to be involved in political matters, many Koreans understood Christianity as part of anti-colonialism, Korean nationalism and pro-*minjung* (or pro-mass). The hostility of the Japanese colonial government to Christianity meant that the time was not ripe for the development of religio-economic entrepreneurship within Christianity in Korea during the first part of the 20th century.

The end of the Second World War led to national independence and the re-opening of the close links between South Korea and the United States. In keeping with the Confucian emphasis on the importance of learning, a large number of Koreans went to America to undertake various types of education and they have formed a significant proportion of leading elites of different sectors in Korea, especially since 1945. Many Koreans undertook theological studies in the United States. Theological graduates with diverse perspectives returned home and they became leading figures in the various factions of Christianity in Korea. The heavy influence of the head office of different denominations in the United States on the American missionaries in Korea, together with the influence of American-educated Korean theologians, fostered denominationalism rather than ecumenism. Although there were attempts at the latter in areas such as the media, schools and church-run hospitals, no significant attempt at ecumenical partnership was made in the area of theological institutions. Every denomination maintained its own college. The American link was one of the prime factors which led to the rise of religio-economic entrepreneurship, especially after the 1960s, when urbanisation and rapid economic development took place and a large number of tertiary educational institutions, including theological colleges, were established. It was also one of the core ingredients producing church schism.

The enormous church growth in Korea over recent decades has been due to the complex interaction of a number of factors, including Korean indigenous religions, industrialisation, and education. This study has shown the ways in which these factors have created a high degree of demand for, and supply of, church activity. Korean society has been rapidly industrialising since the 1960s, and Koreans have tried almost all possible means to achieve this. Part of this change includes a new religious orientation. For example, the clergy, in their preachings and teachings, have offered to churchgoers a better life in the here and now. A prevalent tendency of Korean Christianity is that it accommodates indigenous belief systems, such as totemism, shamanistic fetishism and other kinds of nature worship, through which people are inclined to seek blessings such as material wealth, good health, and general personal and financial well-being. This has appealed in a significant way not only to the poor but also to the middle class who suffer a strong sense of relative deprivation. A church which preaches this doctrine has been, and still is, in demand. This relative deprivation became more obvious when the gap between the rich and the poor widened due to the effects of highly growth-oriented development policies. This complex of social circumstances enabled materialism and religio-economic entrepreneurship to penetrate deeply into Christianity in Korea.

By contrast, Buddhism and Confucianism have not experienced religio-economic entrepreneurship of the same order. Since the coming of Christianity, Korea has undergone westernisation. In this process the traditional education system, based on Confucianism, quickly lost its significance. However, the close tie between Christianity and Western-style education prompted a significant development of education in general and theological education in particular. This injected a high level of institutionalisation into theological training. The nation-wide entrance exam is compulsory and the system of offering a "diploma" to graduates was quickly adopted in theological institutions. A 3-4 year period of formal training became necessary for those who wanted to be clergy. This process has not happened in Buddhism, which has been a "hermit religion" mostly located in the mountains due to suppression by the Chosŏn Dynasty. There are only a few tertiary institutions where Buddhist monks receive qualifications widely recognised in Korean society. Korean Confucianism focused on teaching students to be government officials rather than producing clergy to work for the expansion of Confucianism. Only one Confucian university produces professionally trained graduates. As was the case in the Chosŏn Dynasty, they are regarded as Confucian scholars rather than clergy. Consequently, neither of these two religions have an over-supply of clergy, and relatively little religio-economic entrepreneurship has developed within them.

Other features of religio-economic entrepreneurship in Korean Christianity are as follows. The level of demand for tertiary education, especially since the 1960s, has been extremely high because indigenised Confucianism tends to pay a high degree of respect to the learned and to teachers. This produces enormous difference between economic and social rewards for university graduates and non-graduates. As a part of these changes, a large number of theological colleges have been established. The graduates have had to compete vigorously to begin, and to enhance, their careers. One outcome is that graduates have gone out of their way to establish churches and to recruit members. The specialisation of theological education has been a barrier to obtaining other employment available to university graduates who have obtained an education more directly relevant to the process of industrialisation. Theological graduates in Korea have a high rate of unemployment. This has led some to migrate to other countries.

Although some Koreans had migrated to Hawaii earlier in the century to work on sugar plantations, large-scale immigration of Koreans to mainland USA has occurred mainly since the 1960s, when

Korean society started to develop a number of new socio-political problems, such as instability, unemployment and the political threat from North Korea. The consequent growth of the Korean church in the United States has offered alternative places to minister for theological graduates who were competing to find ministerial positions in Korea. Whilst a large proportion of potential migrants, including ministers, have chosen the United States as destination for the last several decades, other developed countries such as Canada and Australia have also become popular in recent decades.

The major migration of Koreans to Australia started in the early 1970s when the Korean government was withdrawing Korean troops from the Vietnam War. About 500 Korean civilians and technicians from the war formed the first group of Koreans to come to Australia. Due to the lack of employment in their preferred area in Korea, which is highly status conscious because of the culture of deep-rooted Confucianism, many decided to emigrate. They often came as tourists to Australia, known among Koreans as "a heaven on earth in the twentieth century", in the hope of improving their lives. Most obtained permanent residency at the time of the Australian government's amnesty in 1975. Subsequently their families and relatives in Korea also migrated here. The first Korean to minister at a church in Sydney came in 1974 at the invitation of those early Korean migrants. Australia soon became a popular site of migration for Koreans and Korean ministers. There were some Buddhist and Catholic migration, but their organisations have not grown to any significant degree. This is not only because of the tight control over each congregation or temple by higher authorities, but also because of the lack of the development of religio-economic entrepreneurship within these religions in Korea itself.

When Koreans migrate to Australia they bring many cultural aspects of Korean society with them. Their adjustment process in the new country has also caused a high degree of demand for church-related services among Koreans in Australia. At present, there are about two hundred Korean ministers in Sydney. It has not only been a demand for church-related services that has created growth; an abundant supply of such services has also been important.

The significance of the church for Koreans in Australia is that it not only fulfils religious needs but also operates at the ethnic, economic and political level of people's lives. This study has highlighted what Koreans are searching for and the ways in which their needs are met by Korean churches and the clergy. Without religious needs the church growth among Koreans in Sydney would not have been as great as it has. The religious aspects of the Korean churches are what make them distinct from other Korean ethnic organisations. This religious aspect has made it possible for those who were Christians prior to migration to continue their church activities and for non-Christians to convert to Christianity. Some Korean churches in Sydney have been involved in evangelical work in third world countries such as China, Paraguay and the Philippines by providing financial support or sending missionaries. These activities are often a way of expressing religiosity or thanking God for the prosperity of the Korean church .

Migrant theology, a theological perspective developed in overseas Korean churches, has helped Koreans cope with various difficulties that occur in their immigrant life. This theology pays attention not only to other-worldly matters but also to well-being in this world. Korean churches in Sydney hold meetings at least once a week, whereas other Korean ethnic organisations meet monthly or bimonthly, or even less frequently. The frequency of church meetings has also contributed to the heightened interest in church activities among Koreans in Sydney.

However, viewing the Korean church in Sydney as strictly a religious organisation does not provide a full picture of the functions it serves. The Korean church in Sydney is a site of Korean ethnicity or Koreanness, which includes the Korean language, eating habits, and an emphasis on learning. This sense of being Korean is sometimes heightened after migration. Koreans prefer to marry other Koreans and they wish to celebrate traditional Korean festivals and historically important events such as Independence Day and the Foundation Day of Korea. Singing the Korean national anthem as a part of the church service seems to strengthen the feeling of Koreanness. Of the numerous organisations in the Korean community, the church is the most significant instrument for maintaining these ethnic characteristics.

The church operates to teach Australian-born Koreans the Korean language, history and culture, and helps Koreans maintain a sense of identity. The church has made much effort to improve the quality of the life of the Korean elderly through *Kyŏngnodaehak,* the weekend school for the elderly. Many of the elderly spend their weekdays baby-sitting their grandchildren and they look forward to sharing the experiences of the past week with friends at the school. This results in the involvement of more families in church activities. The church has often helped welcome new arrivals at the airport, find accommodation and jobs, and provide interpreting services. Some Koreans, such as lawyers, health professionals and those who run a food store or a restaurant, attract customers for their business activities from among their fellow church members. The Korean church has attempted to ensure the welfare of Koreans, *e.g.,* by helping them gain permanent residency. There have always been a number of illegal migrants in the Korean community.

They usually seek information about immigration through the Korean church.

Thus Korean ministers in Sydney provide social as well as religious services for members of their congregations. Koreans go to the church where they feel they are best served. They drift around the churches until they are satisfied with the services they find. This causes a high level of competition between churches to recruit and maintain a large membership and to best serve their members. This competition is heightened by the large number of churches available and by the surplus of persons with theological training. The latter have made themselves readily available to serve existing churches or to establish new ones. Korean clergy in Sydney are religious leaders, but they are also professional directors of economic and ethnic services. The Korean church in Sydney has been an important source of employment for Korean ministers. The same thing has been observed among immigrant Koreans all over the world.

Whilst the clergy pursues religio-economic entrepreneurship through church activities, church members also try to find various forms of fulfilment. Holding positions such as deacons or elders is one way of doing so. Church elders are considered more powerful than deacons, and they often have a right to discharge the clergy, being aware that replacement clergy are easily available. Sometimes there are conflicts between the clergy and the laity, and these conflicts may lead to church schisms. The competition thus engendered has generally accelerated rather than retarded church growth. It has also been emphasised in this study that church schisms among Korean churches in Sydney have to do with the particular social setting of the Korean community, which is, in turn, influenced by a number of aspects of Korean culture

Christianity in Korea is likely to continue to grow under present social conditions, which might last another few decades. Provided that other countries, such as Australia, continue their migrant intake, Koreans, including ministers and theological graduates, are likely to continue to migrate, and thus overseas Korean churches will also continue to grow. When the Korean community in Australia comes to have a large number of second and third generation Korean-Australians, the functions of the church in Australia may change. It is hard to predict whether this will necessarily lead to church decline.

The application of the perspective developed in this study leads us to understand various aspects of the growth of Korean churches, both within Korea and in other countries. It is important to bear in mind that, as argued throughout this book, the church is a part of society, and thus a study of churches needs to take into account all the relevant social factors in the wider society.

Bibliography

ABERCROMBIE, Nicholas, Stephen HILL and Bryan S. TURNER. 1984. *The Penguin Dictionary of Sociology.* Harmonsworth: Penguin Books.

ABRAMSON, H. 1975. "The Religioethnic Factor and the American Experience: Another Look at the Three-Generation Hypothesis", *Ethnicity* 2: 163-177.

ADELMAN, Irma and Sherman ROBINSON. 1978. *Income Distribution Policy in Developing Countries: A Case Study of Korea.* New York: Oxford University Press.

AHLSTROM, Sydney E. 1970. "The Radical Turn in Theology and Ethics: Why it Occurred in the 1960s", *Annals of the American Academy of Political and Social Sciences* 387: 1-13.

AHLSTROM, Sydney E. 1972. *A Religious History of the American People,* New Haven, CT: Yale University Press.

AHLSTROM, Sydney E. 1978. "National Trauma and Changing Religious Values", *Daedalus* 107: 13-29.

ALBA, R. 1976. "Social Assimilation Among American-Catholic National-Origin Groups", *American Sociological Review* 41: 1030-1046.

ALBA, Richard D. 1990. *Ethnic Identity: The Transformation of White America.* New Haven: Yale University Press.

ALDRICH, Howard E. and Roger WALDINGER. 1990. "Ethnicity and Entrepreneurship", *Annual Review of Sociology* 16: 111-135.

ALLPORT, Gordon W. 1950. *The Individual and His Religion.* New York: Macmillan.

ALLPORT, Gordon W. 1954. *The Nature of Prejudice.* Boston: Addison-Wesley Publishing Company.

ALLPORT, Gordon W. 1966. "The Religious Context of Prejudice", *Journal for the Scientific Study of Religion* 5: 447-457.

AN Chungsik. 1991. "Minjok Kyohoero Chŏngch'ak Haryŏmnida (Towards the Settlement as a Korean Ethnic Church)", *Saenuri Sinmun*, 25 May: 8 (in Korean).

AN Pyŏngmu. 1983. "Minjok, Minjung, Kyohoe (The Nation, The People and The Church)", pp. 342-348 in *Han'gug-ŭi Sinhak Sasang (Korean Theological Thought)*. Seoul: Christian Literature (in Korean).

AUSTRALIAN Bureau of Statistics. 1986a. *1986 Census*.

AUSTRALIAN Bureau of Statistics. 1986b. *1986 Census of Population and Housing: Overseas Born and Other Ethnic Population*.

AUSTRALIAN Bureau of Statistics. 1991. *1991 Census*.

AUSTRALIAN, The. 1993. "The Editorial: A Renewal of Religious Faith", 9 June: 10.

BAINBRIDGE, William Sims. 1990. "Explaining the Church Member Rate", *Social Forces* 68 (4): 1287-1296.

BALCH, R. W. 1980. "Looking behind the Scenes in a Religious Cult: Implications for the Study of Conversion", *Sociological Analysis* 41 (2): 137-143.

BALCH, Robert W. 1985. "What's Wrong with the Study of New Religions and What We Can Do about it", pp. 24-39 in B. K. KILBOURNE. (Ed.). *Scientific Research of New Religions: Divergent Perspectives*. Proceedings of the Annual Meeting of the Pacific Division of the American Association for the Advancement of Science, and the 59th Meeting of the Rocky Mountain Division. San Francisco: AAAS.

BALCH, Robert W. and David TAYLOR. 1977. "Seekers and Saucers: The Role of the Cultic Milieu in Joining a UFO Cult", *American Behavioral Scientist* 20: 839-860.

BALLARD, R. 1976. "Ethnicity: Theory and Experience" (a review article), *New Community* 5: 196-202.

BARKAN. Elliot R. 1991. "A Review Article", *Society* 28 (4): 94-95.

BARRET, David B. (Ed.). 1982. *World Christian Encyclopedia: A Comparative Study of Churches and Religion in the Modern World*. New York: Oxford University Press.

BARTH, Frederick. 1969. *Ethnic Groups and Boundaries*. London: George Allen and Unwin.

BARTON, Josef J. 1975. *Peasants and Strangers*. Cambridge, MA: Harvard University Press.

BATSON, C. D. and W. L. VENTIS. 1982. *The Religious Experience: A Social-Psychological Perspective*. New York: Oxford University Press.

BECKER, Howard. 1932. *Systematic Sociology*. New York: John Wiley & Sons.

BECKFORD, James A. 1973. "Religious Organisation: A Trend Report and Bibliography", *Current Sociology* 21 (2).

BELL, Daniel. 1975. "Ethnicity and Social Change", pp. 141-174 in N. GLAZER and D. MOYNIHAN. (Eds.). *Ethnicity: Theory and Experience.* Cambridge, Mass.: Harvard University Press.

BELLAH, Robert. 1970. *Beyond Belief.* New York: Harper and Row.

BERGER, Peter L. 1961. *The Noise of Solemn Assemblies.* New York: Doubleday & Company, Inc.

BERGER, Peter L. 1963. *Invitation to Sociology.* New York: Doubleday.

BERGER, Peter L. 1967. *The Sacred Canopy: Elements of a Sociological Theory of Religion.* Garden City, N. Y.: Doubleday.

BERGER, Peter L. 1979. *The Heretical Imperative.* Garden City: Doubleday.

BERGER, Peter and Thomas LUCKMANN. 1966. *The Social Construction of Religion: A Treatise in the Sociology of Knowledge.* Garden City, N. Y.: Doubleday.

BLACK, Alan W. 1978. "Religious Socialisation", pp. 282-300 in F. J. HUNT. (Ed.). *Socialisation in Australia.* Melbourne: Australian International Press Publications.

BLACK, Alan W. 1983. "The Sociology of Ecumenism: Initial Observations on the Formation of the Uniting Church in Australia", pp. 86-107 in Alan W. BLACK and Peter GLASNER. (Eds.). *Practice and Belief.* Sydney: George Allen & Unwin.

BLACK, Alan W. 1988. "Pentecostalism in Australia: Some Preliminary Findings", Paper prepared for the Conference of the Australian Association for the Study of Religions, Brisbane, 1-4 September.

BLACK, Alan W. 1991. "Ethnic Diversity, Multiculturalism and the Churches", pp. 160-172 in Peter BENTLEY, Tricia BLOMBERY and Philip J. HUGHES. (Eds.). *A Yearbook for Australian Churches 1992.* Hawthorn: Christian Research Association.

BLACK, Alan W. and Peter E. GLASNER. 1983. *Practice and Belief: Studies in the Sociology of Australian Religion.* Sydney: George Allen & Unwin.

BODYCOMB, John F. 1984. *QUO VADIS, ECCLESIA?* Unpublished Th.D. Dissertation submitted to Melbourne College of Divinity.

BOGARDUS, E. S. 1930. "Race-Relations Cycle", *American Journal of Sociology* 35: 613.

BONACICH, Edna. 1973. "A Theory of Middleman Minorities", *American Sociological Review* 38 (5): 583-594.

BOSCH, Henry G. 1990. "Life-Saving Station", *Our Daily Bread,* 1990, May 20. Grand Rapids: Radio Bible Class.

BOTTOMLEY, Gill. 1988. "Ethnicity, Race and Nationalism in Australia: Some Critical Perspectives", *Australian Journal of Social Issues* 23 (3): 169-183.

BOUMA, Gary D. 1991. "By what authority? An analysis of the locus of ultimate authority in ecclesiastical organisations", pp. 121-132 in Alan W. BLACK. (Ed.). *Religion in Australia: Sociological Perspectives.* Sydney: Allen & Unwin.

BOYLEN, Louise. 1991. "The Corporate Behemoth That is God Incorporated", in *Financial Review* 17 December.

180   *Social Sources of Church Growth*

BROWN, John P. 1982. "Saenggak-hamyŏ Malhamyŏ: Kyohoe Pulli Ch'angp'ihan Irijiyo (Church Schisms are Something to be Ashamed of", *Hoju Sosik*, December: 8 (in Korean).

BROWN, John P. 1988. "A Letter to Rev. Norman McDonald, General Secretary, NSW Synod of the UCA", an official letter.

BROWN, John P. 1991. "Hanin Nohoe Kusŏng Cheŭi-rŭl Pomyŏnsŏ? (Forming the Korean Ethnic Synod?)", *Hoju Tonga*, 2 August: 10 (in Korean).

BROWN, W. O. 1934. "Culture Contact and Race Conflict", pp. 34-37 in E. B. REUTER. (Ed.). *Race and Culture Contacts*. New York: McGraw-Hill.

CARROLL, Jackson W. 1978. "Understanding Church Growth and Decline", *Theology Today* 35: 79-80.

CHANG Hyŏngil. 1991. "Kyop'a Pun'yŏlsang Chŏngmal Ant'akkawŏyo (Tantalising Denominational Splits)", *Saenuri Sinmun*, 18 May (in Korean).

CHANG Insŏk. 1990. "Cholputŏr-ŭi Taehaengjin: Kwasobi Kwangt'ae (The Parade of Overnight Millionaires)", *Sin Tonga*, October: 434-449 (in Korean).

CHI T'aeyŏng. 1983. "Imin-gyohoe-ŭi Hyŏnsil-gwa Kwaje (Korean Immigrant Churches in Sydney, Today and Tomorrow)", *Hoju Sosik*, August: 12, 13 (in Korean).

CHO Insuk. 1982. "Kyop'o Tanch'etŭrŭl Ikknŭn Saramtŭr-ege Kamsahae (Thanks to the Leading Organisations in the Sydney Korean Community)", *Hoju Sosik*, November: 6 (in Korean).

CHO Yohan. 1984. "Han'guk Kidokkyo-ŭi Konan (The Struggles of the Korean Christianity)", pp. 7-102 in *Han'guk Sahoe-wa Kidokkyo (Korean Society and Christianity)*. Seoul: Sungjŏn University Press (in Korean).

CH'OE Pyŏnghak. 1991. "Hoju-nŭn Ch'ŏn'guk Ch'ŏrŏm Choŭnnara (Australia is as Good as Heaven)", *Hoju Tonga*, 8 November: 10 (in Korean).

CH'OE Chŏngbok. 1983. "Iminsaenghwar-ŭi Ppuri (The Roots of Migrant Life)", *Hoju Sosik*, November: 7 (in Korean).

CH'OE Chŏngbok. 1991. "Yŏnhap Kyodan-e Sokhan Hanin-gyohoe-ŭi Samyŏng (Mission of the Korean Immigrant Churches Which are the Members of the UCA)", *Yŏnhap Kidok Sinbo (Younhab Christian News)*, 17 September. Sydney: The Sydney Korean Parish of the Uniting Church in Australia: 7-8 (in Korean).

CHOI, Joon-Sik, 1992. "Shamanism in the Context of Modern Korea Religion", *Koreana* 6 (2): 10-13.

CHŎN Kyut'ae. 1983. "Han'gugin-ŭi ŭisik Kucho (The Structure of Korean Consciousness)", *Hoju Sosik* June: 13 (in Korean).

CHŎN Kyut'ae. 1985. *Hoju-ro Kanŭn'gil: 20 segi-ŭi Chisang Nagwŏn (The Way to Australia: a Heaven on Earth in the Twentieth Century)*. Seoul: Chimundang Publishing Co (in Korean).

CHŎN T'aekpu. 1987. *Han'guk Kyohoe Palchŏnsa (The History of Church Development in Korea)*. Seoul: The Christian Literature Society (in Korean).

CHŎNG Chisŏk. 1991. "Yŏnchung Kihoek Han'guk Kyohoe Chindan: Kukchŏk Innŭn Sinhakkyoyuk Chŏlsilhada (Indigenisation of the Theological Education?)", *Saenuri Sinmun* 9 March (in Korean).

CHŎNG Sŭngguk. 1986. "Segye Ch'eje Iron-gwa Han'guk sahoe (World System Theory and Korean Society)", pp. 61-88 in *Che sam Segyewa Han'gug-ŭi sahoe-hak (The Third World and Korean Sociology)*, KIM Jin'gyun. (Ed.). Seoul: Tolbegae Publishing Company (in Korean).

CHŎNG Uhyŏn. 1980. "Kyosa-ŭi Sahoechŏk Chiwi (Social Status of Teachers in Korea)", pp. 263-281 in KIM Sŏnyang et al. (Eds.). *Han'guk sahoe-wa Kyoyuk (Korean Society and Education)*. Seoul: Scientific Education Publishing Co (in Korean).

CHOU, Sun-Ae. 1983. "Korean Church Growth and Christian Education", pp. 309-317 in Bong-Rin RO and Marlin L. NELSON. (Eds.). *Korean Church Growth Explosion*. Seoul: Word of Life Press.

CHOY, Bong-Youn. 1979. *Koreans in America*. Chicago: Nelson-Hall.

CHRISTIANITY Today. 1968. "News", *Christianity Today* 13 (2): 47.

CHRISTIANITY Today. 1973. "The Korean Christian Phenomena", *Christianity Today* 17 (19): 23.

CHRISTIANITY Today. 1975. "South Korea: Challenge From the Church", *Christianity Today* 19 (9): 24-26.

CHUGAN Saenghwal Chŏngbo (Weekly Korean Life Review). 1991. March 8 (in Korean).

CHUGAN Saenghwal Chŏngbo (Weekly Korean Life Review). 1993. June 18 (in Korean).

CHUNG, Bom-Mo. 1966. "Problems Facing Educational Planning", *Korea Journal* 6 (7): 5-8.

CHUNG, Tai-Si. 1966. "Problems Facing the Enhancement of the Status of Teachers in Korea", *Korea Journal* 6 (7): 13-17.

CLARK, Donald N. 1986. *Christianity in Modern Korea*. Lanham, MD: University Press of America.

CLARK, John. 1979. "Cults", *Journal of the American Medical Association* 243 (3): 279-281.

CLARK, M., S. KAUFMAN and R. PIERCE. 1976. "Explorations of Acculturation: Toward a Model of Ethnic Identity", *Human Organization* 35: 231-238.

CLIFFORD, Mark. 1990a. "Seoul Loses its Nerve: Cabinet Reshuffle Signals Return to High-growth Strategy", *Far Eastern Economic Review*, 29 March: 56-57.

CLIFFORD, Mark. 1990b. "Messianic Mission", *Far Eastern Economic Review*, 1 November: 24-31.

COCHRAN, Thomas C. 1966. "Entrepreneurship", pp. 87-90 in *International Encyclopedia of Social Sciences*, Vol. 5. The Macmillan Company & The Free Press.

COHEN, A. (Ed.). 1974. *Urban Ethnicity* (A. S. A. Monograph No. 12). London: Tavistock.

COHEN, S. 1985. *American Modernity and Jewish Identity*. New York: Tavistock Publications.

CONWAY, Flo and Jim SIEGELMAN. 1978. *Snapping*. New York: J. B. Lippincott.

COUGHENOUR, Milton and Lawrence M. HEPPLE. 1957. *The Church in Rural Missouri, Part II, Religious Groups in Rural Missouri*. Columbia, Mo.: A. E. S. Research Bulletin 633B, September.

COX, David R. 1987. *Migration and Welfare: An Australian Perspective*. New York and Sydney: Prentice Hall.

CROSS, M. 1971. "On Conflict, Race Relations, and the Theory of the Plural Society", *Race* 4: 478-494.

CURRIE, Robert, Alan GILBERT, and Lee HORSLEY. 1977. *Churches and Churchgoers*. London: Oxford University Press.

CURSON, Sheila and Peter CURSON. 1982. "The Japanese in Sydney", *Ethnic and Racial Studies* 5 (4): 478-512.

DANIELS, Michael. 1979. "Confucius and Confucianism in Korea", *Korea Journal* 19 (5): 46-48.

DEARMAN, Marion. 1982. "Structure and Function of Religion in the Los Angeles Korean Community: Some Aspects", pp. 165-184 in Eui-Young YU, Earl H. PHILLIPS, and Eun Sik YANG. (Eds.). *Koreans in Los Angeles: Prospects and Promises*. Los Angeles: Koryo Research Institute.

DEMERATH III, N. J. 1965. *Social Class in American Protestantism*. Chicago: Rand McNally & Company.

DEMERATH III, N. J. and Phillip E. HAMMOND. 1969. *Religion in Social Context: Tradition and Transition*. New York: Random House.

DEMPSEY, Kenneth. 1983. *Conflict and Decline: ministers and laymen in an Australian country town*. North Ryde: Metheun Australia.

DISCUSSIONS and Recommendations of Ten Workshops, a UCA monograph, 1991. May.

DOUGLASS, H. Paul and Edmund DeS. BRUNNER. 1935. *The Protestant Church as a Social Institution*. New York: Institute of Social and Religious Research.

DOWNTON, James V. 1979. *Sacred Journeys: The Conversion of Young Americans to Divine Light Mission*. New York: Columbia University Press.

DOWNTON, James V., Jr. 1980. "An Evolutionary Theory of Spiritual Conversion and Commitment: The Case of Divine Light Mission", *Journal for the Scientific Study of Religion* 19: 381-396.

DRIEDGER, Leo. 1989. *The Ethnic Factor: Identity in Diversity*. Toronto: McGraw-Hill Ryerson Limited.

DURKHEIM, Emile. 1965. *Elementary Forms of the Religious Life*. Tr. J. W. Swain. New York: Free Press.

EBERSOLE, Luke E. 1951. *Church Lobbying in the Nation's Capitol.* New York: The Macmillan Company.

EIPPER, Chris. 1983. "The Magician's Hat: A Critique of the Concept of Ethnicity", *Australian and New Zealand Journal of Sociology* 19 (3): 427-446.

EISENDTADT, S. N. 1963. *The Political Systems of Empires.* New York: The Free Press.

EPSTEIN, A. 1978. *Ethos and Identity.* London: Tavistock.

ETHNIC Link. 1990. November.

ETHNIC Link. 1991. May.

ETZIONI, A. 1965. *A Comparative Analysis of Complex Organisations.* 3rd edition. New York: Free Press of Glencoe.

FAR East and Australasia 1992, The. 1992. London: Europa Publications Limited.

FAULKNER, Joseph and Gordon DEJONG. 1966. "Religiosity in 5-D: An Empirical Analysis", *Social Forces* 45: 246-254.

FOSS, Daniel and Ralph LARKIN. 1978. "Worshipping the Absurd: The Negation of Social Causality Among the Followers of the GuRu Mahari'ji", *Sociological Analysis* 39 (2): 157-164.

FRANCIS, E. K. 1947. "The Nature of the Ethnic Groups", *American Journal of Sociology* 52 (5): 393-400.

FRANCIS, E. K. 1948. "The Russian Mennonites from Religious to Ethnic Group", *American Journal of Sociology* 54 (2): 101-107.

FRAZIER. E. F. 1963. *The Negro Church in America.* New York: Schocken Books.

FUKUYAMA, Yoshio. 1961. "The Major Dimensions of Church Membership", *Review of Religious Research* 2: 154-161.

GANS, H. 1979. "Symbolic Ethnicity: The Future of Ethnic Groups and Cultures in America", *Ethnic and Racial Studies* 2 (1): 1-20.

GEERTZ, C. 1963. "The Integrative Revolution: Primordial Sentiments and Civil Politics in the New States", pp. 105-107 in C. GEERTZ. (Ed.). *Old Societies and New States.* New York: Free Press.

GIDDENS, Anthony. 1973. *The Class Structure of the Advanced Societies.* London: Hutchinson University Library.

GLAZER, Nathan and Daniel P. MOYNIHAN. 1975. *Ethnicity: Theory and Practice.* Cambridge, Mass.: Havard University Press.

GLOCK, Charles Y. and Rodney STARK. 1965. *Religion and Society in Tension.* Chicago: Rand McNally & Company.

GLOCK, Charles Y., Benjamin B. RINGER, and Earl R. BABBIE. 1967. *To Comfort and To Challenge: A Dilemma of the Contemporary Church.* Berkeley and Los Angeles.

GLOCK, Charles. 1964. "The Role of Deprivation in the Evolution of Religious Groups", pp. 24-36 in Robert LEE and Martin MARTY. (Eds.). *Religion and Social Conflict.* New York: Oxford University Press.

GOERING, J. 1971. "The Emergence of Ethnic Interests: A Case of Serendipity", *Social Forces* 49: 379-384.

GOLDSTEIN, S. and C. GOLDSCHEIDER. 1968. *Jewish Americans: Three Generations in a Jewish Community.* Englewood Cliffs: Prentice-Hall.

GORDON, Milton M. 1964. *Assimilation into American Life.* New York: Oxford University Press.

GOUGH, J. W. 1969. *The Rise of the Entrepreneur.* London: B. T. Batsford.

GRAYSON, James H. 1985. *Early Buddhism and Christianity in Korea: A Study in Emplantation of Religion.* Leiden, The Netherlands: E. J. Brill.

GRAYSON, James H. 1989. *Korea: A Religious History.* Oxford: Claredon Press.

GRAYSON, James H. 1991. "Dynamic Complementarity: Korean Confucianism and Christianity", Paper presented at Conference on Religion and the Resurgence of Capitalism, University of Lancaster, 14-17 July.

GREELEY, Andrew. 1971. "Ethnicity as an Influence on Behaviors", pp. 1-16 in Otto FEINSTEIN. (Ed.). *Ethnic Groups in the City.* Lexington, Mass.: Health Lexington Books.

GREELEY, Andrew. 1972. *The Denominational Society: A Sociological Approach to Religion in America.* Glenview and London: Scott, Foresman and Company.

GREELEY, Andrew. 1974. *Ethnicity in the United States: A Preliminary Reconnaissance.* New York: Wiley.

HADAWAY, Christopher Kirk. 1980. "Conservatism and Social Strength in a Liberal Denomination", *Review of Religious Research* 21 (3): 302-314.

HADAWAY, Christopher Kirk. 1981. "The Demographic Environment and Church Membership Change", *Journal for the Scientific Study of Religion* 20 (1): 77-89.

HADDEN, Jeffrey K. 1969. *The Gathering Storm in the Churches.* Garden City, N. Y.: Doubleday.

HADDEN, Jeffrey K. 1980. "Religion and the Construction of Social Problems", *Sociological Analysis* 41: 99-108.

HADDEN, Jeffrey K. 1987. "Religious Broadcasting and the Mobilization of the New Christian Right", *Journal for the Scientific Study of Religion* 26 (1): 1-24.

HAHN, Bae-Ho and Kyu-Taik KIM. 1963. "Korean Political Leaders (1952-1962): Their Social Origins and Skills", *Asian Survey* 3 (7): 305-323.

HAMMOND, Phillip E. 1985. "Introduction", pp. 1-6 in *The Sacred in a Secular Age.* Berkeley and London: University of California Press.

HAN Pyŏngok. 1986. "Sŏn'gyo Isegirŭl Man-nŭn Han'guk Kyohoe-ŭi Chŏnmang (The Retrospection and Perspective of Korean Church for the One Hundred Years Korean Mission)", pp. 25-35 in *Kyohoe Munje Yŏn'gu Che o-chip: Onŭr-ŭi Han'guk Kyohoe Muŏsi Munje-in'ga (Research Journal of Church Affairs, Vol. 5: What are the Problems with Korean churches today),* September (in Korean).

HAN, Sung-Joo. 1982. "Modernisation and Political Development", *Korea Journal* 22 (8): 80-82.

HAN Wansang. 1983. "Han'guk Kyohoe-ŭi Yangjŏk Sŏngjang-gwa Kyointŭr-ŭi Kach'igwan (Quantitative Growth of Korean Church and the Values of Korean Christians)", pp. 121-156 in *Han'guk-ŭi Kŭntaehwa-wa Kidokkyo (The Modernisation of Korea and Christianity)*. Seoul: Sungjŏn University (in Korean).

HAN Yŏngje. (Ed.). 1986. *Han'guk Kidokkyo Sŏngjang Paengnyŏn (100 Years of Korean Churches' Growth)*. Seoul: The Christian Literature Press (in Korean).

HANDLIN, Oscar. 1973. *The Uprooted*. Boston: Little Brown.

HANG'UK Kidokkyosa Yŏn'guhoe (Institute of Korean Church History Studies, The). 1989. *Han'guk Kidokkyosa (A History of Korean Church)*. Seoul: The Christian Literature Press (in Korean).

Hanho T'aimjŭ (Hanho Times, a Korean ethnic newspaper in Sydney). 1989. October 20 — July 13 1990 (in Korean).

HANSEN, M. 1952. "The Third Generation in America", *Commentary* 14: 492-500.

HARGROVE, Barbara. 1979. *The Sociology of Religion*. Arlington Heights, Ill.: AHM Publishing Corp.

HARMAN, Grant. 1990. "Challenges for Higher Education in Asian and Pacific Region", *University of New England Gazette* 6 (9): 3-4.

HERBERG, William. 1955. *Protestant, Catholic, Jew: An Essay in American Religious Sociology*. Garden City, N. Y.: Doubleday.

HERTZLER, J. O. 1948. "Religious Institutions", *Annals of the American Academy of Political and Social Science* 256 : 7-19.

HOJU Sosik (a Korean ethnic newspaper in Sydney). 1982. September — November 10, 1989 (in Korean).

HOJU Tonga (a Korean ethnic newspaper in Sydney). 1991. January 18 — March 25, 1992 (in Korean).

HOGE, Dean R. 1979. "A Test of Theories of Denominational Growth and Decline", pp. 179-197 in Dean R. HOGE and David A. ROOZEN. (Eds.). *Understanding Church Growth and Decline, 1950-1978*. New York: The Pilgrim Press.

HOGE, Dean R. and David A. ROOZEN. (Eds.). 1979b. *Understanding Church Growth and Decline, 1950-1978*. New York: The Pilgrim Press.

HOGE, Dean R. and David A. ROOZEN. 1979a. "Research on Factors Influencing Church Commitment", pp. 42-68 in Dean R. HOGE and David A. ROOZEN. (Eds.). *Understanding Church Growth and Decline, 1950-1978*. New York: The Pilgrim Press.

HOGE, Dean R. and David R. ROOZEN. 1979c. "Some Sociological Conclusions About Church Trends", pp. 315-333 in Dean R. HOGE and David A. ROOZEN. (Eds.). *Understanding Church Growth and Decline, 1950-1978*. New York: The Pilgrim Press.

HONG, Harold S. 1983. "Social, Political and Psychological Aspects of Church Growth", pp. 171-181 in Bong-Rin RO and Marlin L.

NELSON. (Eds.) 1983. *Korean Church Growth Explosion*. Seoul: Word of Life Press.

HONG Kilbok. 1986. *Iminja Yesu (Jesus, the Migrant)*. Seoul: Yang Sŏ Publishing Company (in Korean).

HONG Kilbok. 1988. *Nae Paeksŏng-ŭl Wiro-hara (Comfort My People)*. Seoul: Yang Sŏ Publishing Company (in Korean).

HONG Kŭnsu. 1991a. "Minjok T'ongir-e Taehan Han'guk Kyohoe-ŭi Samyŏng - 1 (Korean Christianity's Responsibility for the Reunification of the Korean Peninsula - 1)", *Saenuri Sinmun*, 9 March (in Korean).

HONG Kŭnsu. 1991b. "Minjok T'ongir-e Taehan Han'guk Kyohoe-ŭi Samyŏng - 2 (Korean Christianity's Responsibility for the Reunification of the Korean Peninsula - 2)", *Saenuri Sinmun*, 6 April (in Korean).

HONG Kŭnsu. 1991c. "Minjok T'ongir-e Taehan Han'guk Kyohoe-ŭi Samyŏng - 3 (Korean Christianity's Responsibility for the Reunification of the Korean Peninsula - 3)", *Saenuri Sinmun*, 23 March (in Korean).

HONG, Kyong-Man. 1983. "Formation of Korean Protestantism and Its Political Nature", *Korea Journal* 23 (12): 18-29.

HONG Pansik. 1986. "Tochŏn-pannŭn Hyŏndae Kyohoe (Modern Korean Church Challenged)", pp. 7-14 in *Kyohoe Munje Yŏn'gu Che o-chip: Onŭr-ŭi Han'guk Kyohoe Muŏsi Munje-in'ga (Research Journal of Church Affairs, Vol. 5: What are the Problems with Korean churches today?)*, September (in Korean).

HOUCHINS, Lee. and Chang Su HOUCHINS. 1974. "The Korean Experience in America, 1903-1924", *Pacific Historical Review* 43: 548-573.

HURH, Won-Moo. 1980. "Towards a Korean-American Ethnicity: Some Theoretical Models", in *Ethnic and Racial Studies* 3 (4) : 444-464.

HURH, Won-Moo and Kwang-Chung KIM. 1979. "Social and Occupational Assimilation of Korean Immigrants in the USA", A paper presented at the Annual Meeting of the Association for Asian Studies. Los Angeles, California, March 30- April 1.

HURH, Won-Moo and Kwang-Chung KIM. 1984a. *Korean Immigrants in America: A Structural Analysis of Ethnic Confinement and Adhesive Adaptation*. Associated University Press, Inc.

HURH, Won-Moo and Kwang-Chung KIM. 1984b. "Adhesive Sociocultural Adaptation of Korean Immigrants", *International Migration Review* 18 (2): 188-217.

HURH, Won-Moo and Kwang-Chung KIM. 1988. *Uprooting and Adjustment: A Sociological Study of Korean Immigrants' Mental Health*. Final Report submitted to the NIMH. Macomb, IL: Western Illinois University.

HURH, Won-Moo and Kwang-Chung KIM. 1989. "The 'success' image of Asian Americans: its validity, and its practical and theoretical implications", *Ethnic and Racial Studies* 12 (4): 512-538.

HURH, Won-Moo and Kwang-Chung KIM. 1990. "Religious Participation of Korean Immigrants in the United States", *Journal for the Scientific Study of Religion* 29 (1): 19-34.

HYŎN Sunho. 1988. *Imin Sahoe-ŭi Chin-P'unggyŏng-tŭl (The Real Features of Korean Ethnic Communities in the USA)*. Seoul: Yeo Woon Sa Publishing Company (in Korean).

IANNACCONE, Laurence R. 1992. "Sacrifice and Stigma: Reducing Free-riding in Cults, Communes, and Other Collectives", *Journal of Political Economy* 100 (2): 271-291.

IM Ch'ŏnil. 1991. "Segye-rŭl Hyanghae Chunŭn Kyohoe-ro (Korean Churches to the World Mission: from receiving to giving)", *K'ŭrisch'yan Ribyu (Christian Review)*, October: 38-39 (in Korean).

IM Tonggyu. 1989. "Imin Kyohoe-ŭi Mokhoe Hyŏnjang (Ministering Field in the Korean Community in Sydney)", *Hanho T'aimjŭ (Hanho Times)*, 20 October (in Korean).

ISAJIW, Wsevolod W. 1974. "Definitions of Ethnicity", *Ethnicity* 1: 111-124.

ISAJIW, Wsevolod W. 1975. "The Process of Maintenance of Ethnic Identity: The Canadian Context", in P. MIGUS (Ed.). *Sounds Canadian: Languages and Cultures in Multi Ethnic Society*. Toronto: Peter Martin Associates.

JENKINS, J. Craig. 1983. "Resource Mobilization Theory and the Study of Social Movements", pp. 527-553 in *Annual Review of Sociology*.

JENKINS, Shirley. 1988. "Introduction: Immigration, Ethnic Associations, and Social Services", pp. 1-20 in Shirley JENKINS. (Ed.). 1988. *Ethnic Associations and the Welfare State; Services to Immigrants in Five Countries*. New York: Columbia University Press.

JI, Won-Yong. 1965. "Christian Church and Sects in Korea", *Korea Journal* 5 (9): 4-11.

JO, Moon H. 1992. "Korean Merchants in the Black Community: Prejudice among the Victims of Prejudice", *Ethnic and Racial Studies* 15 (3): 395-411.

JOHNSON, Benton. 1963. "On Church and Sect", in *American Sociological Review* 28: 539-549.

JOHNSON, C. 1976. "The Principle of Generation among Japanese in Honolulu", *Ethnic Groups* 1: 13-35.

JUPP, J. (Ed.). 1988. *The Australian People*. Sydney: Angus & Robertson Publishers.

KAHOE, R. D. 1974. "Personality and Achievement Correlates of Intrinsic and Extrinsic Religious Orientations", *Journal of Personality and Social Psychology* 29: 812-818.

KAHOE, R. D. and M. J. MEADOW. 1981. "A Developmental Perspective on Religious Orientation Dimensions", *Journal for the Scientific Study of Religion* 11: 240-251.

KANG Chŏnggyu. 1983. *Han'gug-ŭi ch'il-ttae Kyohoe (The Great Seven Churches in Korea: their growth and the present condition)*. Seoul: Chongro Book Center (in Korean).

KANG, Shin-Myung. 1983. "The Dignity of Korean Pastors", pp. 301-308 in Bong-Rin RO and Marlin L. NELSON. (Eds.). 1983. *Korean Church Growth Explosion*. Seoul: Word of Life Press.

KANG, Wi-Jo. 1987. *Religion and Politics Under the Japanese Rule*. Lewiston: Edwin Mellen Press.

KANG Yosep. 1983. "Pogŭmsŏ-wa Minjung-Sinhak (The Gospel and Minjung Theology)", pp. 378-386 in *Han'gug-ŭi Sinhak sasang (Korean Theological Thought)*. Seoul: Christian Literature (in Korean).

KELLEY, Dean M. 1972. *Why Conservative Churches Are Growing*. New York: Harper & Row Publishers.

KELLEY, Dean M. 1977. *Why Conservative Churches are Growing*. New York: Harper & Row Publishers.

KELLY, P. 1988. "Settlement of Vietnamese Refugees", pp. 833-836 in J. JUPP. (Ed.). *The Australian People*. Sydney: Angus & Robertson Publishers.

KIM, Bernice Bong-Hee. 1937. "The Koreans in Hawaii", Master's thesis, University of Hawaii.

KIM, Bok-Lim. 1978. *The Asian Americans: Changing Patterns, Changing Needs*. Montclair, N. J.: Association for Christian Scholars in North America.

KIM Byong-Suh. 1981. "Han'guk Kyohoe Hyŏnsang-ŭi Sahoehak-chŏk Ihae (A Sociological Understanding of the Korean Church Phenomenon)", in *Sinhak Sasang (Theological Thought)*, Winter: 696-724 (in Korean).

KIM Byong-Suh. 1984. "Han'guk Kyohoe-ŭi Chonggyosŏng-gwa Kyech'ŭngsŏng Yŏn'gu (The Religiosity and the Stratification within the Korean Christianity — Protestantism)", pp. 103-170 in *Han'guk Kyohoe-wa Kidokkyo (Korean Society and Christianity)*. Seoul: Sungjŏn University Press (in Korean).

KIM, Byong-Suh. 1985. "The Explosive Growth of the Korean Church Today: A Sociological Analysis", *International Review of Mission* 64 (293): 61-74.

KIM, Chan-Hie. 1982. "Christianity and the Modernization of Korea", pp. 117-127 in Earl H. PHILLIPS and Eui-Young YU. (Eds.). *Religions in Korea: Beliefs and Cultural Values*. Los Angeles, California: Center for Korean-American and Korean Studies, California State University.

KIM Chinyŏp. 1990. *Nae Chogug-ŭi Ch'ŏlch'ang-e Katch'yŏ (In my Mother Land's Prison)*. Seoul: Tolbegae Publishing Company (in Korean).

KIM Chŏngjun. 1983. "Han'guk Sinhag-ŭi Ichŏngp'yo (A Milestone of the Korean Theology)", pp. 12-32 in *Han'gug-ŭi Sinhak Sasang (Korean Theological Thought)*. Seoul: Christian Literature (in Korean).

KIM, Doo-Hun. 1963. "Confucian Influences on Korean Society", in *Korea Journal* 3 (9): 17-21.

KIM, Han-Sik. 1983. "The Influence of Christianity on Modern Korean Political Thought", *Korea Journal* 23 (12): 4-17.

KIM Hyŏngsŏk. 1983. "Han'gug-ŭi Kŭndaehwa-wa Kidokkyo Kyoyuk (Modernisation of Korea and Christian Education)", pp. 279-326 in *Han'gug-ŭi Kŭndaehwa-wa Kidokkyo (The Modernisation of Korea and Christianity)*. Seoul: Sungjŏn University (in Korean).

KIM, Hyung-Chan. 1974. "History and Role of the Church in the Korean American community", *Korea Journal* 14 (8): 26-37.

KIM, Hyung-Chan. (Ed.). 1977a. *The Korean Diaspora: Historical and Sociological Studies of Korean Immigration and Assimilation in North America*. California: ABC — Clio, Inc.

KIM, Hyung-Chan. 1977b. "The History and Role of the Church in the Korean American Community", in *The Korean Diaspora: Historical and Sociological Studies of Korean Immigration and Assimilation in North America*. Hyung-chan KIM. (Ed.). California: ABC — Clio, Inc.

KIM, Hyung-Chan. 1977c. "Korean Community Organisations in America: Their Characteristics and Problems", pp. 65-83 in *The Korean Diaspora: Historical and Sociological Studies of Korean Immigration and Assimilation in North America*. Hyung-chan KIM. (Ed.). California: ABC — Clio, Inc.

KIM, Hyung-Chan. 1981. "Koreans", pp. 601-606 in *Harvard Encyclopedia of American Ethnic Groups*. Harvard University Press.

KIM, Ill-Soo. 1981. *New Urban Immigrants: The Korean Community in New York*. Princeton, N.J.: Princeton University Press.

KIM, Ill-Soo. 1985. "Organizational Patterns of Korean-American Methodist Churches: Denominationalism and Personal Community", pp. 228-237 in *Rethinking Methodist History*, R. E. RICHEY and K. E. ROWE. (Eds.). Nashville: Kingswood Books.

KIM, Jongchol. 1983. "Higher Education Policies in Korea, 1945-83", *Korea Journal* 23 (10): 4-19.

KIM, Kwang-Chung and Won-Moo HURH 1985. "Ethnic resources utilization of Korean immigrant entrepreneurs in the Chicago minority area", *International Migration Review* 19 (1): 82-111.

KIM, Man-Souk. 1988. "Koreans in Australia", pp. 659-660 in *The Australian People*. James JUPP. (Ed.). Sydney: Angus & Robertson Publishers.

KIM, (Mathew) Man-Young. 1983. *A Theology of and Strategy for MInistry among Korean Immigrants in Australia*. Unpublished D. Min. Dissertation submitted to San Francisco Theological Seminary.

KIM Myŏngdong. 1991 (February). "Midŭm-ŭn Haengham-ida (Christian Faith thorough Action)", *K'ŭrisch'yan Ribyu (Christian Review)*, February: 28 (in Korean).

KIM Myŏngdong. 1991 (September). "Hananim-ŭi Ch'angcho-ŭi Sumkkyŏl-gwa Maekpag-i Ttwigo-Innŭn Kyohoe (The Sydney

Korean Parish UCA: in the occasion of the seventeenth anniversary)", *K'ŭrisch'yan Ribyu (Christian Review)*, September: 32-35 (in Korean).

KIM, Sangho J. 1975. *A Study of the Korean Church and her People in Chicago, Illinois*. San Francisco: R and E Research Associates.

KIM, Sin-Bok. 1983. "Recent Development of Higher Education in Korea: Quantity, Quality and Equality", *Korea Journal* 23 (10): 20-30.

KIM Sŏnghwa. 1991. "Hŏlgab-e Hagwi-Sasŏ Chegap-Patkko Yŏnghon p'anŭn Nallip Sinhakkyo (Illegal Theological Seminaries' Selling Degrees: Spiritual Bargain Sale)", *K'ŭrisch'yan Ribyu (Christian Review)*, September: 6 (in Korean).

KIM, Sung-shik. 1962. "Tasks for Korean Education", *Korea Journal* 2 (1): 4-6.

KIM T'aekyong. 1979. *Chaemi Hanin Kyohoe 75 Nyŏn-sa (The History of the Korean Church in the United States for 75 years: 1903-1978)*. Seoul: Word of Life Bookstore (in Korean).

KIM, Warren Won-Yong. 1971. *Koreans in America*. Seoul: Po Chin Chae.

KIM Yongbok. 1984. "Minjok Puntansog-ŭi Han'guk Kidokkyo: Kŭ Sunan-gwa Taeŭng (Christianity in the Divided Koreas)", pp. 257-299 in *Han'guk Sahoewa Kidokkyo (Korean Society and Christianity)*. Seoul: Sungjŏn University Press (in Korean).

KIM Yŏngsŏk. 1991. "Moksanim, Moksanim, Uri Moksanim! (Minister, Minister, Our Minster!)", *Hanho T'aimjŭ (Hanho Times)*, 3 June: 18-19 (in Korean).

KOREA Journal. 1962a. "The Underwood Family and Korean Education", in *Korea Journal* 2 (1): 22-23.

KOREA Journal. 1962b. "Overseas-Trained Students Play Vital Roles", *Korea Journal* 2 (1): 21.

KOREAN National Bureau of Statistics. 1985. *1985 In'gu Chut'aek Sensōsŭ (1985 Population and Housing Census)*. Seoul: The Economic Planning Board, Korean Government (in Korean).

KOREAN Overseas Information Service. 1982. *A Handbook of Korea*. Seoul: Ministry of Culture and Information.

KOREAN Overseas Information Service. 1988. *A Handbook of Korea*. Seoul: Seoul International Publishing House.

KOREAN Society of Sydney. 1990. "Hanin sahoe Sŏlmun-chosa kyŏlgwa mit T'onggye Kyŏlgwa (A Survey of the Korean Community in Sydney)", *Hanho T'aimjŭ (Hanho Times)*, 26 January: 34-35 (in Korean).

KOREAN Youth Movement in Australia. 1990. "Chaeho Hanch'ŏng Kyŏlsŏng-ŭro Hoju Ch'ŏngnyŏn Undong Pakch'a (The Establishment of Korean Youth Movement in Australia)", in *Minju Choguk/ Demokratie in Korea*, 1 May, Berlin: Korean Democratic Movement in Europe (in Korean).

KORNBLUM, W. 1973. *Blue-Collar Community*. Chicago: University of Chicago Press.

KOTLER, Philip and Sidney J. LEVY 1969. "Broadening the Concept of Marketing", *Journal of Marketing* 33: 10-15.

K'ŭrisch'yan Ribyu (Christian Review, monthly Korean church magazine in Sydney). 1991. January — May 1992 (in Korean).

K'ŭrisch'yan Sinmun (Christian Newspaper, a Christian newspaper published in Korea). 1991. 24 November (in Korean).

LAUMANN, E. 1973. *Bonds of Pluralism: The Form and Substance of Urban Social Networks.* New York: West.

LEE, Hyo-Chae. 1977. "Protestant Missionary Work and Enlightenment of Korean Women", *Korea Journal* 17 (11): 33-50.

LEE Sang-Taek. 1982. "Irŏnara, Pich'ul Parhara (Wake up and Be the Light of the World)", *Hoju Sosik,* September: 10 (in Korean).

LEE, Sang-Taek. 1987. *Exploring an appropriate church structure for Korean Speaking Congregations which are members of the Uniting Church in Australia.* Unpublished D. Min Dissertation submitted to the San Francisco Theological Seminary.

LEE Sang-Taek. 1988. *Sidŭni-wa Pangnangja (The Wandering Migrant in Sydney).* Seoul: Yangsŏ Publishing Company (in Korean).

LEE Sang-Taek. 1989a. *New Church, New Land.* Melbourne: Uniting Church Press.

LEE Sang-Taek. 1989b. "Kuchŏn-esŏ Hwalcharo (A Transition of Media: From Information by Word of Mouth to Print Information)", *Yŏnhap Kidok Sinbo (Younhab Christian News),* 10 September (in Korean).

LEE Sang-Taek. 1990. "Sahoehag-ŭro pon Imin Sahoe: Uri-nŭn Haengbok Han'ga?" (Koreans in Australia from a Sociological Perspective), *Sosu Minjok (Minority),* 4: 13-14 (in Korean).

LEE, Sharon M. 1989. "Asian Immigration and American Race-Relations", *Ethnic and Racial Studies* 12 (3): 368-390.

LEE Sŏkryŏl. 1988. *Yangk'i Nara-ŭi K'orian (Koreans in a Yankee Country).* Seoul: Chŏn Ye Wŏn Publishing Company (in Korean).

LENSKI, G. 1963. *The Religious Factor.* Rev. Ed. Garden City, N. Y.: Doubleday.

LEVITT, Thedore. 1960. "Marketing Myopia", in *Harvard Business Review* 38: 45-56.

LEVY, Reuben. 1957. *The Social Structure of Islam.* Cambridge: Cambridge University Press.

LEWINS, Frank W. 1975. "Ethnicity as Process: Some Considerations of Italian Catholics", *Australian and New Zealand Journal of Sociology* 11 (3): 15-17.

LEWINS, Frank W. 1978b. "Religion and Ethnic Identity", pp. 19-38 in H. MOL. (Ed.). *Identity and Religion: International Cross-Cultural Approaches.* London: Sage.

LEWINS, Frank W. 1978c. "Race and Ethnic Relations", pp. 10-19 in A. CURTHOYS and A. MARKUS. (Eds.). *Who are Our Enemies? Racism and the Australian Working Class.* Sydney: Hale & Ironmonger.

LEWINS, Frank W. 1991. "Religion and Ethnicity — A Closer Look", pp. 173-179 in Peter BENTLEY, Tricia BLOMBERY and Philip J. HUGHES. (Eds.). *A Yearbook for Australian Churches 1992.* Hawthorn: Christian Research Association.

LEWINS, Frank. W. 1978a. *The Myth of the Universal Church: Catholic Migrants in Australia.* Canberra: Faculty of Arts, The Australian National University Press.

LEWY, Guenter. 1964. *The Catholic Church and Nazi Germany.* New York: Mcgraw Hill Book Company, Inc.

LIE, John. 1992. "The Political Economy of South Korean Development", *International Sociology* 7 (3): 285-300.

LIGHT, Ivan and Edna BONACICH. 1988. *Immigrant Entrepreneurs; Koreans in Los Angeles, 1965-1982.* Berkeley: University of California Press.

LITT, Edgar. 1970. *Ethnic Politics in America.* Glenview, Illinois: Scott, Foresman and Company.

LOFLAND, J. and R. STARK. 1965. "Becoming a World Saver: A Theory of Conversion to a Deviant Perspective", *American Sociological Review* 30: 862-872.

LOFLAND, John and Norman SKONOVD, 1981. "Conversion Motifs", *Journal for the Scientific Study of Religion* 20: 373-395.

LOFLAND, John. 1977a. " 'Becoming a World-Saver' Revisited", *American Behavioural Scientist* 20: 805-818.

LOFLAND, John. 1977b. *Doomsday Cult.* Enlarged Ed. New York: Irvington Publishers.

LOPATA, H. Z. 1979. *Polish Americans: Status Competition in an Ethnic Community.* Englewood Cliffs, NJ: Prentice-Hall.

LYMAN, S. M. 1974. *Chinese Americans.* New York: Random House.

LYNCH, Frederek R. 1977. "Toward a Theory of Conversion and Commitment to the Occult", pp. 91-112 in J. T. RICHARDSON. (Ed.). *Conversion Careers.*

MACKEN, Deirdre. 1993. "Sydney Carve-up: Our Changing Cultural Map", *Sydney Morning Herald,* 1 May: 37, 42.

MANGIAFICO, L. 1988. *Contemporary American Immigrants: Patterns of Filipino, Korean and Chinese Settlement in the United States.* New York: Praeger.

MARIN, Peter. 1972. "Children of Yearning", *Saturday Review,* 6 May: 58-63.

MARTY, Martin E. 1976. *A Nation of Behavers.* Chicago: University of Chicago Press.

MASUDA, M., G. MATSUMOTO and G. MEREDITH. 1970. "Ethnic Identity in Three Generations of Japanese Americans", *Journal of Social Psychology* 81: 199-207.

MASUDA, M., R. HASEGAWA and G. MATSUMOTO. 1973. "The Ethnic Identity Questionnaire: A Comparison of Three Japanese Age Groups in Tachikawa, Japan, Honolulu, and Seattle", *Journal of Cross-Cultural Psychology* 4: 229-245.

MATIASZ, Sophia. 1989. "Three Parishes: A Study in the Ethnic Use of Religious Symbols", pp. 219-230 in *The Ukrainian Religious Experience: Tradition and the Canadian Cultural Context.* David J. GOA. (Ed.). Edmonton: University of Alberta.

MATSUMOTO, G., G. MEREDITH and M. MASUDA. 1970. "Ethnic Identification: Honolulu and Seattle Japanese Americans", *Journal of Cross-Cultural Psychology* 1: 63-76.

McGAVRAN, Donald A. 1970. *Understanding Church Growth*. Grand Rapids. MI: Eerdmans Publishing Co.

McGAVRAN, Donald A. 1980. *Understanding Church Growth*. Grand Rapids: Wm. B, Eerdmans Publishing.

McGAVRAN, Donald A. and Win ARN. 1976. *Church Growth Principles*. Bayswater, Victoria: Vital Publications.

McGAVRAN, Donald A., and Winfield C. ARN. 1973. *How To Grow a Church*. Glencoe, CA: Regal Books.

McGUIRE, Meredith B. 1981. *Religion: The Social Context*. Belmont, California.: Wadsworth.

McKAY, Jame. 1982. "An Exploratory Synthesis of Primordial and Mobilizationist Approaches to Ethnic Phenomena", *Ethnic and Racial Studies* 5 (4): 395-420.

McKAY, Jame. 1989. *Phoenician Farewell: Three Generations of Lebanese Christians in Australia*. Melbourne: Ashwood House Academic.

McKAY, Jim and Frank LEWINS. 1991. "Religious Conflict and Integration among Some Ethnic Groups", pp. 166-175 in A. W. BLACK. (Ed.). *Religion in Australia: sociological perspectives*. Sydney: George Allen & Unwin.

McKINNEY, William and Dean R. HOGE. 1983. "Community and Congregational Factors in the Growth and Decline of Protestant Churches", *Journal for the Scientific Study of Religion* 22: 51-66.

McKINNEY, William. 1979. "Performance of United Church of Christ Congregations in Massachusetts and in Pennsylvania", pp. 224-247 in Dean R. HOGE and David A. ROOZEN. (Eds.). *Understanding Church Growth and Decline, 1950-1978*. New York: The Pilgrim Press.

MELENDY, H. Brett. 1977. *Asians in America: Filipinos, Koreans, and East Indians*. Boston: Twayne.

MERTON, Robert. 1957. *Social Theory and Social Structure*. revised and enlarged edition. New York: The Free Press.

MILTON, Gordon. 1964. *Assimilation in American Life*. New York: Oxford University Press.

MIN, Pyong-Gap. 1984. "From White-Collar Occupations to Small Business: Korean Immigrants' Occupational Adjustment", *Sociological Quarterly* 25: 333-352.

MIN, Pyong-Gap. 1988. *Ethnic Business Enterprise: Korean Small Business in Atlanta*. Staten Island: Center for Migration Studies Press.

MIN, Pyong-Gap. 1990. "The Structure and Social Functions of Korean Immigrant Churches in the United States", an unpublished paper.

MIN, Pyong-Gap. 1991. "Cultural and Economic Boundaries of Korean Ethnicity: a comprehensive analysis", *Ethnic and Racial Studies* 14 (2): 225-241.

MOBERG. David. 1962. *The Church as a Social Institution*. Englewood Cliffs, N. J.: Prentice-Hall.

MOFFETT, Samuel H. 1973. "What Makes the Korean Church Grow?" *Christianity Today* 18 (4): 10-12.

MOK, Chong-Bae. 1983. "Korean Buddhist Sects and Temple Operations", *Korea Journal* 23 (9): 19-27.

MURVAR, Vatro. 1968. "Russian Religious Structures: A Study in Persistent Church Subservience", *Journal for the Scientific Study of Religion* 7 (1): 1-22.

NAHIRNY, V. C. and J. A. FISHMAN. 1965. "American Immigrant Groups: Ethnic Identification and the Problems of Generations", *Sociological Review* 13 (3): 311-326.

NAM Kiyŏng. 1990. "Ano K'at'o (Anno Caetteau, a serial article about church matters)", *Hanho T'aimjŭ (Hanho Times, a Korean ethnic newspaper)*, 30 April (in Korean).

NELSON, Geoffrey. 1968. "The Concept of Cult", *Sociological Review* 16: 351-362.

NELSON, Marlin L. 1983a. "A Foreigner's View of the Korean Church", pp. 182-197 in Bong-Rin RO and Marlin L. NELSON. (Eds.). 1983. *Korean Church Growth Explosion*. Seoul: Word of Life Press.

NELSON, Marlin L. 1983b. "Korean Church Mission Growth", pp. 88-102 in Bong-Rin RO and Marlin L. NELSON. (Eds.). 1983. *Korean Church Growth Explosion*. Seoul: Word of Life Press.

NEW York Times. 1987. "Boom Time in South Korea: An Era of Dizzying Change", *New York Times*, 7 April: 4.

NIEBUHR, H. R., Daniel Day WILLIAMS, and James M. GUSTAFSON. 1956. *The Process of the Church and Its Ministry*. New York: Harper.

NIEBUHR, H. Richard. 1957. *The Social Sources of Denominationalism*. New York: Meridian Books. (Originally published in 1929 by New York: Henry Holt and Company).

NIEBUHR, Reinhold. 1932. *The Contribution of Religion to Social Work*. New York: Columbia University Press.

NO Ch'ijun. 1987. "Ilcheha Han'guk Kidokkyo Sahoechuŭi Sasang Yŏn'gu (A Study of Christian Socialism of Korean YMCA during the Japanese Colonial Period)", pp. 104-150 in *Han'gug-ŭi Chonggyo-wa Sahoe Pyŏndong (Religion and Social Change in Korea)*. Seoul: Munhakkwa Chisŏng sa Publishing Co (in Korean).

NOLAN, James. 1971. "Jesus Now: Hogwash and Holy Water", *Ramparts* 10 (2): 20-26.

NOTTINGHAM, Elizabeth K. 1971. *Religion: A Sociological View*. New York: Random House.

Ŏ Yun'gak. 1989. "Ch'uksa (The Congratulatory Message)", *Yŏnhap Kidok Sinbo (Younhab Christian News)*, 10 September (in Korean).

OH, Pyeong-Seh. 1983. "Keeping the Faith Pure", pp. 211-230 in Bong-Rin RO and Marlin L. NELSON. (Eds.). 1983. *Korean Church Growth Explosion*. Seoul: Word of Life Press.

OLSON, Daniel V. A. 1989. "Church Friendships: Boon or Barrier to Church Growth?", *Journal for the Scientific Study of Religion* 28 (4): 432-447.

OOSTHUIZEN, G. G. 1972. *Theological Battleground in Asia and Africa: The Issues facing the Churches and the Efforts to overcome Western Divisions.* London: C. Hurst & Company.

PAEK Sihyŏn. 1990. "Hoju Kyop'o Iminsa Kaegwal (An Overview of the History of Korean Migration to Australia)", in *Sosu Minjok* (Minority), 4: 23-26 (in Korean).

PAIGE, Glenn D. 1967. "1966: Korea Creates the Future", *Asian Survey* 7: 21-30.

PAIK, Hyun-Ki. 1968. "The Social Structure of Korea and Its Implications for Korean Education", *Korea Journal* 8 (3): 11-15, 27.

PAK Hyosaeng. 1986. "Han'guk Kidokkyo Ŭiryo Undongsa (The History of Korean Christian Medical Development)", pp. 100-103 in HAN Yŏngje. (Ed.). 1986. *Han'guk Kidokkyo Sŏngjang Paengnyŏn (100 Years of Korean Churches' Growth).* Seoul: The Christian Literature Press (in Korean).

PAK Kyejŏm. 1983. Yesuchaengi-tŭr-ege Ponaenŭn P'yŏnji (*Letters to the Korean Christians).* Seoul: Dong Ho Sŏ Kwan (in Korean).

PAK Sung'yŏng. 1985. "Iminjog-ŭi Kitorŭl Tŭrŭsosŏ! (Listen to the Prayers of this nation!)", in *Minjok T'ongil-gwa Kidokkyo (The Reunification of Korea and the Christianity).* Seoul: Han Kil Publishing Company (in Korean).

PALMER, Spencer J. 1967. *Korea and Christianity: The Problem of Identification with Tradition.* Seoul: Royal Asiatic Society Korea Branch.

PARGAMENT, Kenneth I. 1987. "Indiscriminate Proreligiousness: Conceptualization and Measurement", *Journal for the Scientific Study of Religion* 26 (2): 182-200.

PARK, Robert E. 1950. *Race and Culture.* Glencoe: Free Press.

PARK, Sun-Young. 1983. "Buddhist Schools and Their Educational Ideologies", in *Korea Journal* 23 (9): 38-46.

PARKIN, F. 1974. "Strategies of Social Closure in Class Formation", pp. 1-18 in F. PARKIN. (Ed.). *The Social Analysis of Class Structure.* London: Tavistock.

PARSONS, Talcott and Edward A. SHILS. (Eds.). 1951. *Toward a General Theory of Action.* Cambridge, Massachusetts: Harvard University Press.

PATTERSON, Orlando. 1975. "Context and Choice in Ethnic Allegiance: A Theoretical Framework and Caribbean Case Study", pp. 305-349 in Nathan GLAZER and D. P. MOYINIHAN. (Eds.). *Ethnicity: Theory and Experience.* Cambridge and London: Harvard University Press.

PATTERSON, Wayne. 1988. *The Korean Frontier in America.* Honolulu: University of Hawaii Press.

PATTERSON, Wayne and Hyung-Chan KIM. (Eds.). 1977. *The Koreans in America.* Minneapolis: Lerner Publications.

PHILLIPS, Earl H. and Eui-Young YU. (Eds.). *Religions in Korea: Beliefs and Cultural Values*. Los Angeles, California: Center for Korean-American and Korean Studies, California State University.

PHOTIADIA, John and Jeanne BIGGAR. 1962. "Religiosity, Education, and Ethnic Distance", *American Journal of Sociology* 67: 666-672.

PIDO, A. J. A. 1986. *The Pilipinos in America*. New York: Center for Migration Studies.

PRICE, Charles A. 1991. *Religion and Ancestry in Australia*. Deakin: Australian Immigration Research Centre.

PYŎN Hyosŏp. 1991 (February). "Sidŭni Hanin Kyohoe Saengsŏng-gwa Palchŏn Kwachŏng-ŭl Tŏtŭmŭmyŏ, 3 (The Genesis and the Development of Korean Churches in Sydney, 3)", *K'ŭrisch'yan Ribyu (Christian Review)*, February: 32-34 (in Korean).

PYŎN Hyosŏp. 1991 (April). "Sidŭni Hanin Kyohoe Saengsŏng-gwa Palchŏn Kwachŏng-ŭl Tŏtŭmŭmyŏ, 4 (The Genesis and the Development of Korean Churches in Sydney, 4)", *K'ŭrisch'yan Ribyu (Christian Review)*, April: 38-39 (in Korean).

PYŎN Hyosŏp. 1991 (October). "Chip'ir-ŭl Chungtanhanŭn Sagwa-ŭi Malssŭm (Apology to the Readers of *K'ŭrisch'yan Ribyu)*", *K'ŭrisch'yan Ribyu (Christian Review)*, October: 50 (in Korean).

RAMBO, Lewis R. 1982. "Current Research on Religious Conversion", *Religious Studies Review* 8 (2): 146-159.

READING, Hugo F. 1976. *A Dictionary of the Social Sciences*. London: Routledge & Kegan Paul.

REDEKOP, Calvin. 1974. "A New Look at Sect Development", *Journal for the Scientific Study of Religion* 13 (1): 345-352.

REITZ, Jeffrey G. 1980. *The Survival of Ethnic Groups*. Toronto: McGraw-Hill.

REPORT of Working Group Meeting on the Calling and Settlement of Ministers from Overseas, a monograph.

RHI, Ki-Yong. 1983. "Korea Buddhist Thought", *Korea Journal* 23 (9): 4-11.

RICHARDSON, James T. (Ed.). 1978. *Conversion Careers: In and Out of the New Religions*. Beverly Hills: Sage.

RICHARDSON, James T. 1985. "Studies of Conversion: Secularisation or Re-enchantment?", pp. 104-121 in *The Sacred in a Secular Age, Toward Revolution in the Scientific Study of Religion*. Phillip E. HAMOND. (Ed.). Berkeley, L. A. and London: University of California Press, 1985.

RICHMOND, A. 1974. "Language, Ethnicity and the Problem of Identity in a Canadian Metropolis", *Ethnicity* 1: 175-206.

RO, Bong-Rin. 1983. "Non-Spiritual Factors in Church Growth", pp. 159-170 in Bong-Rin RO and Marlin L. NELSON. (Eds.). *Korean Church Growth Explosion*. Seoul: Word of Life Press.

RO, Bong-Rin and Marlin L. NELSON. (Eds.). 1983. *Korean Church Growth Explosion*. Seoul: Word of Life Press.

ROCHE, J. 1984. "An Examination of the Resurgence of Ethnicity Literature", in *Plural Societies* 15: 157-171.

ROOF, W. Clark. 1978. *Community and Commitment: Religious Plausibility in a Liberal Protestant Church*. New York: Elsevier.

ROOF, Wade Clark, Dean R. HOGE, John E. DYBLE, and C. Kirk HADAWAY. 1979. "Factors Producing Growth or Decline in United Presbyterian Congregations", pp. 198-223 in Dean R. HOGE and David A. ROOZEN. (Eds.). *Understanding Church Growth and Decline, 1950-1978*. New York: The Pilgrim Press.

ROOSENS, Eugeen E. 1989. *Creating Ethnicity: The Process of Ethnogenesis*. London: SAGE.

ROOZEN, David A. and Jackson W. CARROLL. 1979. "Recent Trends in Church Membership and Participation: An Introduction", pp. 21-41 in Dean R. HOGE and David A. ROOZEN. (Eds.). *Understanding Church Growth and Decline, 1950-1978*. New York: The Pilgrim Press.

RUSSO, N. 1969. "Three Generations of Italians in New York City: Their Religious Acculturation", *International Migration Review* 3: 3-17.

SAENURI Sinmun. 1991. June 1 — February 15, 1992 (in Korean).

SAHLIYEH, Emile. (Ed.). 1990. *Religious Resurgence and Politics in the Contemporary World*. Albany: State University of New York Press.

SALAMONE, F. 1976. "Nigerian Children's Games and Ethnic Identity", *Review of Sport and Leisure* 1: 62-92.

SCHERMERHORN, R. A. 1970. *Comparative Ethnic Relations*. New York: Random House.

SELTH, Andrew. 1988. "The Development of Public Education in the Republic of Korea: An Australian Perspective", *Australia-Asia Papers*, No. 46, Centre for the Study of Australia-Asian Relations, Griffith University.

SHIM, Steve S. 1977. *Korean Immigrant Churches Today In Southern California*. San Francisco: R and E Research Associates.

SHIN, Eui-Hang and Hyung PARK. 1988. "An Analysis of Causes of Schisms in Ethnic Churches: The Case of Korean-American Churches", *Sociological Analysis* 49 (3): 234-248.

SIDŬNI Hanin Chusorok, 1991-92 (Korean Directory in Sydney, 1991-92) — (in Korean).

SIN Chunsik. 1991. "Chaeho Tongp'o Ch'ŏngnyŏn Undong-ŭi Hyŏnhwang-gwa Chŏnmang (The Korean Youth Movement in Australia: Yesterday, Today and Tomorrow)", a monograph. Sydney: The Korean Youth Movement in Australia (in Korean).

SIN Kipŏm, 1991a. "Ilbu Yŏnsusaeng-dŭl Munje-It-ta (Some Problematic Korean Language Students in Australia)", *Hoju Sosik*, 15 May: 39 (in Korean).

SIN Kipŏm. 1991b. "Kŭ Pŏrŭt Mot-Kkoch'yŏ (Dark Side of Misled High Fever on Education)", *Hoju Sosik*, 10 April: 39 (in Korean).

SINGER, Margaret. 1979. "Coming Out of the Cults", *Psychology Today* 12 (January): 82-82.

SKLARE, Marshall. 1955. *Conservative Judaism*. Glencoe, IL: Free Press.
SMART, Ninian. 1984. *The Religious Experience of Mankind*. London: Fontana.
SMELSER, Neil. 1963. *Theory of Collective Behaviour*. New York: Free Press.
SMITH, Timothy L. 1978. "Religion and Ethnicity in America", *American Historical Review* 83 (5): 1115-1185.
SNOW, David A. and Cynthia L. PHILLIPS. 1980. "The Lofland-Stark Conversion Model: A Critical Reassessment", *Social Problems* 27: 430-447.
SON, Bong-Ho. 1983. "Some Dangers of Rapid Growth", pp. 333-347 in Bong-Rin, RO and Marlin L. NELSON. (Eds.). *Korean Church Growth Explosion*. Seoul: Word of Life Press.
SON Insu. 1980. *Han'guk Kaehwa Kyoyuk Yŏn'gu (The Start of Modern Education in Korea)*. Seoul: Il Chi Sa (in Korean).
SON Sehwan. 1991. "K'ŭrisch'yan Ribyu P'yŏnchipcha-ege (A Letter to the Editor of *the K'ŭrisch'yan Ribyu)*", *K'ŭrisch'yan Ribyu (Christian Review)*, October: 42 (in Korean).
SON Sŏnghun. 1987. "Han'gugini Sŏnŭngot ... (Where Koreans Stand ... 3)", *Hoju Sosik*, March: 7 (in Korean).
SON Tongsik. 1991. "P'aragwai Indian Pujok Sŏn'gyo-ŭi Imojŏmo (Some Features of Indian Tribal Mission Field of Paraguay)", *K'ŭrisch'yan Ribyu (Christian Review)*, July: 24-26 (in Korean).
SONG Pyŏnggu. 1991. "Yŏnjung Kihoek, Han'guk Kyohoe Chintan: Sahoe Pyŏngni Pan'yŏnghanŭn Muin'ga Sinhakkyo (Illegal Theological Seminaries as a Reflection of the Sick Society)", *Saenuri Sinmun*, 9 February (in Korean).
SONG Pyŏnggu. 1991. "Yŏnjung Kihoek, Han'guk Kyohoe Chintan: Paltŭng-ŭi Pul, Sinhak Kyoyuk (Theological Training in Korea Today)", *Saenuri Sinmun*, 26 February (in Korean).
SOSU Minjok (Minority). 1990. August (in Korean).
STARK, Rodney and William Sims BAINBRIDGE. 1985. *The Future of Religion*. Berkeley: University of California Press.
STARK, Rodney and William Sims BAINBRIDGE. 1987. *A Theory of Religion*. New York; Peter Lang.
STARK, Werner. 1967. *Sectarian Religion, Vol. 2, The Sociology of Religion: A Study of Christendom*. New York: Fordham University Press.
STOKES, HENRY S. 1982. "Korea's Church Milliant", *New York Times Magazine*, November.
STRAUS, Roger. 1976. "Changing Oneself: Seekers and the Creative Transformation of Life Experience", pp. 252-272 in John LOFLAND. *Doing Social Life*. New York: John Wiley .
STRAUS, Roger. 1979. "Religious Conversion as a Personal and Collective Accomplishment", *Sociological Analysis* 40 (2): 158-165.
STRICKLAND, B. R. and S. C. WEDDELL. 1972. "Religious Orientation, Racial Prejudice, and Dogmatism: A Study of Baptists and

Unitarians", *Journal for the Scientific Study of Religion* 11: 395-399.

SUH, David Kwang-sun. 1983. *Theology, Ideology and Culture.* Hong Kong: World Student Christian Federation, Asia/Pacific Region.

SUH Kwang-Sun. 1984. "Kidokkyo-wa Munhwa (Christianity and Culture)", pp. 213-256 in *Han'guk Sahoewa Kidokkyo (Korean Society and Christianity).* Seoul: Sungjŏn University Press (in Korean).

SUTTLES, G. 1968. *The Social Order of the Slum: Ethnicity and Territory in the Inner City.* Chicago: University of Chicago Press.

SYDNEY Cheil Church. 1990. *Kyou Such'ŏp (Fellowship Diary)* — (in Korean).

SIDŬNI Cheil Church. 1992. *Kyou Such'ŏp (Fellowship Diary)* — (in Korean).

SIDŬNI K'orian P'ost (SYDNEY Korean Post, a Korean ethnic nespaper in Sydney). 1991. August 2 (in Korean).

TAEYANGJU Nyusŭ, (a Korean ethnic nespaper in Sydney), 1988. November 1 — August 30, 1991 (in Korean).

THUNG, Mady A. 1976. *The Precarious Organization: Sociological Explorations of the Church's Mission and Structure.* The Hague: Mouton and Co.

THUNG, Mady A. 1977. "Organising Religion: An Exercise in Applied Sociology", *Annual Review of the Social Science of Religion* 1: 145-166.

TONGA Ilbo (a newspaper published in Korea). 1990. August 5 — February 11, 1992 (in Korean).

TROELTSCH, Ernst. 1931. *Social Teachings of the Christian Churches.* translated by Olive Wyon. London: Allen & Unwin.

Tŭlsori Sinmun (a Christian newpaper published in Korea). 1991. November 24. "Haksamo Yugam (The Usage of the Square College Cap Regretted)", (in Korean).

TURNER, Bryan S. 1983. *Religion and Social Theory: A Materialist Perspective.* London: Heinemann Educational Books.

UNITED Nations. 1988. *Demographic Yearbook.* New York: United Nations.

UNITING Church in Australia: Property Policy, a monograph.

VAUGHAN, John N. 1984. *Segye-ŭi Isipttae Kyohoe-tŭl (The World's Twenty Largest Churches),* translated into Korean by Chŏng Myŏngsŏp. Seoul: Yotan Publishing Co (in Korean).

WAGNER, C. P. 1979. "Church Growth Research: The Paradigm and Its Applications", pp. 270-287 in Dean R. HOGE and David A. ROOZEN. (Eds.). 1979. *Understanding Church Growth and Decline, 1950-1978.* New York: The Pilgrim Press.

WAGNER, C. Peter. 1981. *Church Growth and the Whole Gospel.* New York, N. Y.: Harper and Row.

WALDINGER, Roger David, Howard ALDRICH and Robin WARD. 1990. *Ethnic Entrepreneurs: Immigrant Business in Industrial Societies.* Newbury Park, California: Sage Publications.

WALLMAN, S. 1977. "Ethnicity Research in Britain", *British Journal of Sociology* 29 (4): 464-480.
WALRATH, Douglas A. 1979. "Social Change and Local Churches: 1951-75", pp. 248-269 in Dean R. HOGE and David A. ROOZEN. (Eds.). *Understanding Church Growth and Decline 1950-1978.* New York: Pilgrim Press.
WEBER, Max. 1958. *The Protestant Ethic and the Spirit of Capitalism.* translated by Talcott Parsons. New York: Charles Schribner's Sons. (Originally Published in 1904-1905.)
WEBER, Max. 1963. *The Sociology of Religion.* Boston: Beacon Press.
WILKEN, Paul H. 1979. Entrepreneurship: a Comparative and Historical Study. Norwood, N. J.: Ablex Pub. Corp.
WILLIAMS, William M. 1962. "Foreign Assistance to Korean Education", *Korea Journal* 2 (1): 16-18.
WILSON, Bryan. 1970. *Religious Sects.* New York: McGraw-Hill.
WILSON, Bryan. 1982. *Religion in Sociological Perspective.* New York and Oxford: Oxford University Press.
WILSON, Bryan. 1985. "Secularization: The Inherited Model", pp. 9-20 in *The Sacred in a Secular Age.* Berkeley and London: University of California Press.
WILSON, Richard W. 1988. "Wellsprings of Discontent: Sources of Dissent in South Korean Student Values", *Asian Survey* 23 (10): 1066-1081.
WINTER, Gibson. 1962. *The Suburban Captivity of the Churches: An Analysis of Protestant Responsibility in the Expanding Metropolis.* New York: Macmillan.
WINTER, Gibson. 1968. *Religious Identity: A Study of Religious Organisation.* New York: Macmillan.
WITVLIET, Theo. 1985. *A Place in the Sun: Liberation Theology in the Third World.* London: SCM.
WUTHNOW, Robert. 1987. *Meaning and Moral Order.* Berkeley: University of California Press.
YANCEY, W. et al. 1976. "Emergent Ethnicity: A Review and Reformulation", *American Sociological Review* 41: 391-402.
YANG Myŏngdŭk. 1983. "Isipsegi-ŭi Musinron-gwa Sidŭni Kyohoe (The 20th Century Atheism and Korean Immigrant Churches in Sydney)", *Hoju Sosik,* September: 16, 23.
YANG Myŏngdŭk. 1989a. "Hoju Hanin Imin Kyohoe-ŭi Kwaje-wa Chŏnmang (Korean Churches in Sydney: Their Missions and Future)", *Yŏnhap Kidok Sinbo (Younhab Christian News),* 10 September (in Korean).
YANG Myŏngdŭk. 1989b "Tŏpurŏ Sanŭn Iyaki (A Story of Living Together)", *K'ŭrisch'yan T'aimjŭ (Christian Times),* November (in Korean).
YANG Myŏngdŭk. 1990. "Hoju Sog-ŭi Hanin Sahoe (Korean Community in Australia)", *Sosu Minjok (Minority),* no. 4: 14-16 (in Korean).
YANG Myŏngdŭk. 1991. "Han'guk P'yŏnghwa T'ongir-ŭl Wihan Hochu Kyohoe-ŭi Ch'am'yŏwa Chŏnmang (Korean Immigrant Churches'

Concern about the Peaceful Re-unification of Korea)", *Hoju Tonga*, 9 August: 13 (in Korean).

YI Kwanch'un. 1983. "Han'guk Kyohoe Sŏngjang Nunbusitanŭnde (Amazing Growth of Church in Korea?)", *Hoju Sosik*, November: 9 (in Korean).

YI Sam'yŏl. 1984. "Sahoe sŏn'gyo-ŭi Ironjŏk Kŭngŏwa Silch'on Pangbŏp (Theoretical Foundation of Social Mission and Its Implications)", pp. 171-211 in *Han'guksahoe-wa Kidokkyo (Korean Society and Christianity)*. Seoul: Sungjŏn University Press (in Korean).

YI Sanggyu. 1986. "Han'guk Kyohoe-ŭi Pun'yol, Kŭ Yŏksachŏk Yoin (The Schism of the Korean Church and Its Historical Factors)", pp. 103-118 in *Kyohoe Munje Yŏn'gu Che o-chip: Onŭr-ŭi Han'guk Kyohoe Muŏsi Munje-in'ga (Research Journal of Church Affairs, Vol. 5: What are the Problems with Korean churches today?)*, September (in Korean).

YINGER, J. Milton. 1970. *The Scientific Study of Religion*. New York: Macmillan.

YINGER, J. Milton. 1985. "Ethnicity", in *Annual Review of Sociology* 11: 151-180.

Yŏnhap Kidok Sinbo (Younhab Christian News, a Christian news published in Sydney*)*. 1991 September 17. Sydney: The Sydney Korean Parish of the Uniting Church in Australia (in Korean).

YOON, Yee-Heum. 1992. "The Role of Shamanism in Korean History", *Koreana* 6 (2): 6-9.

YU, Eui-Young. 1977. "Koreans in America: An Emerging Ethnic Minority", *Amerasia* 4: 117-131.

YU, Eui-Young. 1987. "Demography and Settlement of Koreans in the United States", pp. 26-41 in *The Korean Community in New York*. New York: The Korean Association of New York.

YU Sŭngguk. 1983. "Han'gug-ŭi Yugyo (Confucianism in Korea)", pp. 77-118 in *Han'guk Chonggyo Kaekwan (Korean Religions)*. Iri: Chonggyo Munje Yŏn'guso (The Research Institute of Religion, Won Kwang University (in Korean).

YUN Sung-Bum. 1963. "Hwan-in, Hwan-ung, Hwan-gŏm-ŭn Kot Hananimida (Hwanin, Hwanung, Hwangom Truly God)", *Sasanggye*, May: 263-264 (in Korean).

YUN, Sung-Bum. 1973. "Korean Christianity and Ancestor Worship", *Korea Journal* 13 (2): 17-21.

YUN Yŏmun. 1991. "Ch'ŏngso-hanŭn Chayuin (The Cleaner with Freedom)", *Hoju Tonga*, 9 August: 17 (in Korean).

Index

About the Author

Gil Soo Han holds a Master of Arts in Sociology from Jawaharlal Nehru University, New Delhi, India and a Master of Arts with Honours in Sociology from the University of New England, Armidale, Australia. Currently he is a doctoral candidate at the University of New England completing his thesis on "The Myth of Medical Pluralism: Health Care Systems among Korean Immigrants in Australia". Other research interests include culture, industrialisation and social change in contemporary Korea; and religious, political and economic aspects of the Korean community in Australia.